DORSET AT WAR
Diary of WW2

RODNEY LEGG

dpc

Dorset Publishing Company
at the WINCANTON PRESS
National School, North Street, Wincanton, Somerset BA9 9AT

*'I vow to thee, my country —
all earthly things above —
entire and whole and perfect
the service of my love . . .*

*And her ways are ways of
gentleness, and all her
paths are peace'*

— Sir Cecil Spring-Rice [1859-1918]

The motivation for this book was to research the stories of two of The Few,
those of Warmwell's Battle of Britain hero **Eric Simcox 'Boy' Marrs** (1921–41),
and 152 Squadron's great survivor, **Roland Beamont** who progressed from Dorset
and Spitfires to become the fastest Briton in the post-war sky.
That it has expanded into the potted history of so much more was the realisation
via Bournemouth fireman **Ted Hughes** that my home town had such a lively war,
more of which will be revealed in his own book *Bournemouth Firemen at War*.
He unearthed the unique series of photographs of the town's Sunday lunchtime blitz
of 23 May 1943 which left dozens dead. In tribute to them, **Sir Adrian Boult**
took the Bournemouth Municipal Orchestra through the 'Nimrod' passage of
Elgar's *Enigma Variations* at the orchestra's golden jubilee concert in the Pavilion,
just a couple of hours after the Focke-Wulf 190s had turned tail for Cherbourg.
He recalled that day when he helped me put *The Bournemouth Symphony Orchestra*
into print for **Geoffrey Miller**, the source of more memories, in 1970.
Then came the encouragement of Somerset & Dorset Notes and Queries editor
Dr Jim Davies of Weymouth that he positively welcomed references to the
twentieth century and was just a little bored with those scholars who think
that something has to be mediaeval, preferably in Latin, to be worth writing about.
Practical help with information and photographs has always been cheerfully
forthcoming from **Leslie Dawson**, the author of *Wings over Dorset*, who charitably
regarded me as producing work that was complementary rather than competitive.
Similarly **Lieutenant-Colonel George Forty** of Bovington Camp, author of its
Bovington Tanks standard history, helped with Lulworth photographs.
The Pentagon was generous with its abundant archival material on a scale
that only the United States and its defence budget can manage.
Last minute doubts on anything military were checked out with a knowledgeable
unbellicose seventeen-year-old, **Andrew Fudge** at Anchor Hill Service Station,
whilst filling up with petrol just outside of Wincanton.
John Pitfield is mentioned in the Foreword for being a similar information bureau
at the time of the *Dorset's War* predecessor to this book in autumn 1985.
The typesetting was put on computer by **Reg Ward**, beneath the oaks of the
Blackmore Vale, though my thanks there go particularly to **Vera Ward**
for tolerating gross intrusions on their seclusion and hospitality.
Those are the people past and present to whom I would like to dedicate the book —
to **Eric** and **Roland** for inspiration, and to **Ted, Sir Adrian, Geoffrey, Jim, Leslie, George,
Andy, John, Reg** and **Vera** for their interest and support.

First published as *Dorset's War 1939-45*, by Wincanton Press in 1986. This expanded second edition retitled *Dorset at War — Diary of WW2* and published by Dorset Publishing Company in 1990. Copyright Rodney Legg © 1986-90.

Main typesetting by Ian R. Pratt with additional material input by Reg Ward. Output in 11/12 point ITC Clearface at PCS Typesetting, Stoke House, Christchurch Street West, Frome, Somerset BA11 1EB.

Printed in Great Britain by the Eastern Press Limited, at Katesgrove Lane, Reading, Berkshire RG1 2NE. Distributed by Dorset Publishing Company from the Wincanton Press, National School, North Street, Wincanton, Somerset BA9 9AT, telephone 0963 32583.

INTERNATIONAL STANDARD BOOK NUMBER 0 948699 16 7

This is Dorset's war diary.

It is the definitive account of the thousand major events – on land, sea, and in the air – that were the county's contribution and sacrifice towards winning the Second World War.

Each entry is set out with the reality as it was at the time, as seen by those in the 'know' rather than the general population, with any hindsight or comment being reserved for a footnote. The cumulative effect of this mass of information is to show what a close-run thing it all was – and how Dorset was in the front-line for the duration.

It is no exaggeration to say that there is no other single county in the British Isles that contributed to victory in so many decisive ways on such a variety of levels and fronts:

- **shipping losses off Dorset were enormous – the Channel was one big minefield and battleground for both Allied and German convoys.**

- **fliers from Warmwell, in their Spitfires, were in the thick of the battle of Britain.**

- **boffins at Worth Matravers won the secret war and gave the RAF its victory by perfecting radar equipment and devising anti-bomber countermeasures.**

- **old Shirburnian Alan Turing, creator of the world's first programmed electronic digital computer, perfected the technology that cracked the German top-secret 'Enigma' machine-coded radio traffic, to give the Allies advance notice of enemy actions throughout the war.**

- **civilians at Bournemouth, Poole, Christchurch, Weymouth and Sherborne took a hammering from enemy bombs but few were to fall on the vital military installations and factories.**

- **German invasion, had it come, could have been here – the sandy coastline between Studland and Christchurch was a prime target.**

- **as the tide of war began to turn, commandos from Poole raided the French coast.**

- **Poole flying boats restored the air links across the Atlantic and to the Empire.**

- **invasion when it came was an occupation by the United States Army, who used Portland and Weymouth as the springboard for Omaha beach and the bloodiest of the Normandy landings.**

- **American fliers, from Warmwell and Christchurch, paid a heavy price to harry the German lines.**

- **gliders from Tarrant Rushton took British airborne forces to victory at Caen – they were the first Allied soldiers to land in France on D-Day – and a disastrous 'Bridge too Far' at Arnhem.**

- **RAF Typhoons flew from Hurn against anything that moved in northern France, whilst the home skies were protected by Mosquito night-fighters directed by Sopley radar station.**

- **prefabricated steel Bailey Bridges, which speeded the war across Europe, were developed at Christchurch.**

- **overseas, battalions of the Dorsetshire Regiment were the spearhead of the British infantry, recovering from retreat to Dunkirk to carry out assault landings in Sicily, Italy and Normandy. They were the first infantry to cross the Seine and enter the Reich. Three battalions found themselves defending a salient in the Netherlands and showed heroism en masse in their valiant struggle to rescue the remnants of the airborne divisions from Arnhem. On the other side of the globe, the Dorsets fought the Japanese in the Burma jungle and went on to provide the guard for the Imperial Palace in Tokyo.**

- **Christchurch scientists test-fired captured V2 rockets and began Britain's guided weapons programme.**

Also by Rodney Legg

Editor *Dorset — the county magazine* [issues 1 to 114, 1968-87]

Purbeck Island [two editions: 1972, 1989]

A Guide to Dorset Ghosts

Ghosts of Dorset, Devon and Somerset

with Mary Collier, Tom Perrott

Afterword *Coker's Survey of Dorsetshire* [for the 1980 second edition of the 1732 work]

Editor *Steep Holm — a case history in the study of ecology*

Annotator *Monumenta Britannica* with John Fowles [first edition as two volumes 1980, 1982: volume one re-issued as an expanded first American edition, 1981]

Exploring Ancient Wiltshire with George Osborn

Old Portland with Jean M. Edwards

Romans in Britain

Purbeck Walks [three editions: 1983, 1985, 1988]

Old Swanage

The Dorset Walk with Ron Dacombe, Colin Graham

Stonehenge Antiquaries

Guide to Purbeck Coast and Shipwreck

Hardy Country Walks

The Steep Holm Guide

Lulworth and Tyneham Revisited

Walks in West Dorset

The Blandford Forum Guide

Dorset's War 1939-45 [original edition of this work, 1986]

Cerne's Giant and Village Guide

East Dorset Country Walks

Blackmore Vale and Cranborne Chase Walks

Exploring the Heartland of Purbeck

Brownsea — Dorset's Fantasy Island

Purbeck's Heath — nature, claypits and the oilfield

Wincanton's Directory [two editions: 1987, 1988]

Mysterious Dorset

Walks in Dorset's Hardy Country

National Trust Dorset with Colin Graham

Lawrence of Arabia in Dorset

Steep Holm Wildlife with Tony Parsons

Dorset Encyclopaedic Guide

Literary Dorset

Note about ranks.

Ranks, titles, commands and decorations are as they were at the relevant date — rather than those which were attained later in careers.

Foreword

I HAVE no qualifications for writing this book; I was not alive at the time. Even when I came along in the post-war baby boom it was as a probable mistake to an almost middle aged Bournemouth ex-ARP warden rather than one of those infantrymen who was commemorating his first home leave from the Dorsetshire Regiment in six years.

As I grew up the physical signs of war were part of daily life. There was the air-raid shelter beneath the garden shed at 21 Easter Road in Moordown. Its timbers came from Bournemouth Pier, breached as was Boscombe Pier to prevent utilisation by invading Germans. A stirrup pump and bucket provided the fun way to water the plants and anyone venturing out of the house.

Opposite Alma Road Schools was a gaping bomb site with rose-bay willow herb seeding from the basement brickwork. There were similar holes in the central townscape around the Square, in Richmond Hill, Exeter Road, Old Christchurch Road and the Lansdowne.

My first lengthy free-choice writing at school was about the war, chronologically like this except we knew next to nothing then of local events and thought of everything interesting as belonging to distant places. It appalled Miss Thomas, my second teacher. Left-handed writing was enough to do that in itself; she would not have us writing about the war, and certainly not with a left-hand. The other thing I remember from her is the promise that we shall be reunited with our pets when we go to heaven. I would like that.

In those days I could draw a passable Spitfire that no one then would mistake for a Hurricane, though I had seen neither. We envied those who had. Nine-year-old Fred Pitfield of Bere Regis had watched the Warmwell pilots winning the Battle of Britain and in 1944 shown his future double destiny as a draughtsman and historian by etching a Spitfire for posterity in the wet cement of a wall by the watercress beds.

Twenty-five years later and his left-handed son, John, at a similar age would be making his streaks directly in the sky with practical rocketry. It was friendship with John Pitfield that made this book possible because he alone among the younger people I know does not share the fashionable view that war is somehow vulgar and unmentionable. Perhaps that's because he also has brown eyes. He pointed out that war is a human failing but it can bring out the best in people. It was enough encouragement, not that I needed much as I feel at ease with active history and find lively doing minds much more stimulating than the lumpish proletariat who have come to be regarded as the true meat of the past.

To write another book was to resume a self-imposed exile from life and it was somehow reassuring to know that John was also lying on his bed scribbling away in private. His research, in rocket propulsion, has the discipline of precision that I now try to bring to local history. Having listened for years to a general muddle of folktales I decided that with this book I would curtail the material to hard information. There could still be anecdotes, but they would be ones to which someone could put a date and a place.

Disappointingly, I found that upon the slightest degree of questioning the majority of informants became vague and inconsistent. Worse were those who implied they had information of a higher quality but cultivated a reluctance to reveal anything at all. One West Howe worker who had made airborne H2S radar apparatus determindly took his non-secrets to the grave. In 1966 he refused even to admit the apparatus was a radar set—though the Commander-in-Chief of Bomber Command, Sir Arthur Harris, had published pages on it in 1947. In 1966 I never knew the right reply: "Their lipstick stinks!" For airborne radar was codenamed H2S, a chemical notable for its smell, and by that time the wartime factory was producing cosmetics for Max Factor.

My other reservation about selective memories is that a scientific survey has shown how faulty they can become after four decades. War records of semi-prominent people, some of the good and locally great who are the mainstay of parochial society, were compared with what they now remembered having done during the war. Not only had major decisions, which were preserved above their signatures, been purged from their minds but a high proportion had forgotten the titles or even the existence of posts they had held and committees on which they served. Separate incidents had been merged, condensed and transposed to produce a rounded story. It is the stuff of a Viking saga; but we no longer live in imaginative times.

That said, I am nonetheless hoping that some readers will write to me via the publishers with experiences or documents to which they can provide a date so that these can be incorporated in a future reprint. There is also scope for detailed recollections that can flesh-out some of my terseness.

One of my little satisfactions has been to learn something about the occasional quiet hero of my chance acquaintanceship. "I'd like to see it in print before I go," Eric Wilson told me about a manuscript of his. "Why," I asked, "won't you get a third chance?" To his surprise I knew that he had returned from the dead in British Somaliland to find he had been awarded a posthumous VC.

As for my opinions about the war there are none in the body of the book. Anything that sounds like comment is contemporary and therefore pre-dates me. I shall, however, inflict a few thoughts here that are entirely hindsight.

To grossly over-simplify the whole thing I believe that the British won the Second World War by cheating and the Russians with blood. Our secret game was deciphering the enemy's coded communications, enabling strategic anticipation and giving Churchill the smug satisfaction of knowing his opponents' minds. The other great contribution, under-estimated from our Atlantic viewpoint, was the practical one of the Soviet Union in clogging two-thirds of the German war-machine with their contribution of seven million dead and fourteen million wounded. That's not to belittle the Americans and their 290,000 dead and armaments on a scale that only they can produce. It is to think that all else in reality was a sideshow; though if there is another life George Patton will have fitted out Saint Michael with the finest tank division of the celestial skies.

Even with defeat the Second World War would make this Hitler's century. His visions have prevailed. Poland was no more free on VE Day than it had been when Britain declared war on its behalf. A barrier on political thought came down across the centre of Europe and communism could no longer expand—as we so often delude ourselves—but was henceforth under siege. Likewise imperialism. The Victorian dream of a British Empire was sadly shown to be a monumental bluff. The Jews, converted by Hitler into Zionists, gained their own state in the Holy Land. The successors to the V2 rocket would let men walk on the moon. Hitler's Germans would be rewarded by the highest living standards in Europe and out of anger could come reconciliation, to the extent that Swanage families such as Bob and Merle Chacksfield would twin their town with Rüdesheim-am-Rhein.

Western technology, if you want me to acknowledge an American contribution, provided a couple of atomic bangs but by then the other war in the Far East was already ending. I will not, however, condemn those bombs with our specious current morality. For if you send fighting men thousands of miles to risk death on your behalf there is an obligation to do anything in your power that may help to bring them back alive.

The descendants of those weapons are set to give us fifty years of peace in Europe and the North Atlantic. They were perfected in time to remove the threat that was hanging over my childhood: "Wait till your call-up papers come. National Service is going to sort you out!" I cannot claim that we have become the generation that renounced war, but by conscious decision or otherwise we make it in other ways and in other continents.

R.L.

1944. Warmwell Spitfire etched in wet cement by Bere Regis boy Fred Pitfield.

Frontispiece. The picture that sums up England and Dorset at war
in 1940 — Warmwell Aerodrome and its Spitfires fought the Battle of Britain.

Avro Anson:
flying from Warmwell.

January **Hawks and doves.**

The politicians have split into the hawks and the doves. Viscount Cranborne, South Dorset's MP, cautions Wyke Regis Women's Institute about the threat posed by Hitler and Mussolini: "These dictators have tasted blood and have applied a policy of force and had considerable effect with it. We must make England an impregnable fortress."

Clement Attlee, the leader of the Labour opposition, was a little less specific when he addressed farm workers in the Corn Exchange, Dorchester: "People may ask what I would have done at Munich. Suppose you had a man who was driving a heavy lorry. He drove it mile after mile on the wrong side of the road, and after narrowly missing other vehicles, came to a position where a collision seemed inevitable, swerved and ran over a child. You might ask me what I would have done had I been driving. I would not have driven on the wrong side of the road. The trouble is that the government has been driving on the wrong side. I would remind you that the right side for an Englishman to drive on is the left." It is not, however, a time when Europe is keeping to the left.

18 February   **Khaki, not hosepipes, for Bournemouth's young men.**

Speaking tonight at a Territorial Army dinner in the Christchurch Drill Hall, Lieutenant-Colonel Arthur Malim, second in command of the 5th and 7th Battalions, the Hampshire Regiment, was unequivocal that "the duty of every young man who is patriotic is to be in the Territorial Army".

He was particularly scathing at a suggestion that the Auxiliary Fire Service had no shortage of recruits because of the attractions of the blue and scarlet uniform:

"We can supply the uniform, not blue with scarlet facings, but His Majesty's khaki. That is where the young men of Bournemouth ought to be—not running around with hosepipes.

"It will be a bad day for Bournemouth and other towns if they cannot get men to take an active part in a battalion of His Majesty's Army, as part of the field force that will defend the lives and liberties of the people when the time comes. Fit young men of the right age ought to be in the Territorial Army—not in those civilian organisations which are all very well for old men who are not fit."

18 March   **Dorchester Evacuation Committee prepared for 4,612.**

A survey of parishes in the Dorchester Rural District, in which Abbotsbury and Maiden Newton are the only significant places that have failed to respond, shows that a total of 4,612 evacuees could be accommodated in the area. Dorchester Evacuation Committee has reservations, however, and will tell the Ministry of Health that water supplies and sanitary facilities are inadequate.

2 June   **Reception Areas prepare for evacuees.**

Billeting Officers met with local government officials for a conference at Dorchester today to discuss how the Reception Areas would handle their expected influx of children evacuated from London. The local reception centre is Maud Road School in Dorchester, which will provide light refreshments and disperse the youngsters with a bag of food each that is sufficient for forty-eight hours. Quite where to house them aroused deeper discussion.

It was agreed to send 1,600 children into the borough of Dorchester, 1,900 to the surrounding rural district, and 1,300 into the Beaminster area.

June   Anti-aircraft guns issued at Poole.

The 310th Anti-Aircraft Battery, which has 130 recruits training at the Mount Street drill hall in Poole, has been issued with the new 3.7 inch AA guns.

June   Territorial gunners reorganised.

The 375th and 376th Queen's Own Dorset Yeomanry Batteries, with recruits from Shaftesbury, Blandford and Sherborne, have been amalgamated. The new Territorial Army unit will retain the historic name, as the 141st (Queen's Own Dorset Yeomanry) Field Regiment, Royal Artillery.

Likewise the 218th Field Battery, based in the Drill Hall at the Lansdowne, Bournemouth, has merged with the Dorchester and Bridport 224th (Dorset) Field Battery to form the 94th (Dorset and Hants) Field Regiment, Royal Artillery.

June   1st Dorsets garrison Malta.

The 1st Battalion of the Dorsetshire Regiment have arrived in the Grand Harbour, Valetta, aboard the troopship *Neuralia* from Bombay. They had been serving in India since 1936. These Regular Army soldiers are to man the south-eastern sector of the island's defences.

9 July   Dorset tests the black-out.

04.00 hours. The lights have gone out all across Dorset and fourteen other southern counties of England. Aeroplanes are overhead to monitor the results. Air Raid Precautions directives state that even a light of one candle-power can be seen from a height of two miles on a clear night.

Urban kerbs, posts and poles are to be painted white to lessen the need for street lighting. The weather has co-operated with this Sunday morning's experiment.

July   Huge tented camp sprouts across Blandford downland.

Race Down, to the east of Blandford, is smothered with more than a hundred marquees and five hundred smaller tents concentrated across the former hutted lines around Cuckoo Clump that were used in the Great War to train the Royal Naval Division who landed at Gallipoli in the Dardanelles.

It was here, it is said, that Sub Lieutenant Rupert Brooke wrote those immortal lines: "If I should die, think only this of me: That there's some corner of a foreign field that is for ever England."

The mobilisation this time is for a Militia Camp to provide volunteers with basic physical and weapons training in a gentler introduction to the military life.

1 August   5th Dorsets reformed.

The 5th Battalion of the Dorsetshire Regiment, a Territorial unit many of whose volunteers are from Poole, has been reformed under the command of Colonel Sir John Lees. It is part of the 43rd (Wessex) Division. Sir John was wounded twice in the Great War.

Footnote   He would serve as an honorary bodyguard to King George VI.

1939. Chickerell Camp. 4th Battalion Dorsetshire Regiment queue for the cookhouse.

1939. Bovington Camp. Toast from the tank crews.

1939. Radipole. Weymouth boys carry gas-masks.

3 August 'War today . . . is unlikely'—Defence Minister.

"War today is not only not inevitable but is unlikely. The Government have good reason for saying that."—Sir Thomas Inskip, the Minister of Defence.

9 August The King at Weymouth—'It's raining everywhere.'

Thousands of visitors pack Weymouth to see King George VI visit the town for a review of the Reserve Fleet which is being mobilised in Portland Harbour. For most in the Royal Navy Volunteer Reserve the last summer of the Thirties has already ended, but on shore the holidaymakers are having their last fling. An estimated 45,000 converged on the station and the situation was worsened by the delay to trains that the royal visit caused. Many fainted in the crush and the St John Ambulance Brigade commandeered the waiting room and parcels office as a field hospital for casualties.

As for the King, he failed to see the ships off Bincleaves because of mist and drizzle. The Mayor expressed regrets about the rain. "Don't worry, Mr Mayor," the King replied, "it's raining everywhere."

11 August Bournemouth Auxiliary Fire Service in action.

04.00 hours. The second major test of the effectiveness of the black-out has been postponed for twenty-four hours due to continuous rain. Bournemouth's eleven zones of the Auxiliary Fire Service, each with its own local emergency station, are going ahead as planned with their own mass turn-out.

Fifty-four mock incidents have been devised. Five hundred firemen are involved. The exercises are being watched by Home Office Assistant Secretary F.W. Smith and the Inspector of Fire Brigades, Tom Beakes, together with the Mayor of Bournemouth and council officers.

12 August Radar exercises: 'Eastland' intercepted.

Sustained exercises for the past four days, involving 1,300 aircraft of the Royal Air Force split between 'Westland' defenders and 'Eastland' attackers, have shown that the country's twenty-five Radio Direction Finding [radar] stations detected almost every attacking formation. This was despite appalling weather, including rain, wind and fog, which caused frequent suspension of both attacking and interception flights.

The taller aerials of the radar stations sent out radio waves from 350 feet, which were then reflected back from the intruding aeroplanes and received on the station's lower set of 250 feet aerials. The fractional difference of time between the transmitted and returned signal was measured on a calibrated cathode-ray tube to indicate the altitude and direction of intruding aircraft whilst they were up to 150 miles offshore.

Air Chief Marshal Sir Hugh Dowding today broadcast on the BBC wireless to tell the nation that the exercise had been successful, though he stopped just short of directly mentioning the art of Radio Direction Finding:

"It only remains for us to see that our technical equipment keeps ahead of that of our potential enemy. What we have been doing is to work at increasing interception towards one hundred per cent which is our goal. I am satisfied with our progress, and I confidently believe that a serious attack on these islands would be brought to a standstill within a short space of time."

Footnote Prophetic words. "Our technical equipment" now included secrets of the German 'Enigma' military cipher machines, courtesy Polish cryptanalysts in July.

13 August Blackout, sirens and Portland mock battle.

Air raid sirens have sounded across south Dorset at 00.15 hours this Sunday and a blackout is being enforced. The lights have gone out on the ships of the Reserve Fleet at anchor in Portland Harbour and there is the drone of air activity. Destroyers are being deployed as 'enemy' vessels to test the defences at the entrance to the harbour. In the villages the death-bells tolled and bewildered country people staggered out of bed to find out what was happening. In Weymouth the news had already got around, or at least among those who had been out on the town, dancing and drinking or laughing with Elsie and Doris Waters. There was a noticeable absence of sailors about last night.

30 August Dorchester councillors consider 'war imminent'.

Dorchester Rural District Council has decided that "in view of the imminent outbreak of war, that the whole power of the council so far as allowed by law, be delegated to an Emergency Committee until further orders".

August Imperial Airways becomes BOAC and moves to Poole.

The amalgamated Imperial Airways and British Airlines are to be known from next year as the British Overseas Airways Corporation, which will operate under the chairmanship of Lord Reith, the founder of the BBC. Its fleet of Short Sunderland C-class 'Empire' flying boats is being moved with their support facilities from Hythe on Southampton Water to Poole Harbour.

Here Salterns Pier and its club rooms have been requisitioned from the Poole Harbour Yacht Club and water runways, or 'trots' as they are called, are being marked out by lines of tyres in the Wareham Channel off Hamworthy and the Main Channel between Salterns and Brownsea Island. The yacht club is now the Marine Terminal.

Footnote Airways House was opened in a Poole shop, 4 High Street, and the showrooms at Poole Pottery became the reception area and customs clearance point for incoming passengers. Harbour Heights Hotel was to become the rest centre for those due to embark from Salterns Pier on early morning flights.

August Ansons bomb Warmwell 'factory'.

217 Squadron, flying Avro Ansons, is now operational for coast patrols at the aerodrome to the east of Dorchester near Warmwell, where the Royal Air Force set up its school for air firing in May 1937. Their last public display as the Warmwell Armament Training Squadron was a bombing exercise for a 10,000 crowd at the open day. Five Ansons came in and a bomb was dropped on a make-believe factory, a building on the other side of the grass airfield, as the attacking planes were buzzed by three Hurricanes. One of the Ansons was 'disabled' and forced to land. Forty planes took part in the day, including a squadron of Singapore reconnaissance flying boats from Southampton Water.

There will be more practice bombs heard in Dorset as the Air Ministry has announced that sixteen square miles of Lyme Bay, lying six miles off Lyme Regis, will be designated as a bombing range for daylight use. A limit of 120 lb has been imposed on the live bombs that can be dropped.

An inland bombing range is being established on Crichel Down, in the parish of Long Crichel, on the foothills of Cranborne Chase.

August Christchurch 'death-rays' zap the newspapers.

Sensational stories are appearing in the national newspapers that the Air Defence Research and Development Establishment at Somerford, Christchurch, has perfected the "death ray". This is an intensely strong electromagnetic wave which, it is said, can heat up anything in its path—

including living tissue—to the point at which it explodes.

Footnote This was no precurser of the laser or star-wars. As long ago as 1935, Skip Wilkins had demonstrated at the Radio Research Establishment, at Slough, that the energy needed for death rays was way beyond present technology. It was, on the other hand, a convenient cover story for the development of radar systems.

August   **Horse-drawn wagons bring out Blandford spoil.**

Contractors with convoys of horse-drawn wagons are removing thousands of tons of earth and chalk from the site of the military encampment that is to be constructed across Race Down to the east of Blandford.

1 September   **The lights go out.**

A full blackout will be enforced from today. All street lighting and illuminated advertisements are being turned off and curtaining must be made light-tight to prevent any seepage through windows. Regulation masks are to be fitted to car headlights and sidelight lenses must also be dimmed with double sheets of paper.

3 September   **Mobilisation as Bournemouth floods.**

The mobilisation of the Armed Forces took place yesterday as the rains fell. In Bournemouth the 750 men and 26 women of the Auxiliary Fire Service were called-up to their places of duty and found themselves answering fifteen flood calls between 21.45 last night and 01.35 today.

Bobby's department store in the Square had to be pumped out, with the loss of two tons of sugar, as did an air-raid shelter. Electrical transformers exploded and the Pier Approach Baths found itself with an embarrassment of water in its basement this Sunday morning. Ironically it is now regarded as an emergency reservoir for fire-fighting purposes, with 150,000 gallons being held, so this was an exercise which may have to be repeated.

3 September   **War is declared at 11.15.**

This Sunday morning war hums through military communication lines from 10.00 hours as all units are informed that unless Germany pledges to remove her troops from Poland, war is to be declared by Great Britain. At 11.15 the Prime Minister, Neville Chamberlain, broadcasts to the nation on the wireless from the Cabinet Room in Number Ten Downing Street:

"This morning the British Ambassador in Berlin handed the German Government a final Note stating that unless we heard from them by eleven o'clock that they were prepared at once to withdraw their troops from Poland a state of war would exist between us.

"I have to tell you now that no such undertaking has been received, and that consequently this country is at war with Germany.

"You can imagine what a bitter blow it is to me that all my long struggle to win peace has failed . . ."

4 September   **Dorset's first 4,000 evacuees.**

There are already four thousand evacuees in Dorset, mainly children from London, and the number is increasing by every train. Billeting allowances are 8s 6d a head to the host families. Many schools are so overcrowded that shift systems are being introduced, the local children coming for the mornings and evacuees in the afternoon.

1939. Corfe Castle (above) and Bere Regis (below). War games became serious stuff, drawing a Territorial Army unit to Corfe and the 76th Heavy Field Regiment, Royal Artillery, to Bere. In both cases the enemy turned out to be the wet weather.

13 September   **Dorchester girls deliver 14,000 gas-masks.**

Volunteers at Dorchester are distributing 14,000 gas-masks and twenty-four men came to the council's depot in Poundbury Road and offered to fill sandbags. By the end of the day they had stacked five thousand.

The ladies are helping too, particularly the staff and pupils of the Dorset County School for Girls who are cycling the district delivering gas-masks. Many have been assembled by the inmates of Dorchester Prison.

16 September   **Belgian steamer blown up off Portland.**

The 6,000 ton Belgian passenger liner *Alex van Opstal*, empty and homeward bound to Antwerp from New York, was blown up today by a German mine south of the Shambles, Portland. All forty-nine crew and eight passengers were saved though six have been detained in hospital in Weymouth. They were rescued by a Greek steamer.

The explosions, heard in Weymouth, are the first to be experienced in Dorset from the current hostilities.

23 September   **2nd Dorsets on their way to France.**

The 2nd Battalion of the Dorsetshire Regiment today left Aldershot on their way to join the British Expeditionary Force in France.

24 September   **Prayer is the best weapon.**

It is three Sundays on from the declaration of war upon Germany. Adela Curtis, the Christian mystic writer, has told her sisters of the Christian Contemplatives' Charity at St Bride's Farm, Burton Bradstock, that she abhors pacifism and regards "the most effective of all weapons in our warfare" as "faithful prayer".

September   **Training for AA duties (without a gun).**

A Royal Artillery anti-aircraft regiment is giving basic training to recruits at Blandford Camp; very basic training, in fact, as it lacks any operational gun with which to put them through their paces.

1 October   **Hitler's coffee beans impounded at Weymouth.**

In the first four weeks of war a thousand tons of contraband cargo that was intended for Germany has been confiscated, mainly from neutral vessels, and impounded at Weymouth. A total of 513,000 tons had been searched in seventy-four ships that were bound for European ports.

The prize must go to ten bags of fine coffee beans from a Danish vessel. They are labelled: "Adolf Hitler." The little dictator is teetotal.

6 October   **Bournemouth fireman dies in exercise.**

Auxiliary Leading Fireman Reg Cooper slipped from a moving Auxiliary Fire Service van and was killed by its wheels in an accident today outside a disused church in Nortoft Road, Bournemouth. The building is a fire station operated by number 7 zone of the town's AFS. An exercise was being held.

Bournemouth has eleven such auxiliary fire stations. Eighty emergency fire pumps have now been delivered to the town.

Twenty-five pumps are required to turn-out for a major wartime incident.

7 October **Dutch freighter sinks off Portland.**

Another ship has been sunk by a German mine off the Shambles lightship, Portland. She was the Dutch steamship *Bynnendyk*, returning to Rotterdam from New York.

The forty-two crew were able to abandon the blazing wreck and watched her gradually sink from the bows, from the rescue vessel that was taking them into Weymouth.

12 October **More survivors brought into Weymouth.**

The *Alex Andrea*, a Belgian oil tanker, has docked at Weymouth to bring home the crew of a Whitby steamer, the *Sneaton*, that was torpedoed by a German U-boat in the South Western Approaches. She was carrying coal, to the Argentine. A stoker was killed.

The U-boat commander surfaced his boat to watch the men abandoning ship and called to them in English: "So long, boys. Sorry I had to do it, but it was my duty."

14 October **Dorset sailors die in the 'Royal Oak'.**

A German submarine [U-47] has slipped into the naval anchorage of Scapa Flow in the Orkney Isles and torpedoed the 29,000 ton battleship HMS *Royal Oak*. She turned over and went down into the cold, grey waters with 810 men inside her. The whole country is stunned and there is hardly a town in the land that doesn't have a wife or a mother who is not suffering personal grief.

In Weymouth, Petty Officer William Helmore left a widow in Hillcrest Road with three children, the youngest of whom he had never seen. Seventeen-year-old Billy Savage came from Holton Heath, near Wareham. Petty Officer Charles Beeling's parents live at Plush, near Piddletrenthide. Twenty-year-old John Hocking had been living with his grandfather at Martinstown. East Dorset's losses include Dennis Brown of Broadstone and Vernon Fay of Branksome Park.

For others, however, the knock on the door that night brought relief after a day of despair. Able Seaman Victor Ayles and Stoker Cecil Lucking, both with Weymouth parents, had survived. So too had Ronald Kenny of Ackerman Road, Dorchester, though the news was not brought to his mother until 2 am the following morning. A call in the early hours of Sunday was also made to St Helens Road, Broadwey, where police were able to tell Mrs Barrett that she still has a husband, Petty Officer W. Barrett.

Footnote Leutnant Prien and his U-boat crew were feted as heroes on their return to Berlin.

October **Swimming hero distributes Poole's gas-masks.**

Harry Davis, who in his sixty-six years has saved numerous people who were drowning, is taking an active part in Poole's Air Raid Precautions and has made himself responsible for the distribution of 7,500 gas-masks to local residents.

11 November **The Armistice service takes on a new meaning.**

This Armistice Day is different. Throughout the decade the November services marking the end of the Great War have been expressions of pacifism. They were a communal revulsion at the memory of the carnage in the trenches. Now however they are having a military flavour as the country once more steps back into uniform.

"Once war seems inevitable again, a million martyrs will have died again," Ramsay MacDonald said at the Cenotaph in 1934.

Few will have experienced similar thoughts during this minute's silence. The picture houses concentrate on newsreel coverage for civilian air-raid precautions. The public is being reintroduced to warfare. Joining the armed services had also been out of fashion. Even with high unemployment the level of Army recruitment remained inadequate.

All that has now changed. These days the only partially acceptable pacifists are the "chocolate soldiers" of the Friends Ambulance Unit that has been re-formed by the Quaker Cadbury and Rowntree families.

18 November   Poole firm celebrates its silver jubilee.

Hamworthy Engineering's three hundred employees are marking their firm's silver jubilee with a dance at the Woodlands Hall, Parkstone. The company was formed at the start of the last war so it does not seem inappropriate to be celebrating the occasion at the beginning of another one.

22 November   Portland mines claim another ship.

The German mines floating off the Shambles, to the south-east of Portland, have claimed yet another vessel, the Greek steamship *Elena R*.

Footnote   The British destroyer HMS *Kittiwake* also hit a mine in the Channel but though listing she was able to make it back to Portland. Five of her crew had been lost.

31 December   Year in perspective (and Dorset girl weds a Churchill).

The song of the year on both sides of the Atlantic is *There'll Always Be an England* by Ross Parker and Hughie Charles: "There'll always be an England/While there's a country lane/Wherever there's a cottage small/Beside a field of grain."

In Germany the Luftwaffe test the world's first turbojet aircraft, Hans von Ohain's Heinkel 178. German physicists split the uranium nucleus with neutron bombardment, causing Albert Einstein to write to President Roosevelt that a "nuclear chain reaction in a large mass of uranium" would "lead to the construction of bombs". Britain and Germany hoard food. The Germans have 8½ million tons of grain in store, with the promise of a million tons from Russia in 1940.

Britain is the largest global buyer of food—taking forty per cent of world trade. Rationing is planned and state intervention extends to the enrichment of bread and margarine with vitamins and trace elements; though only in that is Britain ahead of American food fads.

The Birds Eye label of General Foods introduce precooked frozen foods. Nylon becomes a commercial product. In Connecticut the Warner Brothers Company introduce cup-sizes for bras. Igor Sikorsky flies the first American helicopter. Al Capone leaves prison, a vegetable from syphilis. German physician F.H. Muller publishes *Tabakmissbrauch und Lungencarcinom*; the world has been told smoking causes lung cancer. Another Muller, Paul, develops DDT for the Geigy Company and saves the Swiss potato crop from Colorado beetles. Batman and Robin join the comic strips.

"This is London," Ed Murrow says nightly to most of the 27½ million US families who listen to the radio. His closing line is always the same: "Goodnight and good luck."

Ten per cent of Britons own 88 per cent of the nation's wealth.

The wedding of the year for Dorset's social set came after Mr Churchill had stepped back into Whitehall as First Lord of the Admiralty; his son, Randolph, married the Hon. Pamela Digby, daughter of Lord and Lady Digby of Minterne Magna.

7 February **Bournemouth ARP now have 11 fire stations.**

Bournemouth's Air Raid Precautions are organised from the basement of the Town Hall, telephone 7220. All reports of damage of whatever character are to be made to there. The town has been split into eleven zones, each with its own fire station. Some such as the Central Fire Station and Pokesdown Fire Station are regular fire service establishments but most are auxiliary depots set-up in buildings such as the San Remo Towers at Boscombe and Lee Motor Works in Winton.

26 February **Young scientists arrive in Purbeck.**

Several young radio research scientists are being posted to the Isle of Purbeck. Alan Hodgkin and Bernard Lovell have arrived at Worth Matravers with the advance party from the Air Ministry's Telecommunications Research Establishment at Dundee, which is to set up a new base between Worth Matravers village and Renscombe Farm. They will be joined by Dr Robert Cockburn.

Footnote All three would go on to be knighted in their eminent post-war careers. By 5 May 1940 the whole of the Telecommunications Research Establishment had been evacuated to Worth.

2 March **Luftwaffe attack Channel shipping.**

Long-range aircraft from Kampf Gruppe 26 today attacked shipping in the English Channel east of St Alban's Head. The steamship *Domala* was set on fire.

Footnote Heinkel bomber 1H+AC of Kampfgeschwader 26, shot-down in March, contained a navigational note confirming the existence of a beam-bombing system: "Radio Beacon Knickebein from 06.00 hours on 315 degrees."

20 March **Steamship 'Barnhill' sunk off Purbeck.**

Shipping in the Channel has again been attacked by bombers from Kampf Gruppe 26. The 5,439 ton freighter SS *Barnhill* sank off the Isle of Purbeck.

31 March **Paper into shells at Holton Heath.**

Paper is being consumed by the Royal Naval Cordite Factory at Holton Heath and made into nitro cellulose. This guncotton pulp is mixed with nitroglycerine; the basis of cordite SC which is the propellant for the Navy's shells.

The factory has used 4,279,141 lb of paper in the past year.

12 April **Narvik wreath at Hardy Monument.**

A laurel wreath hangs on the door of the Hardy Monument, the memorial to Nelson's flag captain on the hills above Portesham—the village known to Thomas Hardy as 'Possum'—in memory of the men of the Royal Navy who lost their lives two days ago in Narvik fjord, Norway.

A card reads: "To the unfading memory of Captain Warburton-Lee, RN, HMS *Hardy*, and the gallant men who died at Narvik. Nelson's Hardy and Hardy's Possum salute you."

24 April   **Holton Heath munitions factory hit.**

An oil incendiary bomb exploded at 22.10 hours tonight beside the wash-water settling house of the nitroglycerine complex at the Royal Naval Cordite Factory, Holton Heath. The wooden settling house began burning but Walt Dominey and his fire-fighting team brought the fire under control and averted a major disaster.

4 May   **Two Poole flying boats destroyed in Norway.**

Two Short Sunderland 'Empire' flying boats, the *Cabot* and *Caribou*, which had been seconded to 119 Squadron at Invergordon, have been attacked at anchor by a Heinkel floatplane in Bodo fjord. They had arrived today to bring radar equipment to the beleagured British troops at Harstadt in northern Norway.

Footnote The equipment was lost in the attack though the injured crews were rescued and brought home by a British destroyer. A further raid, the following morning, sank the planes. They had been scheduled to operate BOAC's peacetime Atlantic service in 1940.

5 May   **Telecommunications Research Establishment moves to Worth Matravers.**

The Air Ministry's Telecommunications Research Establishment, which has pioneered the development of early warning radio-direction finding equipment known as radar, has been evacuated from Dundee to Dorset.

It is being housed in a hutted encampment on a plateau beside Renscombe Farm, a short distance from Chapman's Pool, at Worth Matravers in the Isle of Purbeck.

Telecommunications Research Establishment was previously known as the Air Ministry Research Establishment and used to be based at Bawdsey in pre-war days. It is headed by A.P. Rowe and Robert Watson-Watt.

Footnote   RDF, originally the initials for Radio Direction Finding, came to be regarded as Range and Direction Finding but both would be replaced by the American description Radio Direction and Ranging, thanks to its catching palidrome nmemonic — radar.

8 May   **Special Duty Flight arrives at Christchurch.**

The Air Ministry's Special Duty Flight is arriving at Christchurch Aerodrome from St Athan, near Barry, in Glamorgan. It at present comprises six Ansons, four Blenheims, two Harrows, two Fairey Battles and three adapted "Special Aircraft". These are a Hurricane, an Anson and a High Altitude Machine.

The aeroplanes, which are to be augmented by other arrivals of a variety of types, carry experimental radar aerials and other items of secret equipment. They will be at the disposal of the scientists of the Telecommunications Research Establishment at Worth Matravers.

10 May   **2nd Dorsets in the Belgian front-line.**

The 2nd Battalion of the Dorsetshire Regiment, in the Belgian front-line to the east of Genval, awoke this morning to the drone of enemy aeroplanes and have been told to prepare for battle.

10 May   **Attlee recalled to London from Bournemouth.**

Labour leaders Clement Attlee and Arthur Greenwood have been recalled to London today from their party conference in Bournemouth, as the Chamberlain government is in crisis following the invasion of the Low Countries. Chamberlain has offered them posts in a new national government.

1939—40. Images from six months of war. Neville Chamberlain; black-outs; evacuees; gas-masks; Lord Gort (below, second from right) leading the British Expeditionary Force in France.

They have accepted the posts (Attlee as Lord Privy Seal; Greenwood as Minister without Portfolio) but rejected Chamberlain's continued leadership—which with Parliament's present mood will cause the Premier's instant resignation and a call to Winston Churchill to form the new government.

10 May **Churchill's Dorset ancestry.**

With the fall today of Neville Chamberlain's government and Mr Churchill's appointment as Premier it is noted with approval in Dorset that his most distinguished ancestor, John Churchill, the first Duke of Marlborough, was the son of Winston Churchill of Glanvilles Wootton, "of a good Dorset family". Winston Spencer Churchill is the grandson of the seventh Duke of Marlborough.

Last year his son, Randolph, married the Hon. Pamela Digby of Minterne Magna.

14 May **Three thousand Dutch refugees camp on Brownsea.**

Following the sudden Nazi invasion into the Low Countries, which also delivered the coup de grâce to the Chamberlain government, an armada of dozens of overloaded Dutch vessels is being shepherded by the Royal Navy into Poole Harbour. The refugees will be temporarily camped on Brownsea Island where they can be properly screened by doctors, police and the security services before being admitted into the country.

An estimated three thousand are on their way.

16 May **2nd Dorsets withdraw towards France.**

"Où est la route pour France?" a Dorsetman heard as Algerian troops were beaten back by the German advance and the 2nd Battalion of the Dorsetshire Regiment found itself under further orders to withdraw in the face of overwhelming odds.

19 May **2nd Dorsets see civilians bombed and strafed.**

For the first time the Dorset soldiers serving in Belgium, now pulled back to Tournai near the French border, have seen the bodies of civilians who were bombed and strafed by German aircraft. The town is on fire.

24 May **2nd Dorsets invited to desert.**

With German radio announcing that the ring around the French, Belgian and British armies has "definitely closed" the 2nd Battalion of the Dorsetshire Regiment—now withdrawn to La Bassee, south-west of Lille—has been showered from the air with leaflets: "You are surrounded—why fight on? We treat our prisoners well."

29 May **Observers told not to fraternise with Local Defence Volunteers.**

Too much fraternisation is taking place with other civilian units, local commander of the Observer Corps, Wing Commander Stewart, has told his men: "Head observers must consult their officers before making any commitments with the Local Defence Volunteers. No instruction has been received with regard to co-operation and any tendency to mingle at posts should be discouraged."

Opposite—May/June 1940. The British Expeditionary Force, including the 2nd Battalion of the Dorsetshire Regiment, is evacuated from Dunkirk.

31 May **Churchill flies from Warmwell to Paris.**

Prime Minister Winston Churchill has flown in a twin-engined de Havilland Flamingo transport aircraft from Warmwell Aerodrome to Paris for secret discussions on the deteriorating military situation. Nine Hurricanes from 601 (County of London) Squadron were deployed to escort the Premier's aeroplane. They waited overnight to bring it safely home.

Churchill met the French Premier and talked with Major-General Edward Spears, the British Prime Minister's personal representative with the French government and armed forces. The clutch of young pilots, even after their night on the town, reminded him of "the angels of my childhood".

Among those escort pilots was Flying Officer William Rhodes-Moorhouse, whose father was the first airman to win the Victoria Cross, in 1915, and is buried on a Dorset hillside, at Parnham above Beaminster.

Footnote As is son Willie. He was awarded the Distinguished Flying Cross during the Battle of Britain and would be killed in Hurricane P8818 during a complex dog-fight with Me109s above Tonbridge, Kent, on 6 September 1940. 601 Squadron grieved, and lost its aggressive spirit, according to Squadron Leader Max Aitken.

War artist Captain Cuthbert Orde wrote that all were affected from the commanding officer to the humblest aircraftman: "They couldn't believe it—it just couldn't have happened. His extraordinary combination of gaiety, joie de vivre, personal attraction and fighting qualities was something that just didn't disappear suddenly."

31 May **2nd Dorsets evacuated from Dunkirk.**

After five days and nights of marching and fighting as they made their way north towards the Channel coast, the main contingent of the 2nd Battalion of the Dorsetshire Regiment last night completed an orderly withdrawal, under fire, to the Mole at Dunkirk where they boarded a Thames dredger. They were appalled to see that she seemed to be half full of water but heard that dredgers are always like that.

May **Local Defence Volunteers: six Dorset units.**

Major-General Harry Marriot-Smith is organising the Local Defence Volunteers under instructions from the War Office. Dorset is being covered by six battalions.

Footnote Churchill would have them renamed—the Home Guard. The 3rd Dorset Battalion was later split to create another, the 7th (Wareham) Battalion, and a Motor Transport Company was also formed as part of the Hants and Dorset Transport Column.

1 June **Fleeing French troops arrive in Weymouth.**

The first train carrying Free French soldiers into Weymouth arrived at 05.00 hours. They are being taken to the former Christ Church, opposite the station, which has been converted into a refugee Welcome Club. There they are being issued with their first rations, half a loaf and a tin of bully-beef, and dispersed to various schools, halls and private accommodation.

2 June **Hardy and love of England.**

Thomas Hardy was a patriot, speakers emphasised at the ceremony in Dorchester to mark the centenary of the author's birth. It was held beside his memorial statute in Colliton Walks. Earl Baldwin of Bewdley, the former Conservative prime minister, laid a wreath and commented that he felt reservations during the week that the celebration should be postponed.

On further consideration, however, he thought there was nothing unseemly even at a moment like the present for English people to gather together in the part of England made famous by a very great Englishman to express their sense of what they owed to him. He had for many increased their knowledge and love of England, for which her sons today were laying down their lives.

4 June   Poole and Weymouth craft help evacuate Dunkirk.

Pleasure craft from Poole and Weymouth are in the armada of Operation Dynamo that today completed the evacuation of the British Expeditionary Force from the beaches of Dunkirk.

Among the craft taken to Dover from Poole were Harvey's *Ferry Nymph* and *Southern Queen*; Davis's *Felicity* and *Island Queen*; Bolson's *Skylarks VI, VIII* and *IX*; and *Thomas Kirk-Wright*, the harbour's inshore lifeboat. These craft were comandeered by the navy and the lifeboat, with its shallow draught, has the distinction of being used to go into the beaches. She has survived shore-fire from Germans positioned less than forty yards away.

The pleasure craft have proved ideal for taking aboard soldiers by the dozen but Poole's fishing fleet, which had also loyally turned up in response to the Admiralty's appeal, was summarily rejected by the navy. Its boatmen, who consider themselves to be the port's only true seamen, were sent home by train and their vessels impounded for possible reserve uses. They are unsuitable for this kind of mass transit.

A third of the 330,000 soldiers who have been brought out are French and 6,000 of these, from Flanders, have been sent to Weymouth. At Dorchester, however, the concern has been of a civilian influx, with news of a further 2,300 evacuees earmarked for the district. Only now are air-raid shelters being constructed in the town.

Footnote Of the local boats, the *Island Queen* and *Southern Queen* were sunk off Dunkirk, and *Skylark VI* abandoned with bomb damage. She was later salvaged, towed back to Bolson's shipyard at Poole and refitted with a larger engine as an Air-Sea Rescue craft. The fishermen returned by train for their boats a few days later.

9 June   Germans mine the channel into Poole.

Last night the Germans mined the Swash Channel that leads into the entrance to Poole Harbour, in anticipation of its use in some relief operation to bring out the beleagured units of the British Army struggling in Normandy.

12 June   Poole boats rescue troops from St Valery.

Overall, Operation Cycle failed to live up the Admiralty's expectations of a second mini-Dunkirk, but for some of the small Poole boats taking part it was a triumph. They last night played a key role in bringing 3,321 soldiers, a third of them British, from the salient at St Valery-en-Caux.

This time the Germans were ready for a maritime rescue mission, though it was the fog that disrupted the efforts of the early hours of the 11th and sent six thousand Scottish troops into prisoner-of-war camps. As part of their counter-measures the Germans mined the Swash Channel into Poole Harbour. It has been rendered at least partly clear by navy divers from Portland.

Not completely, however, as the *Princess Juliana*, found. She was sailing out of Poole last night when she hit a mine off the Training Bank and was lifted clear of the water. George Brown, the pilot, was rescued together with three of the Dutch crewmen.

Footnote Ivor Holland, instrumental in the rescue of *Princess Juliana's* survivors, was to be awarded the Order of the Red Lion by the Netherlands.

13 June   **Eleven killed as 'Abel Tasman' is blown up off Poole.**

Three of the fifteen craft returning from St Valery with remnants of the British and French armies successfully ran the gauntlet of the Swash Channel into Poole Harbour today. The fourth and unlucky craft was the *Abel Tasman*, fortunately returning empty. She hit a mine and was blown to pieces, killing all eleven of her complement from the Royal Navy Volunteer Reserve. An order was then flashed to the remaining ships to turn and sail to Southampton.

13 June   **'British Inventor' mined off St Alban's Head.**

The steam tanker *British Inventor* struck a mine off St Alban's Head. Although she stayed afloat long enough to be put under tow the line had to be released as the stricken vessel began to go under.

   Channels into the ports of Weymouth and Poole are being kept open through the efforts of two Portland-based minesweepers, HMS *Kindred Star* and HMS *Thrifty*.

15 June   **Swash Channel has first magnetic mines.**

The mines that have claimed two ships in recent days in the Swash Channel at the outer entrance to Poole Harbour include some, at least, of a new magnetic type that explode when they come close to a steel ship. These C-type mines have not yet been retrieved intact for examination and today the first attempt burst into a spectacular failure on Studland beach.

   Harold Cartridge with the Poole fishing boat *Smiling Through*, under navy orders, managed to tow one on a seven hundred foot line from the Bar Buoy to the shallows of Studland beach—where for some unknown reason it decided to explode, though without more than a shock and a shake for Cartridge and his craft.

   Footnote   The Germans were slow in deploying this potentially devastating weapon. The first to be dismantled by the British would be recovered from Shoeburyness, Essex, on 22 November; the Germans had been lax in not incorporating an anti-handling device.

19 June   **Highcliffe sighting of French refugees.**

Two boats, apparently carrying French troops fleeing from Cherbourg, have been spotted by the Local Defence Volunteers from their Highcliffe lookout, the Cliff Top Café. The craft are heading for Steamer Point, Christchurch.

20 June   **First air raid warning.**

Condition Red: this is the first air-raid warning at Christchurch, though there have been earlier alerts for Condition Yellow, the precautionary message from Fighter Command that enemy air activity is to be expected. With Condition Red the activity has been monitored and appears to be coming our way—it is a warning to take to the shelters, given as a two-minute warbling blast on the sirens.

   Later there was a continuous two-minute wail from the siren to declare that it was All Clear. Nothing, thank God, happened in the interim.

   Footnote   Christchurch would experience 956 air raid warnings, the vast majority of them being of as little consequence. The last would be on 15 July 1944.

20 June   **Weymouth tears as the French leave.**

Tearful farewells marked Weymouth's parting with the French soldiers, the last of whom have now left to resume the war with fighting units. They were taken to heart, in a way that perhaps the Londoners and others weren't—but the town has experienced an influx unprecedented for anywhere in England. John Murphy has recorded one sad incident where a Catholic priest tried to say something kind to an unhappy Belgian woman but utterly failed.

"Are they all yours?" joked Father Jules Ketele when he saw she had three children with her. A good Catholic should have known better!

She burst into tears and sobbed that she had seven children when she left home eight days ago; those were all she had left.

The total number of arrivals for the past week has been 27,400 refugees, of which the bulk—23,743 of them—have come from the Channel Islands which faces impending German invasion.

Footnote The Germans took over the Channel Islands at the end of the month, on 30 June and 1 July.

21 June Christchurch Ansons fly in search of the 'beam'.

The Telecommunications Research Establishment, Worth Matravers, has organised a special mission tonight for three Anson aeroplanes from the Special Duty Flight at Christchurch. They will try, in poor weather, to use American radar receivers, to track the course of a German radio direction signal, intended to aid the navigation of bombers, that appears to lead from Spalding, Lincolnshire, and cross with another similar 'beam' above the Rolls-Royce aero-engine factory at Derby. The Anson tracking this signal is being flown by Flight Lieutenant H.E. Bufton, with Corporal Mackie as radio operator.

Footnote The Special Counter Measures Unit was to function as part of 109 Squadron.

23 June Wooden glider blips on Worth's radar.

A British Avro 504N biplane today took off from Christchurch Aerodrome to tow a German Minimoa glider into the middle of the English Channel and released the wooden craft at 10,000 feet for it to glide back towards Purbeck. The glider pilot, Philip Wills, returned below cliff level at St Alban's Head and prepared for impact but was saved by the phenomenon of currents rising beside vertical surfaces.

The object of the exercise was for the Telecommunications Research Establishment at Renscombe, Worth Matravers, to establish with its radio direction finding aerials [RDF, now known as radar] whether short-wave radiation that bounced off metal bombers would also reflect from wooden gliders. Worth houses the country's principal radio research unit.

The answer was affirmative; to the relief of the scientists as the country is in fear of a mass invasion of German gliders.

25 June 69th Infantry Brigade takes over.

The 69th Infantry Brigade, late of France and the Dunkirk beaches, is now back in the front-line at Poole and east Dorset where it has taken over the anti-invasion defences from the Queen's Bays. The Officer Commanding, Brigadier Barstow, is at Bovington Camp.

The Brigade comprises the 7th Battalion of the Green Howards, the 5th Battalion of the East Yorkshire Regiment and the 6th Battalion of the Green Howards, who are dispersed into the countryside. The Adjutant of the Green Howards has found that the unit no longer possesses a duplicator—and is to ask Poole Corporation if he may borrow theirs.

June Anti-ship guns emplaced around Poole Bay.

The 554th Coast Regiment of the Royal Artillery, with its headquarters at the Conningtower,

**June 1940. England alone—
the Dorset beaches are now the front line.**

West Road, Canford Cliffs, has sited naval guns, taken from warships and armed merchantmen at the end of the Great War and put into store, as the teeth of the anti-ship defences in Poole Bay. The positions are:

Two × 6-inch guns, Battery Hill, Brownsea Island—347th Battery.
Two × 5.5-inch guns, Hengistbury Head—172nd Battery.
Two × 6-inch guns, Mudeford—175th Battery.
Two × 4-inch guns, Swanage—386th Battery.

Each set of emplacements has a complement of about a hundred men.

1940 (photographed, after some subsidence, by Colin Graham in 1983). Abbotsbury, across the Chesil Beach beside the West Fleet. Dragon's teeth anti-tank obstacles and a pillbox (seaward, left). The concrete cubes are 3½ feet high and four feet apart, in a double row with nine feet between the parallel lines set on a continuous concrete base.

1940. East Lulworth. Semi-obsolete medium tank from Lulworth Camp, pointing seawards from between the dragon's teeth that block Arish Mell, the gap in the chalk cliffs of Worbarrow Bay.

1940. The invasion coast: barbed wire and soldier at Seatown, with Golden Cap beyond. The 6-inch gun is on Brownsea Island, manned by 347 Battery.

June   Ship and boom defence for Poole Harbour entrance.

An Examination Ship is positioned in the Swash Channel at the entrance to Poole Harbour. The duty is being undertaken by the ex-Belgian trawler *Rosa Arthur*, now His Majesty's Trawler XVI, with her sister craft HMT XVII (*Roger Robert*) and HMT XVIII (*Marguerita Marie Louisa*). The alert code for the sighting of enemy forces is "Blackbird". That for a landing of troops is "Gallipoli". For a landing of tanks it is "Caterpillars".

Once a warning of invasion had been radioed and received on the mainland the craft's duty is to suspend the watching brief with a final signal—"Finish"—and head to sea to intercept enemy vessels.

As for the harbour entrance, it has a steel boom with suspended torpedo heads that have been provided by the Royal Naval Cordite Factory at Holton Heath. There is a passage open at the centre in daytime but in the evening this is closed by boatman George Mitchell.

Inside the harbour six pleasure craft have been requisitioned by the Royal Navy and armed with machine guns. They are H1 to H6; the boats of the Poole Harbour Patrol.

In the Main Channel of Poole Harbour an old steamship, the *Empire Sentinel*, has been packed with explosives and in the event of invasion the harbour patrol will sink her to block the approaches to the port. Their prime duty is to ensure the closure of this channel.

Footnote Only one of the pleasure boats, *Etrillita* in civilian days, was retained as a patrol craft. The others were phased out and replaced.

June   British mines laid in Poole Harbour.

The Naval Officer-in-Command, Poole, is completing the laying of a minefield between Sandbanks and Brownsea Island to prevent the intrusion of German submarines or surface vessels. Anti-tank "islands" of urban coastal areas impregnable to tank attack have been established behind concrete obstacles, minefields and flame traps at the Old Town in Poole and at Christchurch. The Garrison Headquarters is also strongly defended in the centre of Bournemouth.

The whole of the area from Upton to Mudeford is under the control of the Garrison Commander at Bournemouth.

June   Royal Naval Air Station Sandbanks.

Seaplane training for Fleet Air Arm pilots is now based at Poole, from the middle of this month, with the removal from Calshot on Southampton Water to Sandbanks of 765 Squadron, the Royal Navy Seaplane School. At Calshot they had been heavily bombed.

The squadron trains its pilots on the air-sea rescue Walrus, which is distinctive with a chugging sound and floats on its wings. It is known as the 'Shagbat'.

On the Sandbanks slipway the machines are stored with their wheels down and wings folded back. The unit also has the Swordfish torpedo-reconnaissance biplane (known as the 'Stringbag') and Kingfisher and Seafox floatplanes.

The base is known as Royal Navy Air Station Sandbanks.

Footnote But to Poole people it was HMS Tadpole—because it handled beginners with seaplanes that were dwarfed by the Short Sunderlands operating from the harbour with BOAC and Coastal Command. The name was later adopted by the Navy for real, in 1943, for a pre-invasion landing craft training establishment.

June   Bovington's tank collection scrapped or used as pillboxes.

The collection of the world's first tanks at the Armoured Fighting Vehicles School, Bovington

Camp, has been dispersed to help the war effort. Many have been taken away for scrap and others are in strategic positions as stationary pill-boxes.

The vehicles had been put in a shed after Rudyard Kipling visited Bovington in 1923 and expressed disappointment that nothing was being done to preserve them.

June   Four hundred French soldiers rest in Bournemouth.

As the exhausted armies are dispersed from the reception ports a detachment of four hundred French soldiers is told to go to Bournemouth for a short recuperation whilst billets are located. Canon Hedley Burrows found they had been sent to St Peter's Hall in the centre of the town.

He telephoned the Town Clerk to ask who was in charge of these men. "You are!" he was told. Canon Burrows is arranging their accommodation.

Thousands more are to pass through Bournemouth like refugees. It is said the only fully equipped division in Britain is Canadian.

1 July   Ration books and identity cards.

Ration books for food came into force today, with green coupons for meat, yellow for butter and margarine, and orange for cooking fat.

Identity cards are being issued to all those living in the Military Control areas, which in Dorset include the entire coast and its towns and stretch twenty miles inland. The Commissioner responsible for the control of civilians in the South-west Region is Sir Geoffrey Peto but the National Registration Identity Cards, each carrying the individual's photograph, are issued locally. In the case of Sandbanks, for instance, they will be signed by the Officer Commanding Troops, Poole Defence Area.

Those without cards have to give reasons for entry into the Military Control areas when they encounter vehicle check points and police also carry out spot-checks inside the zone on bus passengers and in public places.

2 July   Green Howards wiring up the Bournemouth beaches.

All beach chalets and huts are to be removed from the beaches of Bournemouth and Poole, having been considered to have been requisitioned by the military. Their clearance has been demanded to ensure a proper field of fire across the sands. Wire barriers are to be erected by the Green Howards along the low-tide line and emplacements built at intervals. Particular strong-points will be at the Haven Hotel and Sandbanks Pavilion. Sandbanks is being sealed-off.

3 July   Bournemouth gets its first bomb.

Southampton received its first enemy bombers early on 19 June and today, at 00.12 hours, came Bournemouth's turn. A single high-explosive bomb fell at Cellars Farm Road, Southbourne. It set a house on fire and damaged eighteen other properties.

The explosion and blaze caused considerable consternation. Rumours followed and at 02.45 hours, on the other side of the River Stour, Christchurch police issued a warning that German parachutists had landed.

4 July   Control points surround Sandbanks.

Effectively, from today, Sandbanks is sealed with military control points in operation at Shore Road and the Haven Hotel crossing point, and on the Studland road at Shell Bay. From the 6th the position will be regularised by the issue of permits to the 544 inhabitants who will have to gather at the Haven Hotel to have their photographs taken and undergo an interview before they are accredited with official clearance documents.

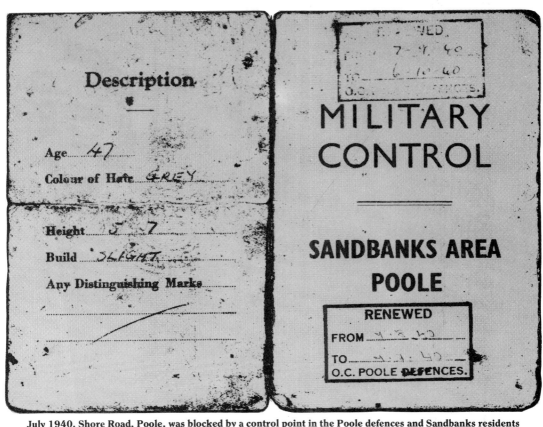

Description

Age 47

Colour of Hair GREY

Height 5 7

Build SLIGHT

Any Distinguishing Marks

MILITARY CONTROL

SANDBANKS AREA POOLE

RENEWED
FROM
TO
O.C. POOLE DEFENCES.

July 1940. Shore Road, Poole, was blocked by a control point in the Poole defences and Sandbanks residents required a passport to reach their homes. Louie Dingwall was to experience less suspicion than most as she converted her guest house into a canteen for the soldiers. She also ran a taxi service for VIPs who came to Poole on the BOAC flying boats.

Serial No. 61

National Registration Identity Card N. WAEF 32 2

Issued to Mrs. ~~Mr.~~ ~~Miss~~ Dingwall
SURNAME

Eileen
CHRISTIAN NAME(S)

Address

Occupation GARAGE PROPRIETRESS

Nationality BRITISH

Available From July 2nd 1940
To August 2nd 1940

Issued by
O.C. Troops Poole Defence Area.

On 6.7.40

Signature of Holder P. Dingwall

3 July 1940 (left). Bournemouth's first air raid was visited upon Cellars Farm Road, Southbourne, and the fire and commotion caused reports that German parachutists had landed.

4 July 1940 (below). Portland Harbour. 'Stuka' dive-bombers left a pall of black smoke rising from the stricken anti-aircraft gunship HMS 'Foylebank'.

1939. Portland Harbour. The destroyer HMS 'Brazen' would have a short war— the Germans sank her in the Channel in July 1940.

4 July 1940. Portland Harbour. Daylight dive-bombers left sixty dead in this wreckage of HMS 'Foylebank', including Leading Seaman Jack Mantle who stuck to his pom-pom, firing at the 'Stukas' as he and the ship were torn apart. He would be posthumously awarded the Victoria Cross: the first the Royal Navy had won from an action inside British territorial waters. A year earlier, 'Foylebank' (below) had been a civilian steamship.

4 July   Dozens killed and Portland hero keeps firing as he dies.

Ninety Junkers 87 'Stukas' today attacked Convoy OA 178 between Portland and Hengistbury Head, sinking the steamship *Elmcrest* and three other vessels. A further nine ships were damaged.

The dive-bombers then attacked Portland Harbour where they sank two ships, including the anti-aircraft auxiliary HMS *Foylebank*. A dozen 'Stukas' came at her and one of the first casualties was 23-year-old Leading Seaman Jack Mantle from Southampton. Despite having his legs shattered as bombs tore the ship apart, causing loss of electrical power, he stayed at his pom-pom and continued firing even as he suffered further wounds, and must have known he was mortally injured.

Fifty-nine of his comrades were also killed and a total of sixty were injured—the other sixty somehow came out of it unscathed.

Perhaps the unluckiest people on Portland that day were nine contractors from McAlpine's, who had been digging a tunnel. They sheltered inside it during the raid and came out when it was thought to be over; to be killed by a last bomb from a single German plane that turned back from the sea. Four of those workers were boys.

Footnote There were repercussions. The Admiralty closed the English Channel to ocean-going merchant vessels, though coastal convoys would continue.

Jack Mantle was gazetted with the first Victoria Cross that the Royal Navy had won inside territorial waters. He is buried in Portland's Naval Cemetery on the Verne Common hillside.

Open air gatherings were henceforth restricted. Only family mourners could attend the funerals that resulted from the day's events. At one the Fortuneswell Methodist minister, Rev F. Jowett, said: "We owe a tribute of gratitude and affection to the one who has departed. He has given his life for his King and country, and those things for which we Englishmen stand."

5 July   E-boats maul Convoy OA 178.

The remnants of Convoy OA 178, which suffered considerably from a Junkers 87 'Stukas' onslaught yesterday, were harassed last night by E-boats off Poole Bay. One ship has sunk and two more are damaged.

5 July   'Hartlepool' sinks in Weymouth Harbour.

SS *Hartlepool*, a British steamship, has sunk at the entrance to Weymouth Harbour as a result of enemy action.

5 July   Bournemouth's piers are blown-up.

In view of the possibilities they offer, not only for German airborne landings, but also as supply points for any conventional invasion force, the precaution has been taken of 'blowing' the seaside piers at Bournemouth and Boscombe. The Royal Engineers today carried out a series of explosions to demolish the central sections of both piers.

The seaward ends, the scene of the famous end-of-the-pier shows, are being left as islands. It is a sad epitaph to those years of joy and a reminder, not that one is now needed, of the state of siege that has descended upon southern England. It is going to shock anyone who cherishes memories of the Victorian bathchairs.

6 July   Warmwell taken over by Fighter Command.

Warmwell has become a front-line defensive aerodrome with the arrival of the Spitfires of 609 (West Riding) Squadron under Squadron Leader H.S. (George) Darley. The squadron

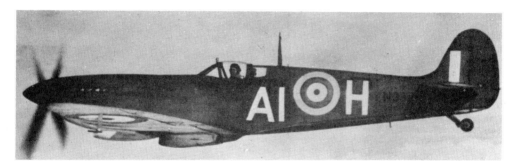

1940. About to become a legend—the Supermarine Spitfire in its Mark IX version. There were 187 in squadron service in Britain when war was declared. A month later 4,000 were on order.

code letters are "PR". Control of the airfield has been transferred to No. 10 Group of Fighter Command, the headquarters of which is at Box, near Bath, and its sector base and home aerodrome is Middle Wallop, near Andover, Hampshire. The pilots return there in the evening and come back to Dorset the following morning.

Scramble time is fifteen minutes and the accommodation is tented.

The advent of the eight-gun fighter has revolutionised aerial warfare. There were 187 Spitfires in squadron service on the Sunday war was declared—by the end of that month 4,000 were on order and their production has the highest priority.

Footnote   There was an inflexible meals timetable at Warmwell that often caused friction and Darley would damn Dorset for its treatment of his men. Once he started the day with a row with the cooks and had to prepare his own breakfast, breaking off to take to the sky to fight off some 'Stukas'. Back on the ground he rang the Station Commander to say he wished to be spared any thanks "for saving the hangars, personnel, and planes, not to mention the officers' mess and kitchens".

Lance Corporal Tony Hollister, later of Swanage, witnessed a gratuitous insult from an ex-Indian Army major to a couple of Warmwell pilots. "Take your bloody hands out of your pockets and salute a senior officer." They deflated him with unprintable public school drawl. There used to be a simple phrase for causing apoplexy amongst such persons: "I always regarded the terrorists as the cream of Bengal."

9 July   Warmwell pilot and 'Stuka' leader killed off Portland.

Dive-bombers today attacked Channel shipping off Portland and 609 Squadron was scrambled from Warmwell Aerodrome.

Three Warmwell Spitfires closed in on two Junkers Ju87 'Stukas' but then at least nine Me110s dived on the British fighters from above.

The attacking Me110s were spotted by Pilot Officer David Moore Crook in Spitfire P9322 (PR-L).

He yelled a radio warning to his two companions. Pilot Officer Michael Appleby switched his radio from transmit just in time to be told "Messerschmitts" and pull his Spitfire clear.

The third Spitfire, flown by Pilot Officer Peter Drummond-Hay, must still have had its radio on transmit and was lost in the action over the sea.

Then, David Crook writes in his log: "I found myself very near to a Ju87 so stalked it through cloud and when it emerged into clear sky I fired all the rest of my ammunition at very close range. He turned over and dived in flames into the sea."

This dive-bomber was piloted by Hauptmann Friedrich-Karl Freiherr von Dalwigk zu

Lichtenfels, the 33-year-old Staffel-Kapitän of I Gruppe, Stukageschwader 77.

Footnote Von Dalwigk, who had joined the Luftwaffe in 1933, would be posthumously awarded the Knight's Cross on 21 July 1940.

9 July **Poole now a sealed-off town.**

Poole is now part of the Defence Area, with access restricted to those with reason for entering the town, under a regulation signed by Regional Controller Harold Butler.

10 July **Poole flying boat arrives in Sydney.**

The British Empire's air link resumed today with the arrival in Sydney of a BOAC flying boat from Poole. Another has reached Durban. They have flown a horseshoe-shaped route to Lisbon and across the southern Sahara.

The Australian plane then travelled northwards via Khartoum and Cairo on to the usual peacetime flight path across Palestine, the Persian Gulf, India and Malaya.

The South African route is via Lagos and Leopoldville.

11 July **Anti-glider precautions erected at Poole.**

Among the various anti-landing traps being laid to discourage enemy glider forces are rows of telegraph poles which are being cut into sections and dug into the fairways of Parkstone golf links and across Branksome playing fields. The poles are ten feet apart and form rows every hundred yards.

11 July **Two more Warmwell losses and a German crashes near Lulworth.**

Two more Spitfires from Warmwell's 609 Squadron have been lost in action over the English Channel, whilst fighting off a 'Stuka' bombardment of a convoy of British merchant ships.

The attacks were in Lyme Bay, by fifty enemy aircraft, and 609 Squadron went to the aid of the hard-pressed Hurricanes from Exeter which had battled alone against an attack earlier in the day by twenty bombers and forty fighters. The steam yacht *Warrior II* was sunk in the first attack and another ship damaged in the second raid.

It is reported that as a result of this action an Me110 has crashed on Povington Heath, between East Lulworth and East Holme, and that this is the first German aircraft to be brought down on Dorset soil.

The two Spitfire pilots who have failed to return to Warmwell are Flight Lieutenant 'Pip' Barron and Pilot Officer Gordon Mitchell.

12 July **More Spitfires for Warmwell.**

An unblooded support squadron, 152 (Hyderabad) Squadron, has flown into Warmwell Aerodrome, led by Squadron Leader Peter Devitt who learnt to fly at the age of nineteen in 1930. Their markings are "UM". The squadron is equipped with Spitfires and has had its practice flights in the north of England.

12 July **Northumberland Fusiliers to prepare Bournemouth's defences.**

Veterans of Dunkirk, the 4th Battalion of the Royal Northumberland Fusiliers have arrived in Bournemouth after a short stay at Yeovil followed by a few days in tents at Piddlehinton. Here in the seaside resort they are taking over the coast defences from the Royal Artillery and will lay mines and erect wood, steel and concrete anti-invasion obstacles.

Invasion 1940. Weymouth, on the Nothe promontory. As with everywhere along the Dorset coast, all who could be found guns were pointing them seawards. Regular army soldiers, territorials, reservists and those who declared themselves de-retired joined with the newly enlisted Home Guard and evacuated units of invaded allied forces.

13 July 'Stay-put if the Germans invade'—mayors order.

Learning from the chaos brought to France and Belgium by refugees blocking the roads in the hours that preceded the arrival of the Germans, the mayors of the Bournemouth conurbation have emphasised that there is to be no civilian evacuation if the enemy invades. All major roads would be sealed off for the use of the Army and if the enemy comes he will in the Bournemouth area take on the burden of an army of occupation with a quarter of a million population to control and support. Resistance will continue from the 'fighting boxes' garrisoned by upwards of fifty armed men, and in some cases two hundred or more. These, it is said, are "fortified, supplied and organised to withstand siege without outside assistance".

13 July German aircraft suffer in dog-fights off Portland.

Spitfires from 609 Squadron, whilst flying a convoy protection patrol over the English Channel, today encountered German aircraft at 15,000 feet off Portland. Flying Officer John Dundas, in R6634, came out of the sun at an Me110 which he claimed to have destroyed, and had a dog-fight with other German fighter-bombers. He then landed at Warmwell Aerodrome.

Meanwhile, Pilot Officer R.F.G. ('Mick') Miller, in Spitfire L1065, took on and damaged an Me110, and then found a Dornier. The coup de grâce for the latter was executed by the Hurricanes of 238 Squadron, from Middle Wallop on the Hampshire Downs.

Footnote   Dundas's claimed Me110 kill was not in fact destroyed but managed to limp back to France.

13 July Australian Hurricane pilot killed at West Knighton.

An Australian volunteer, Flight Lieutenant J.C. Kennedy from Sydney, was killed today when his damaged Hurricane P2950 failed to clear power lines that obstructed his attempted crash-landing at Little Mayne Farm, West Knighton.

It is thought he was wounded during the afternoon encounter off the Chesil Beach in which a Dornier Do17 (4U+DK) was intercepted by the Hurricanes of 238 Squadron, from Middle Wallop, and brought down. Kennedy turned towards Warmwell Aerodrome, to the north-east, but lost too much height and crashed two miles short of the airfield. He was twenty-three.

17 July 1940. Below and opposite—Winston Churchill sees the invasion coast at Sandbanks. It is the day after Hitler issued his directive ordering preparations for landings in England.

These photographs sum up the national spirit of resistance, as expressed by Churchill to Parliament on 4 June 1940 in the best war leader's speech this side of Shakespeare: 'We shall defend our island, whatever the cost may be, we shall fight on the beaches, we shall fight on the landing grounds, we shall fight in the fields and in the streets, we shall fight in the hills; we shall never surrender.'

16 July 'I have decided to prepare a landing against England' — Hitler.

Luftwaffe Enigma machine-coded radio messages have today carried a directive from Hitler. The translation of the deciphered intercept, passed to Churchill by the Government's Code and Cipher School at Bletchley Park, reads: "I have decided to prepare a landing operation against England and if necessary to carry it out."

17 July Churchill visits the Dorset invasion coast.

Winston Churchill today saw the invasion precautions along the most vulnerable beaches of the South Coast when he inspected units at Branksome Chine and Sandbanks. At Branksome he showed his skill as a bricklayer by making a practical contribution to the defences that are taking shape.

He recalled to General Alan Brooke, the chief of Southern Command who had driven with him from Gosport, that it was from the rustic bridge at Alum Chine that he had fallen twenty feet in 1892, at the age of seventeen, very nearly plunging to his death.

They dined at the Armoured Fighting Vehicles School, Bovington, and were at Wool Station at 20.00 hours for Churchill's train back to London. Brooke is less than confident with what he has seen, he confides to his diary: "What has been going on in this country since the war started . . . The ghastly part is that I feel certain that we can only have a few more weeks before the Boche attacks." For all that, he admitted, he realised it was imperative to "maintain a confident exterior".

Footnote Brooke was unimpressed by his men's equipment and means but Churchill realised he had a considerable asset in Brooke—two days later he was promoted Commander-in-Chief Home Forces; on Christmas Day 1941 he became Chief of the Imperial General Staff.

18 July **Warmwell celebrates revenge.**

Warmwell's Spitfire pilots have returned with their first kills. Two enemy aircraft have been shot down by 609 Squadron, which has done much to restore morale after their own recent losses.

One of the kills, a Dornier bomber which crash-landed close to Fleet church, became the second German aircraft to be brought down in Dorset. It had been attacking shipping in Lyme Bay. The pilot, who was the only survivor, passed looted Players cigarettes to his captors.

On the other hand, the station has lost another Spitfire, and has a second machine awash on a beach, but both pilots are safe. Flight Lieutenant Howell parachuted into the sea from Spitfire R6634 during a mid-afternoon dog-fight five miles from Swanage. A Royal Navy launch picked him up, and also Flying Officer Edge, whom they found on Studland beach. He had brought Spitfire R6636 down on to the sands after machine-gun fire from a Junkers had smashed his engine cooling system. As the tide came in the fighter was covered by the sea.

Footnote   R6636 was salvaged and would fly again.

20 July **Warmwell pilot killed.**

Pilot Officer Posner, a young South African volunteer flying a Spitfire from Warmwell with 152 Squadron, has been lost in an engagement with enemy planes off the Isle of Wight. Only yesterday the squadron flew its first operational sortie from Warmwell Aerodrome.

21 July **Hurricanes shoot down Dornier at Blandford.**

The Hurricanes of 238 Squadron, from Middle Wallop, claim the Dornier Do17 (5F+OM) which was shot down at 15.00 hours over Nutford Farm, a mile north of Blandford. Its three crew were wounded in the crash and taken into the farmhouse for treatment before being driven to hospital.

24 July **Liner torpedoed off Portland.**

The *Meknes*, a French liner, has sunk after being torpedoed off Portland.

25 July **Two German planes and Spitfire shot down.**

Squadron Leader Peter Devitt today led the Spitfires of 152 Squadron from Warmwell in their first successful interception. Calling "Tally ho!" and hearing an "Achtung, Spitfire" response his fighters attacked a Dornier with Junkers 87 'Stuka' dive-bombers over Portland.

The Dornier crashed near Weymouth, killing one of the crew, and a 'Stuka' was seen plunging burning into the sea. Both kills were claimed by Ralph ('Bob') Wolton flying UM-F for Freddie with the coup de grâce being delivered to the Dornier by Flying Officer E.C. 'Jumbo' Deanesley who then went after a 'Stuka' but ended up baling out wounded as his Spitfire crashed into the sea. He was picked up by the SS *Empire Henchman* and dropped off at Lyme Regis.

26 July **E-boats sink three ships off Dorset.**

An E-boat Flotilla, comprising three German motor torpedo boats—Schnellboote S19, S20 and S27—have sunk three merchant vessels in attacks in the Channel between Portland and the Isle of Wight.

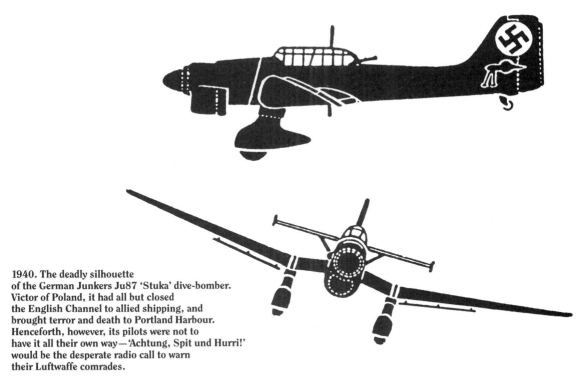

1940. The deadly silhouette
of the German Junkers Ju87 'Stuka' dive-bomber.
Victor of Poland, it had all but closed
the English Channel to allied shipping, and
brought terror and death to Portland Harbour.
Henceforth, however, its pilots were not to
have it all their own way — 'Achtung, Spit und Hurri!'
would be the desperate radio call to warn
their Luftwaffe comrades.

1940. Squadron
Leaders of
the Warmwell
Spitfires—George
Darley of 609
Squadron and
Peter Devitt (far
right) of 152
Squadron.

27 July   **Warmwell Spitfire lost off Weymouth.**

Pilot Officer J.R. Buchanan of 609 Squadron, flying Spitfire N3023 from Warmwell Aerodrome, lost his life today over Weymouth Bay when his fighter was attacked by Me109s.

29 July   **Destroyer loss shock—Germans have radar.**

HMS *Delight*, a 1,375 ton destroyer of the 'Defender' class was today dive-bombed by Junkers 87 'Stukas' and sank twenty miles south of Portland Bill.

Footnote Shortly after she had gone down an intercepted German radio message in the 'Enigma' code was deciphered by the British Code and Cipher School at Bletchley Park. It stated that the warship "had been sunk with the aid of Freya reports".

'Freya' was the codename for some device. Her name was plucked from Norse mythology and Dr Reg Jones, head of scientific intelligence at the Air Ministry, had already heard of "Freya Gerät" (Freya apparatus).

Jones writes in *Most Secret War* that seeing a mention of "Freya-Meldung" on 5 July (Freya reporting) he had bought a book on myths from Foyle's and found that "Freya was the Nordic Venus who had not merely sacrificed, but massacred her honour to gain possession of a magic necklace, Brisinga-men. The necklace was guarded by Heimdall, the watchman of the Gods, who could see a hundred miles by day or night."

The last phrase is the crucial one—making Heimdall a wholly appropriate code for radar, though rather too obvious. Freya was chosen, by association, in its place.

Twelve days before the loss of *Delight*, Jones had used this reasoning to predict the existence "of a coastal chain and detecting system with a range of a hundred miles". The sinking of the destroyer removed any possibility that Freya was detecting associated objects in the sky—for *Delight* had neither balloon protection nor a fighter escort.

"The apparatus must have been able to detect her directly," Jones concluded. "It appeared to be sited near the village of Auderville on the Hague peninsula north-west of Cherbourg, but it had to be very different from our own coastal chain stations, since it was completely undetectable on the best air photographs that we possessed of the area.

"This confirmed the idea that Freya was a fairly small apparatus, which had already been suggested by the fact that it had been set up so quickly after the Germans had occupied the Channel coast."

The story would resume on 24 February 1941.

29 July   **Admiralty bans Channel convoys and destroyers.**

The English Channel has been placed off-limits to destroyers in daytime as a result of today's loss of HMS *Delight*. It brings to four the losses of destroyers in the mid-Channel area this month—the others being HMS *Brazen*, *Codrington* and *Wren*.

Thirty-six merchant ships have also been sunk, five of them when Convoy CW8 was mauled by Junkers 87 'Stuka' dive-bombers. As a result of these awful losses the Admiralty suspended coastal convoys in the English Channel, as from two days ago.

Invasion 1940. Southern Command had its Camouflage School at Poole and practised with the defences at Canford Cliffs. These are at the end of Shore Road (seen before the building of the promenade and cafe).

July **Poole camouflage requests rejected.**

The Air Ministry has turned down requests from Dorset County Council for the camouflaging of prominent buildings in Poole, saying that this would make attacks more likely: "Low flying aircraft would easily see these buildings even if they were camouflaged, and, if they were seen to be camouflaged they would be taken to be more important targets than they really were. Thus camouflaging them would attract attack rather than avoid it."

July **'British Resistance' guerrilla hideouts in Dorset.**

Thirty-two underground hideouts have been established secretly by the Royal Engineers in woods and commons scattered through the Dorset countryside to conceal the weapons, explosives and food necessary for Auxiliary Units of British Resistance to operate behind German lines in the event of an invasion.

This is considered most likely to take place on the sandy beaches between Studland and Hurst Castle, with secondary landings perhaps in Lyme Bay. The plan is that these élite units of the Home Guard should have the local knowledge and connections to sustain a campaign of harassment against the occupying forces. Each unit is under the control of regular Army officers to ensure the necessary level of expertise and professionalism.

July **Fascist Dorset landowner interned.**

A major Dorset landowner has been arrested and imprisoned with the round-up of pre-war members and supporters of Sir Oswald Mosley's British Union of Fascists. He is Captain George Henry Lane Fox Pitt-Rivers of Hinton St Mary, who was last in the news when he opposed the billeting of city children in rural Dorset. Pitt-Rivers is being held under Defence Regulation 18b.

Footnote By August there were 1,600 detained in prison without trial; three out of four of them were Mosley's members. All but four hundred would be released during the winter of 1940–41. Pitt-Rivers was among those who were still held.

July **Dorset Heavy Regiment redesignated.**

The Dorset Heavy Regiment of the Royal Artillery, which includes the gunners responsible for the defence of the naval anchorage at Portland, has been reformed as the 522nd (Dorset) Coast Regiment. They have 9.2 inch guns in the batteries at East Weares, four hundred feet up on the Portland cliffs, and on the other side of Weymouth Bay at Upton Fort, to the east of Osmington Mills.

1940. Opposite and below. 9.2 inch anti-ship gun being emplaced and loaded at East Weares, Portland, by 102 Coast Defence Battery of the 522nd (Dorset) Coast Regiment. 'Ever ready,' ran the original captioning. 'Men on duty keep watch as a searchlight sweeps the sea.' The gun then opened fire across the night.

July   Home Guard cover-up the Cerne Giant.

Members of the Home Guard have dragged scrub and branches across the hillside north of Cerne Abbas to cover the famous 180-feet high chalk-cut figure of a naked man that is etched into the turf of the Dorset Downs. It was considered that this ancient curiosity, known as the Cerne Giant, might be of practical use as a navigation marker for German aircraft, particularly any making northward across the Dorset coast from Portland towards Bristol.

Likewise the prominent marble obelisk on Ballard Down, above Swanage, has been toppled.

Local authority workmen are busily digging up milestones and taking down road signs so that German invaders will not find their routes spelt out on the ground. It will still, however, be relatively easy to identify the major conurbation as it would be impractical to remove all clues, such as the hundreds of cast-iron drain covers that proclaim "County Borough of Bournemouth".

July   Boulogne award for Dorset hero.

Major 'Billy' Fox-Pitt, who was awarded the Military Cross for gallantry whilst commanding a Welsh Guards company at Ginchy on the Somme in 1916, has been gazetted for the Distinguished Service Order in recognition of his leadership and example in holding out against strong German armoured attacks for two days in the attempt to defend Boulogne. The two battalions of the 20th Guards Brigade had been sent to France at short notice.

Footnote   Fox-Pitt would be ADC to the King, 1945-47, and in retirement in Dorset he hunted with the Blackmore Vale until the age of seventy-nine; he died in 1988 at the age of ninety-two.

4 August   Poole flying boat crosses the Atlantic.

The Short Sunderland 'Empire' flying boat *Clare*, which took off early yesterday from the 'Trots' in Poole Harbour as the water runways are known, today landed on the east coast of the United States and thereby resumed the transatlantic service. She carried three American government VIPs and will return with ferry pilots.

The flying boat's pilots are Captains J.C. Kelly Rogers and G.R.B. Wilcockson, with crewmen White, Burgess and Rotherham.

Footnote   See 14 August 1940 for *Clare* pictured on her return.

5 August   French general leaves Poole to arrange a coup.

General Edgard de Larminat, the high commissioner of Free French Africa, has flown from Poole in the 'Empire' flying boat *Clyde* to arrange a coup d'état in the Vichy controlled French colonies in the Congo basin. They are flying via Lagos to Leopoldville in the Belgian Congo from where the general and his staff officers will begin their programme for the repossession of French Equitorial Africa.

Footnote The Free French army, led by General Carretier, walked back to power after taking Brazzaville by complete surprise.

8 August   More mines laid off Dorset.

The Channel shipping lanes have been subject to further German minelaying in the past thirty-six hours. The Raumboote of the enemy's 3rd Mine Laying Flotilla have been active off Dorset, protected by Schnellboote of the 5th E-boat Flotilla.

1940. Portland's
Home Guard, in
Easton Drill Hall.

1940–44. Bere Regis Air Raid Precautions wardens, in their later uniforms of the Wareham and Purbeck Civil Defence Corps, photographed beside the pavilion on the village recreation ground in North Street. They are (front row) Ken Woolfies, Charles Kellaway, Evelyn Lys, Jock Strang, Gertrude Miller, Fred Lys, Edward Hewitt, (centre row) Frank Applin, Henry Hann, Charles Davis, Jack Legg, Louis Joyce, 'Nobby' Bartlett, Harry Pitfield, (back row) Denis Skinner, Leslie Barnes, Percival Pitfield and Michael Miller.
Kellaway would give the air raid warning on his whistle from an ancient Morris Minor. He used a handbell for the all-clear.

8 August   More losses as another convoy tries to get through.

Convoy CW9 has broken through the enemy's blockade of the English Channel, westwards from the Thames, but with severe losses. Three ships were sunk and one damaged by E-boat attacks off the Isle of Wight and two destroyers were called out from Portsmouth to give help. An air attack by sixty planes was intercepted and driven off but the convoy then fell victim to a second wave of more than 130 enemy aircraft off Bournemouth.

Here three more ships were lost and thirteen damaged. The Germans lost fourteen aircraft.

Spitfire R6811 of 152 Squadron, from Warmwell, was damaged in the dog-fights and headed for home. It crashed at Bestwall, on the east side of Wareham, and was burnt-out, but the pilot, Sergeant Robinson, had a lucky escape. Another Spitfire of 152 Squadron was successfully brought down by Pilot Officer Roland Beamont in a field at Spyway, on top of the Purbeck cliffs at Langton Matravers.

10 August   Bournemouth cyclist killed in air raid.

Bombs fell last night on Bournemouth. At 47 Alyth Road, which was demolished at 23.24 hours, the lady of the house fell back into her bath as the roof collapsed.

Less fortunate was a cyclist in Meon Road where five high explosive bombs dropped at about 06.30 this morning. He was killed. Thirty-eight houses suffered damage.

11 August   Air raids at Weymouth and Portland.

Portland Harbour and Weymouth again came under enemy air attack today.

11 August   Five Me 110s claimed by Warmwell's Spitfires.

Five twin-engined Me110s of the Lufwaffe's ZG/2 were accounted for this morning by the Spitfires of 609 Squadron from RAF Warmwell, in a fast-moving action that swirled high above Portland from 10.10 to 10.35.

Pilot Officer David Moore Crook, flying R6986 (PR-S), records in his log: "We took off at 09.45 and after patrolling round Warmwell saw some smoke trails out to sea. Investigated and found a large force of Me110s flying round in circles at 25,000 feet, Hurricanes already engaging them. We all attacked separately. I climbed well above the scrum and then saw an Me110 some distance from the others. I dived on him and fired a burst from the rear quarter which missed as I could not get sufficient deflection. I then came into very close range and fired. I hit him and he did a climbing turn to the right, stalled and started to turn over. I narrowly missed colliding with him and did not see him again. Found myself with Messerschmitts all around so dived away as hard as I could and returned to Warmwell."

Most of the kills fell into the sea, but one crashed near Swanage. It has been credited to Flying Officer John Dundas, whose Spitfire, R6769, took shots through the starboard wing and rudder from the gunner of the stricken Me110.

11 August   Junkers lands on Portland.

Flying Officer Strickland, in a Hurricane of 213 Squadron from Exeter, bagged a twin-engined Junkers Ju88 (B3+DC) in style this afternoon. The German pilot almost succeeded in bringing his crippled bomber down upon "The Castles" as the Portlanders call the flat top of the 275 feet cliffs at Blacknor Fort, Portland. This spot overlooks Lyme Bay from the centre of the western side of the stony island.

The sheer cliffs and the rocks were outmanoeuvred but not the fort's line of telephone

1940. Portland's submarines slipped away to war, particularly the Mediterranean theatre, as the home-base became inoperable for torpedo training or repairs. Many of the latter are these days carried out at sea, from parent ships such as HMS 'Forth' (left). Cast-iron ingots are seen running in her foundry. Rejoining the silent service is His Majesty's Submarine 'Thunderbolt' (above). She last served as HMS 'Thetis' — until 2 June 1939 when she sank in Liverpool Bay in the worst peacetime submarine tragedy. Ninety men drowned. Restored, refitted and renamed, 'Thunderbolt' is joining the British Mediterranean Fleet. Sir Andrew Cunningham's forces chased the Italian Fleet out of the eastern Mediterranean in July 1940, preventing Mussolini from landing an expeditionary army in Syria.

wires. These retracted the undercarriage. The pilot was seriously hurt as the aircraft bounced to a halt but his three comrades had only superficial injuries.

By the end of the day there was also serious damage to 213 Squadron. Two Hurricanes had been lost, with their pilots. Two other Hurricanes had made forced landings though both their pilots were unhurt and the machines repairable.

Sergeant Snowdon brought P3585 down on to C Range at Lulworth Camp. He had been hit by return fire from a Bf110 which he was shooting down. The second damaged Hurricane managed to limp back to Exeter.

Hurricane P3598 of 87 Squadron also crash-landed in Dorset, not quite making it to Warmwell Aerodrome, and injured Pilot Officer McLure in the process. His aircraft will fly again.

12 August   **Heinkel shot down at Sturminster Marshall.**

A Heinkel He111 (1G+AC), heading homeward via Dorset's Stour valley after a raid on Bristol docks, was intercepted at 02.00 hours today by a British night-fighter. The bomber was raked with cannon fire and the pilot, who has been identified as a "Gruppe Kommandeur", parachuted to captivity along with his four crewmen.

Their aircraft crashed in flames at Sturminster Marshall.

13 August **Warmwell Spitfires have five Dorset kills.**

Eagle Day: the Luftwaffe's Adler Tag attack of nearly three hundred aircraft against military targets in central southern England has been routed. At noon a Bf110 (L1 + FZ) crashed in flames at Swalland Farm, Kimmeridge. The two crew baled out and were taken prisoner.

Warmwell's Spitfires were scrambled at 15.30 hours. "Achtung, Achtung, Spit und Hurri", Pilot Officer David Moore Crook, flying R6699 (PR-L), heard repeatedly as he approached the German formations.

One of the twenty-seven Junkers Ju87 'Stuka' dive-bombers of II Gruppe Stukageschwader 2 that had been targeted on Middle Wallop Airfield, Hampshire, was shot down between Portesham and Rodden at 16.00 hours, killing its two crewmen, Feldwebel Linderschmid and Gefreiter Eisold. The kill was claimed by Flight Lieutenant Derek Boitel-Gill of 152 Squadron. At the same time Pilot Officer Crook of 609 Squadron sent an Me109 smoking into the cloud and descended to see the debris of a crash near the Hardy Monument. This, however, was that of another enemy aircraft, which came down two hundred yards from the railway station at Grimstone, killing both crew. They were Feldwebel Erich Haach of Krossen, and Gefreiter Henrich Myer, or Meir, from Oberhausen. The two crew and the discovery of an unexploded 250 kilogram bomb in the wreckage confirm that it was a 'Stuka' or an Me110 fighter-bomber.

None of the enemy aircraft deployed today reached its target.

As for the Messerschmitt Bf109 E1 escort fighters being chased by 609 Squadron, as they turned for the coast short of fuel, Crook's kill ended up in Poole Harbour. The pilot, Unteroffizier Wilhelm Hohenseldt, was rescued and made a prisoner of war. Another was shot down into the sea off Weymouth. Its pilot, Leutnant Heinz Pfannschmidt, was also saved and taken prisoner. This kill was claimed by Pilot Officer T. Nowierski, who is avenging the rape of Poland.

The Hurricanes of 238 Squadron, from Middle Wallop, also took part in the dog-fights but two were lost in the process. One of the pilots, Sergeant Little, was driven away unhurt after P3805 had crashed at Bredy Farm, a mile east of Burton Bradstock.

There were few lucky Germans, but the day's most fortunate Briton was Flying Officer John Dundas of 609 Squadron from Warmwell. His Spitfire, N3113, narrowly pulled clear from collision with a 'Stuka' and in the process he found his oil system ruptured by a bullet from its gunner. His propeller stopped. Dundas skilfully used his height, from off Portland, to glide down to a successful forced-landing at Warmwell Aerodrome.

Footnote Eyewitness E.G. Read of Stratton recalled the Grimstone crash for me in 1981: "My neighbours and I had been watching an aerial battle and machine gun ammunition clips had fluttered down around us. Suddenly there was a bloodcurdling banshee wail. It was heart stopping as it approached us.

"Right over our heads came the stricken plane [from the north-east]. There was dense black smoke pouring from its starboard engine [the Stuka was single-engined, so if remembered correctly this indicates an Me110] and the two young airmen were clearly visible. They had just seconds to live. Later came the news that a German plane had crashed behind Grimstone viaduct. We went there immediately on our bikes, but a sentry was there on guard with fixed bayonet. Beneath two white parachutes were the crumpled bodies of the airmen.

"The next day the sentry was gone and we went souvenir hunting. I pulled off a small electrical bakelite plug that was stamped 'Made in England'. The two young fliers were interred in a green unploughed curve at the side of a field. Later two ornately carved and inscribed wooden crosses appeared at the spot. The bodies remained there from that sunny afternoon

1940. Wave of Junkers Ju87s, the dive-bombers generally known as 'Stukas'—short for 'Sturzkampfbomber'. On 4 July 1940 they sank the 'Foylebank' anti-aircraft gunship in Portland Harbour and on 13 August were back for the Adler Tag ('Eagle Day') attacks on military targets in central southern England. That day's events were a setback for the fearsome reputation they had gained, which pre-dated the Second World War and had been established by cinema newsreels of its preview, the Spanish Civil War.

in 1940 until the late 1960s when they were reburied at the Brookwood military cemetery, Surrey.

"I found their crosses in a dilapidated shed at Frampton churchyard in 1964. The galvanised roof was holed and they were covered in wet lichen. Since then both shed and crosses have disappeared. So, too, has my souvenir component, which I inadvertently threw out with an unwanted box of oddments before moving house in 1978."

1940. One of ours. A Warmwell Spitfire approaches the Observer Corps post at Poundbury Camp, on the edge of Dorchester.

13 August **An entry in the Dorchester Observer Corps log.**

Time: 16.35. Location: Poundbury Camp, north-west of the town. Area of activity: South of sector R4, Dorchester. Report: "Confirmed hostile and friendly pilots approaching the post. Much machine gun and cannon fire. Fierce contest going on. Plane shot down believed Me110, another plane down, much confused sound-plotting and heavy firing for a considerable period. One plane believed friendly, flying low east. Believed forced landing this side of the Maiden Castle House and in neighbourhood of the Fever Hospital."

Footnote John Norman of the Royal Observer Corps remembered that emergency Spitfire touch-down for me in 1980: "It landed in the field at Maiden Castle Farm at the back of the cottages and I cycled over in time to see it take off."

14 August **Second transatlantic crossing from Poole.**

The Air Ministry Under-secretary, Harold Balfour, is flying today from Poole to the United States on the second wartime transatlantic flying boat crossing by *Clare*.

Footnote The flying boat was back in Poole on the 18th. Balfour bought three Boeing 314s—'Clipper' flying boats—from the Americans. These long-range boats will be delivered to British Overseas Airways at Poole early next year.

1940. Spitfire trails in the sky over Dorchester, photographed from the Observer Corps lookout at Poundbury Camp.

August 1940. Flying boat 'Clare' on her return to Poole from the first wartime transatlantic air crossing.

15 August   'Many enemy aircraft'—Spitfire pilot swims home.

Nine Spitfires of 152 Squadron, from Warmwell Aerodrome, were at 15,000 feet above Portland at 17.15 hours when they heard over the radio: "Many enemy aircraft approaching Portland from the south."

Two minutes later a cloud of black specks became visible in mid-Channel, at about the same height as the British fighters. There were an estimated one hundred or more enemy aircraft, with Junkers Ju87s in tight V-formations each of three 'Stukas', surrounded by Me110 escorts.

The Spitfires climbed to 18,000 feet in a wide circle that brought them out of the sun to descend through the German ranks about five miles south of Portland Bill. The resulting mêlée, which was joined by Hurricanes from Exeter, had a mixed outcome.

Ralph ('Bob') Wolton of 152 Squadron was shot down in the engagement with the 'Stukas' and fell out of his Spitfire seconds before it crashed into the sea. He managed to swim to one of the offshore marker buoys of the Chesil Beach bombing range, from which he was rescued by an RAF launch from Lyme Regis.

15 August   A pilot dies a hero at Abbotsbury.

Twenty-seven year old Squadron Leader Terence Lovell-Gregg of 87 Squadron, from Exeter, failed in a desperate attempt to make a crash landing in The Fleet lagoon late this afternoon. The Hurricane came in blazing from over the sea but was brought into a controlled

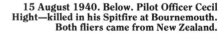

15 August 1940. Left. Squadron Leader Terence Lovell-Gregg—killed in his Hurricane at Abbotsbury.

15 August 1940. Below. Pilot Officer Cecil Hight—killed in his Spitfire at Bournemouth. Both fliers came from New Zealand.

descent for a forced landing. P3215 then clipped a tree beside Abbotsbury Swannery and its wounded pilot fell to his death.

Roland Beamont, one of the Warmwell Spitfire pilots, returned with the story of how Lovell-Gregg had led his squadron into the midst of a mass of German aircraft at 18,000 feet over the English Channel: "We saw the 'Beehive' almost straight ahead at the same height, and with his Hurricanes, Lovell-Gregg flew straight at the centre of the formation without hesitation or deviation in any way."

One hundred and twenty enemy aircraft were heading towards Portland. Lovell-Gregg was a quiet pre-war professional, from Marlborough in New Zealand, who had taught many of the emergent generation of fliers. His courage was never in any doubt, though he had led his squadron for only a month, since 12 July. The pilots knew him as 'Shovel'.

There were only four of them with him when they scrambled at 16.00 hours today. Five Hurricanes were all the air-worthy machines that 87 Squadron could muster. Undaunted by the adverse odds of fifteen-to-one that loomed in front, Lovell-Gregg asked the impossible of his men: "Come on chaps, let's surround them!"

Two of the other Hurricanes were also crippled but their pilots lived. P3465 crash-landed at Symondsbury, near Bridport, and R2687 was forced down at Field Barn Farm, beside the marshland of Radipole Lake at Weymouth.

Footnote William Dunford, then an Abbotsbury schoolboy, described for me how he put out the flames on the Squadron Leader's burning body. "Lovell-Gregg's Hurricane was shot down in flames, at about 6 to 6.30 pm, but he recovered control to put the plane into a perfect glide and attempted to land in The Fleet lagoon at Abbotsbury Swannery. He came low over a small wood but was not quite high enough. The underside of the Hurricane hit the top of an oak tree, and Lovell-Gregg was thrown out of the cockpit. The plane went on through the trees and crashed.

"With another schoolboy I ran to the spot where the pilot had fallen. He was badly shot about and burning. We put out the flames with two buckets of water. About two hours later a truck came from Warmwell and we were then told the flier's identity. Though he had those wounds, I am sure, had he made it into the water, that he would have survived."

Lovell-Gregg is buried in Warmwell churchyard.

15 August   Spitfire crashes at Bournemouth.

The eastern side of the Middle Wallop Sector also saw action today with a formation of bombers approaching Bournemouth. The Spitfires of 234 Squadron were scrambled at Middle Wallop at 17.05 hours and intercepted the bombers, which were heading homeward, over the town. A sustained air battle took place at 4,000 feet, during which Spitfire R6988 was hit by fire from one of the German rear gunners.

It spiralled into Leven Avenue, to the west of Meyrick Park golf links, leaving a crater and wreckage across a wide area. One of the wings fell on a hedge in Walsford Road. Pilot Officer Cecil Hight fell from the aircraft but his parachute did not open. The New Zealander had been seriously wounded and apparently passed out before he could pull the rip-cord. His body was found in Mr and Mrs Hoare's garden; his stomach had been ripped open by machine-gun bullets.

Footnote The town has named Pilot Hight Road in his memory. Cecil Hight was the only allied airman to die over Bournemouth. He is buried at Boscombe and a memorial tablet was unveiled at St Peter's church in the town centre on 7 April 1943.

Mr and Mrs Hoare's house was again to be visited by the war. Ian McQueen records in *Bournemouth St Peter's* that it was hit by a German bomb. Canon Hedley Burrows recalled that it was the house where Hight's Spitfire had crashed.

"The dear old man, Mr Hoare died," Canon Burrows said, but then they heard Mrs Hoare. "Who is that?" she asked. "I am Canon Burrows; keep still; they are going to get you out."

"Canon Burrows," she repied, "how kind of you to come and see me today."

16 August   152 Squadron's two firsts, and a doubtful.

Pilot Officer Roland Beamont, flying a Spitfire with 152 Squadron from Warmwell Aerodrome, has scored his squadron's first kills with two Me109s brought down over the Isle of Wight at lunchtime.

In the evening, as the second patrol of the day was about to head for home, two Heinkel He111s were spotted below, at 3,000 feet over the Solent. The rear one was attacked at 18.15 hours by Pilot Officer Eric Simcox Marrs. 'Boy' is his nickname; he is aged nineteen.

As the Heinkel came out of a bank of mist he shot it up: "I left it with smoke coming from both engines and my own machine covered in oil from it. I don't think it could have got home and I'm pretty sure it didn't."

His claim is not being accepted, because a radio transmission was misunderstood, and no one else in the squadron had seen the action. Marrs, however, is in no doubt, and he is writing to his father: "I am counting that as my first."

8 December 1940, the drawing is dated. The subject is Pilot Officer Eric 'Boy' Marrs of 152 Squadron, who flew a Spitfire from Warmwell. He would become the station's hero and win the Distinguished Flying Cross—which would save his life by taking him to London for the day. But there is a saying about those 'whom the gods love'.

18 August   Warmwell's 'Boy' Marrs has his first confirmed kill.

Formations of more than a hundred Ju87 'Stuka' dive-bombers, escorted by Messerschmitt Me109 fighters, crossed the Channel to attack the radar station at Poling and aerodromes at Ford, Thorney Island and Gosport. Eleven Spitfires of 152 Squadron were scrambled from Warmwell.

The Spitfires dived from 4,000 feet on the 'Stukas' as they swept back to sea after dropping their bombs. Pilot Officer Eric 'Boy' Marrs claimed a kill, his first that would be confirmed:

"We dived after them and they went down to about a hundred feet above the water. Then followed a running chase out to sea. The evasive action they took was to throttle back and do steep turns to right and left so that we would not be able to follow them and would overshoot. There were, however, so many of them that if one was shaken off the tail of one there was always another to sit on. I fired at about six and shot down one. It caught fire in the port wing petrol tank and then went into the sea about three hundred yards further on."

The 'Stukas' were from I and II Gruppen of Stukageschwader 77. They suffered sixteen losses as 43, 601 and 602 Squadrons joined 152 Squadron in the action. The Me109 escort fighters were routed by the Spitfires of 234 Squadron from Middle Wallop.

18 August Marrs goes 'Tally-ho' again.

17.25 hours. On his second combat patrol of the day, Eric 'Boy'Marrs of 152 Squadron from Warmwell Aerodrome has led the three Spitfires of Blue Section in a "Tally-ho" after a German Dornier Do17 which was flying towards Portland.

The interception took place from 16,000 feet and the bomber dropped into cloud at about 5,000 feet. Marrs has emptied his guns and the third Spitfire is claiming a share in the kill.

Footnote Apparently it was not that decisive and the bomber managed to return to France.

19 August Enigma decrypt gives warning of Warmwell attack.

01.52 hours."From a reliable source, information has been received of an impending attack on Warmwell aerodrome this morning. Aircraft are to be ready to leave at 07.00 hours." [From a German 'Enigma' radio signal decoded by the Government Code and Cipher School, at Bletchley Park, Buckinghamshire].

Battle of Britain. 1940.
Somewhere in the west Dorset countryside
one hot summer day, with villagers young
and old and at least one dog swarming
over the wreckage of a German fighter.
The scene is in the Frome valley,
photographed by the Observer Corps
unit from Poundbury Camp, Dorchester.

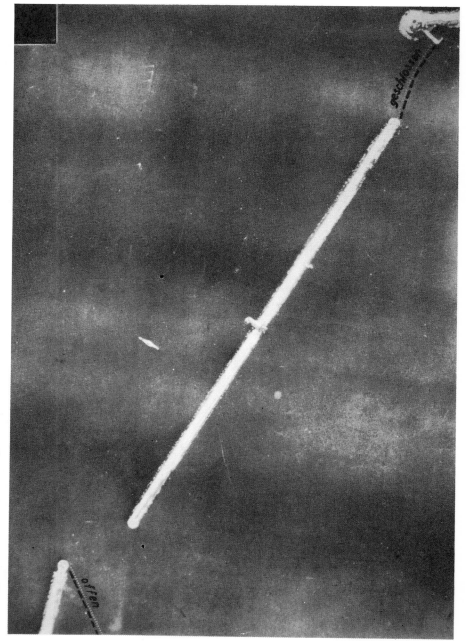

1940. German reconnaissance photograph of 'Netzsperren von Portland'. The central breakwater of Portland Harbour is seen from the north-west. The East Ship Channel (top) is blocked by anti-submarine nets. The North Ship Channel (bottom) is open but also has a line of nets that could be closed.

1940. Portland. Opposite. Luftwaffe photograph of its bombs raining down on the fort guarding the East Ship Channel into Portland Harbour (east is at the top of the picture and north to the left). Note the anti-submarine nets, the floats of which show as a double line of dots extending towards the North Eastern Breakwater. These are the 'geschlossen' [closed] nets of the other German photograph (above, top right).

1940. 5th Battalion of the Northants Regiment put the Bren gun carrier amongst the turkeys during a little mock warfare in the Christchurch countryside.

1940. Poole. School for Junior Leaders with unarmed combat practice in the tennis court of the Sandbanks Hotel (name removed in accordance with Defence Regulations). They used dummies for the finer points of bayonet training in the sand dunes at the back (since built on).

1940. 12th Battalion of the Hampshire Regiment in cliff exercises at Hengistbury Head, Bournemouth.

21 August   **Two killed by afternoon bombs at Poole.**

Mrs Pauline Fairbrother of 38 Market Street and Frederick Landrey of 18 South Road were killed this afternoon when a single German raider, a Junkers 88, came in low over the Old Town area of central Poole from Sandbanks. It dropped six bombs. The one that killed Mr Landrey destroyed the National School air-raid shelter, thankfully unoccupied, and the others hit shops and timber stores.

23 August   **Two killed by Lulworth raider.**

A lone German raider attacked Lulworth Camp today a few minutes after the All Clear had sounded. Recruits had resumed their infantry training and were in the open as the aircraft approached. Sergeant J. Thompson shouted to them to get down and stay still.

Eight bombs were dropped on the sportsfield, the ranges and at St Andrew's Farm which is inside the camp complex. Two men were killed and seven injured, the latter including Sergeant Thompson who received severe leg wounds. He had been in the stores when he heard the aircraft approaching and but for his instant and brave response, when he put himself into the line of fire to warn the men, there would have been a greater number of casualties.

1940. Lulworth Camp. Sharpening firing procedures at the Gunnery Wing of the Armoured Fighting Vehicles School to the painted backdrop of Dorset pines and telegraph poles in a realistic representation of the road across the nearby heath.

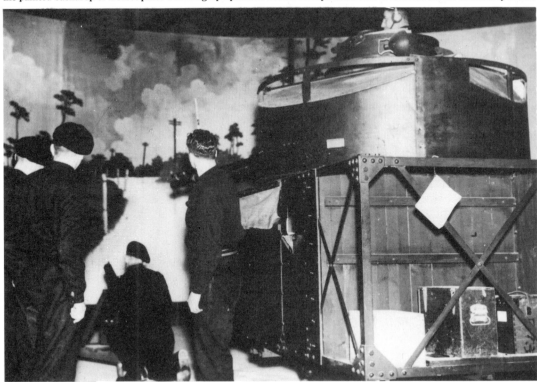

25 August   **Shops bombed at Poole.**

Early this morning a single German bomber attacked the Ashley Road and Constitution Hill area of Upper Parkstone, Poole, destroying three shops and a house. Two people were injured.

25 August **Decoded signals warn of another Warmwell bombing.**

07.40 hours. "It is reliably reported that air attacks are to be expected during the course of today 25th August 1940 at Warmwell, Little Rissington and Abingdon aerodromes and reconnaissances by a single aircraft in the area Southampton-Aldershot-Brighton." [From German 'Enigma' machine-coded radio signals deciphered by the Government Code and Cipher School at Bletchley Park.]

By 17.00 the twelve Warmwell Spitfires of 152 Squadron were airborne. Half an hour later the station was rocked by twenty bombs, which destroyed the sick quarters and damaged hangars. Delayed action bombs went off over the next couple of days. The Spitfires had met Luftflotte 3 over Portland but despite the advance warning it was a more or less even match.

Hurricanes of 213 Squadron joined in the dog-fights from Exeter. They lost two fighters and a third, N2646, crash-landed at Burton Bradstock but is repairable and the pilot, Sergeant Snowden, unhurt.

Sergeant S.R.E. Wakeling of 87 Squadron, aged 21, was killed when his Hurricane plunged in flames at New Barn, on the hillside south of Bradford Peverell, near Dorchester.

There are also a number of German crashes. A Bf109 has crashed on the Chesil Beach at Chickerell and its pilot, Hauptmann Maculan, apparently fell out and drowned. A Bf110 has exploded at Tatton House, between Langton Herring and Buckland Ripers, killing both crew. A Bf109 came down in an adjoining field on Tatton Farm and its pilot escaped with wounds as it was engulfed in flames. He was taken prisoner.

Shortly after 18.00 hours, a Bf110 was reported crashing at Creech Barrow, the conical shaped summit in the Purbeck Hills south of Wareham, and another Bf110 (3M+KH) came down at Priory Farm, East Holme. Both sets of crew parachuted into captivity. A third Bf110 (3M+CH) was taken on by two 609 Squadron Spitfires, those of Squadron Leader H.S. (George) Darley and American volunteer 'Red' Tobin, and put down at East Chaldon, to the west of Lulworth. It became a fireball and both crew died in the explosion.

This Sunday evening, to balance those kills, there is a report that two Spitfires have not returned to RAF Warmwell.

Both pilots have survived, though one is wounded.

Squadron Leader Darley, the commanding officer of 609 Squadron, accounted for the first Messerschmitt to be brought down. In all, the squadron claims eleven, and certainly several Me110 fighter-bombers from II Gruppe ZG/2 and V Gruppe ZG/1 were destroyed, and Me109 fighters from II Gruppe JG/2, though these escorts had succeeded in keeping the Spitfires from the Junkers Ju88 bombers.

Of the Germans on the ground, one has been identified. It was Gefreiter Josef Bröker's Bf109 of JG/53 that belly-landed by a wood at Tatton Farm, Buckland Ripers, to the north of Chickerell. The credit is claimed by Roland Beamont of 152 Squadron who has driven out from Warmwell and arrived "in shirtsleeves and sweat" at the scorched scene of his triumph. Bröker has been taken prisoner of war and will survive his burns.

29 August **Extensive bomb damage at Poole.**

04.00 hours. Though no one has been injured, high explosive and incendiary bombs have caused considerable damage to buildings in the Longfleet, Oakdale and Parkstone suburbs of Poole.

29 August **Bombs miss Christchurch.**

Early this morning incendiary bombs landed near the Priory, Millhams Street and at Queens Avenue in Christchurch. One was on the roof of the air-compressing station. There were also the thuds of high explosive bombs but daylight revealed they had dropped on the north side of the town into heathland and woods at St Catherine's hill. Ten had gone off and one had failed to explode.

August **Burton Bradstock call for Hitler prayers.**

Writing in *The Two Edged Sword*, Adela Curtis, leader of the Christian Contemplatives' Charity at St Bride's Farm,[1] Burton Bradstock,, advises on methods of furthering the war effort through positive prayer: "We are to summon each enemy leader by name. For cumulative effect the message should be spoken three times—Adolf Hitler! Adolf Hitler! Adolf Hitler! Hear the Truth!"

1940. Lulworth Castle grounds. Vickers Mark VI light tanks, on manoeuvres with the Armoured Fighting Vehicles School, Lulworth Camp, were key elements of the thin green line which General Sir Alan Brooke, Commander-in-Chief Home Forces, fielded against the threatened German invasion. Some, however, were being handed over, with the 3rd Hussars, to General Sir Archibald Wavell, Commander-in-Chief Middle East. They would arrive in Egypt in September 1940.

August **Cranborne Chase motor-cycle exercises.**

The 4th Battalion of the Royal Northumberland Fusiliers have been reorganised as a motor-cycle reconnaissance column and are based at Blandford Camp. Their sidecar patrols are seemingly everywhere in the Cranborne Chase villages.

The 2nd and 8th Battalions of the Fusiliers are also in Dorset, dispersed through the Blackmore Vale.

August–October 1940. Opposite. 4th Battalion of the Northumberland Fusiliers—veterans of the British Expeditionary Force, Dunkirk and defending Bournemouth beach—fitted out with motor-cycles and sidecars as a reconnaissance column and training across the rolling downlands of Cranborne Chase.

August–October 1940. From Blandford Camp the 4th Battalion of the Northumberland Fusiliers rode out into the Dorset countryside, with frequent stops to manhandle their Nortons across ditches, trenches and other obstacles.

4 September   Another Warmwell pilot killed.

Spitfire pilot John Barker failed to return to Warmwell Aerodrome today after 152 Squadron had been scrambled for an operational sortie.

5 September   Bomb hits Druitt's House, Christchurch.

Druitt's House, the solicitors' offices and former residence of one of the town's leading families—which produced Montagu James Druitt who was a suspect for Jack the Ripper, the Whitechapel murderer—was destroyed by a German bomb at 01.30 hours this morning. Just after midnight a bomb had dropped on Iford golf course but that one failed to explode.

7 September   Spitfire crashes near Dorchester.

Ralph ('Bob') Wolton, flying at the rear of a flight of Spitfires with 152 Squadron from Warmwell, today lost control of his fighter whilst attempting a sudden dive. He jumped from the falling plane at 13,000 feet though he estimates that it was not until nearly a thousand feet from the ground when he managed to sort out the cords and activate the chute. The Spitfire crashed near Dorchester.
   No enemy plane was involved.

7 September   The great invasion scare.

The German invasion appears to have started. Reports have been received of a seven-mile convoy heading towards the Dorset coast and there is a general flap on that Operation Sealion is taking place and Field Marshal Feodor von Bock is on his way with the victors of Poland, the Wehrmacht's Army Group B. The fuel tanks are to be fired to set the beaches ablaze and an aircraft from Gosport is dropping incendiaries to start them off.
   Troops at Bournemouth have manned the cliffs and keep emphasising that this is not an exercise.
   The Home Guard at the Supermarine aircraft factory in Southampton has been alerted to enemy landings at Portsmouth.

7 September   Invasion expected tonight.

20.07 hours. A national alert has been issued by the War Office: 'Condition Cromwell'. An invasion is regarded as imminent and probable within twelve hours.

   Footnote Nothing happened! One set of 'Fougasse' tanks ignited a beach but the plane was recalled to Gosport before it set alight to any more. There was no landing in Dorset or anywhere else. Despite that, invasion fears had reached fever-pitch and not only in the popular imagination, for aerial reconnaissances were showing concentrations of ships and barges in harbours from Brest to Calais.

10 September   Fourteen bombs at Christchurch.

Fourteen bombs landed in the Christchurch area last night, at about midnight, fracturing water mains and bringing down telephone wires. There was serious blast damage to Hoburne Farm. Six of the bombs fortunately exploded harmlessly on Chewton Common.

14 September   Another Warmwell pilot killed.

A further fatal casualty has been inflicted upon RAF Warmwell, taking the life of Flying Officer C.O. Hinks.

1940. German air reconnaissance photograph of the northern part of Portland Harbour. The coastal features (bottom to top) are the Chesil Beach, Small Mouth and the Ferrybridge, Wyke Regis, Bincleaves and the Northern Arm of the Breakwater, the Nothe promontory and Weymouth Harbour. Ships are identified by numbers and anti-aircraft gun sites by letters.

The picture also shows a munitions factory—Whitehead Torpedo Works, on the Weymouth side of the Small Mouth opening at the Ferrybridge. It occupies the land nearest the shore, between the road (left bridge) and the railway line (right bridge).

15 September Warmwell's Spitfires defend London.

The Spitfires of 609 Squadron from Warmwell were drawn into the air defence of London today as the Battle of Britain reached its climax. Total claims for the day were 186 enemy aircraft shot down.

Footnote The Air Ministry was warned by its own intelligence department that 'kill' claims were being overstated and that no more than 76 planes could have been destroyed on 15 September. Post-war examination of German records showed that even this was exaggerated; the real figure was 62.

For all that it was a victory. Air Chief Marshal Sir Hugh Dowding had handled his forces with precision and economy. They had not been wasted on pointless patrols. A combination of radar and decoded German radio traffic meant that the sectors that were going to have a quiet day—as with Middle Wallop and Warmwell on the 15th—could provide planes for an area where the resident defenders would be outnumbered. Dowding's achievement was to deny the Luftwaffe its one prerequisite for winning the Battle of Britain. This was done by ensuring there were always planes in reserve and that something could be done about the following day's attack.

Göring was frustrated by this and had ordered his commanders: "You must bring the RAF up to battle."

15 September **Heinkels turn back from Portland Bill.**

Intercepted by a flight of six Spitfires of 152 Squadron from RAF Warmwell, led by Pilot Officer Eric 'Boy' Marrs, thirty Heinkel He111 bombers dropped their bombs from 16,000 feet over Portland Bill and turned back towards France.

The Spitfires harried them for ten miles, claiming to have shot down two and damaged others. Marrs writes: "If we had had the whole squadron up we could have broken their formation and knocked down quite a number. The extraordinary part about this raid was that there was no fighter escort."

15 September **Cattistock carillon destroyed by fire.**

14.30 hours. The tall 1873-built tower of Cattistock church has been gutted by fire, destroying its famous carillon of thirty-five bells. The village will miss the tunes. Officially the cause is not known, but locally it has been blamed on a cigarette discarded by a member of the Home Guard who was in the tower for fire-watching.

17 September **Marrs gets a Junkers but loses his 'Old Faithful'.**

Pilot Officer Eric 'Boy' Marrs was leading Blue Section of 152 Squadron, from Warmwell Aerodrome, over Portland early this afternoon. He was then told to rise to 20,000 feet on a course of 350 degrees, which eight minutes later was changed to 280 degrees. This brought him in sight of a lone Junkers Ju88 bomber above Shepton Mallet, Somerset.

"Tally-ho" he called over the radio as he led the three Spitfires in line astern. The first burst from his guns hit the radiator of the bomber's starboard engine and had it streaming with white ethylene glycol coolant. The bomber descended into thick cloud, heading east, and would crash near Imber, Wiltshire, only three miles from Dauntsey's which was Marrs's old school.

Marrs, however, then suffered engine failure. 'Old Faithful', in which the young pilot had flown 130 hours, was coaxed down from 12,000 feet on to the concrete runways of a disused aerodrome that had been partly obstructed to prevent German landings.

A bullet had smashed the air cooler and caused the Merlin engine to lose its oil. A maintenance squad removed the Spitfire by road and Marrs will never fly it again; probably it will go back into service with a training unit.

17 September **Operation Sealion postponed indefinitely.**

Hitler today postponed Operation Seelöwe [Sealion], the planned invasion of England, which should give the country's nerves a reprieve until next spring. Winston Churchill has read out a deciphered German Enigma machine-coded radio message to the Chiefs of Defence Staff—a minor order of huge significance, for the dismantling of loading equipment on Dutch airfields. Churchill refers to Sealion as Operation Smith, to lessen the risk of compromising the Enigma intercepts that revealed its name.

19 September   Bournemouth Garrison stood down.

With the abandonment of Operation Sealion any immediate prospect of a German invasion has receded and accordingly the Bournemouth Garrison has stood down. The Garrison Commander has been replaced by a new posting, that of Officer Commanding Troops, Bournemouth.

1940. Badge of Southern Command, adopted after the Dunkirk evacuation, based upon a representation of the constellation of the Southern Cross. A rectangular version appeared on Dorset's military vehicles.

20 September   Steamship sinks in Lyme Bay.

SS *Trito*, a British steam freighter, has sunk after being bombed by German aircraft in Lyme Bay.

25 September   Heinkels shot down at Poole and Studland.

A German mass bombing force of 220 attacking planes and their escorts passed over Portland and flew to the Bristol Channel coast where they turned between the islands Steep Holm and Flat Holm and made an approach across the water towards the Bristol Aeroplane Company's works at Filton. This was devastated by 350 bombs and from 15,000 feet the aerodrome rippled with flashes.

On the way home, however, the raiders were harried by the RAF. Five aircraft were brought down and a further three had to crash-land in France. The two shot down in Dorset were both claimed by Hurricanes of 238 Squadron from Middle Wallop. One Heinkel 111 (markings

25 September 1940. Wreckage of 'Underwood' and the Branksome Park Heinkel.

G1 + LR) ploughed into 'Underwood', a house at Westminster Road, Branksome Park, and all but one of its five crewmen were killed.

The second Heinkel 111 (G1 + BH) crash-landed at Westfield Farm, Studland. Josef Attrichter, the flight mechanic, was taken from the wreckage but died half an hour later. The other four crewmen had aching backs from the impact but survived. Wine waiter Theo Janku took them prisoner with the aid of an unloaded Home Guard rifle and relieved them of their Lugers. On seeing there were casualties the Studland villagers then tried to help the Germans and provided cigarettes and tea.

Footnote Later the Heinkel was salvaged and reassembled for Cardiff's war weapons week. Before it was removed from Studland it had been guarded by a detachment of the Suffolk Regiment. "This is war, not a bloody peepshow," one of the sentries snapped at onlookers. It seems to have been from this bomber that a document was found forbidding the use of explosive ammunition against troop concentrations and other human targets.

The burial of the Branksome Park Germans in Parkstone Cemetery, next to graves of British seamen, enraged the Poole Herald which protested that "Nazi murderers and British heroes" were "placed side by side" and a week later felt utterly let down by one of its readers: "Someone has put flowers on the grave!"

26 September **Warmwell pilots in action again.**

Flight Lieutenant Derek Boitel-Gill led a section of 152 Squadron from Warmwell into combat against a formation of Junkers 88s over the sea to the west of the Isle of Wight. One was seen to fall into the water, the kill being the work of Ralph ('Bob') Wolton.

Footnote Boitel-Gill was no mean shot, having been credited with five kills in a week in August. He became Commanding Officer of 152 Squadron early in 1941 and Wing Commander in June. He then lost his life in a flying accident, in July 1941.

27 September **Marrs puts his Junkers down in the Bristol Channel.**

Pilot Officer Eric 'Boy' Marrs from 152 Squadron, flying a Warmwell Spitfire, started what was going to be an active day by finding a lone Junkers Ju88 at 23,000 feet over Somerset. He followed it in a running fight across Exmoor, flying at only fifty feet in places, and had ethylene glycol streaming from both engines of the bomber.

The German pilot headed for the coast, but by a different channel from that over which the Dorset Spitfires usually patrol: "As I expected both engines soon stopped. He made for the south coast of the Bristol Channel and landed about twenty feet from the beach in the water, running his machine up on to the beach. I circled round and watched the crew get out. They waved to me and I waved back, and then hordes of civilians came rushing up. I watched the crew taken prisoner, beat up the beach, and then climbed away."

The tiny seaside resort treated to this excitement was Porlock, west of Minehead. It is unusual for anything to happen here, the village's single claim to fame being "a person from Porlock" who interrupted Samuel Taylor Coleridge as he was recalling and writing down his dream-poem *Kubla Khan* and who remains unknown to this day.

27 September **Lulworth AA gunners get an Me110.**

Anti-aircraft gunners at Lulworth Camp are jubilantly celebrating their first definite kill. The unlucky German aircraft was an Me110 which had come low over the huts. There had been an air raid warning and a red alert was in force. The stricken fighter crashed to ground about a thousand yards from the sea.

27 September **German planes crash all over Dorset.**

This Friday has been the day when German planes crashed all over Dorset, plus Mick Miller and his Spitfire from 609 Squadron. The full account of the abortive raid on the Parnell Aircraft Company—makers of gun turrets—at Yate, near Chipping Sodbury, was told in 1979 by Kenneth Wakefield in his *Luftwaffe Encore*.

Ten fighter-bombers of Erprobungsgruppe 210 from Cherbourg, led by Hauptmann Martin Lutz, had the support of eighty-nine fighters. The Gruppe's aircraft have as their crest a red map of the British Isles superimposed with a yellow ring-type gun sight.

The German bombers, coming in fast over north Bristol on their attacking run at 11,000 feet, were met head on by Murray Frisby in a Hurricane. He scored a hit that damaged Lutz's plane, and the others too were forced to turn. The rest of 504 Squadron, scrambled from Filton, chased after the scattering planes and forced them to jettison their bombs. Escape was now the only German objective.

One of the Bf110s was shot down over Fishponds, Bristol. Another came down at Haydon Hill, near Radstock.

That was 11.45 in the morning. At the same moment, over Bellamy's Farm, Piddletrenthide, there was a similar bang as one of the rearguard manoeuvres went wrong. Pilot Officer Mick Miller, in Spitfire X4107 and leading 609 (West Riding) Squadron—scrambled from Warmwell, where they arrived each morning from Middle Wallop—had collided with a Bf110 (number 3U+FT) at 24,000 feet. Miller and the Messerschmitt's wireless operator, Emil Lidtke, were

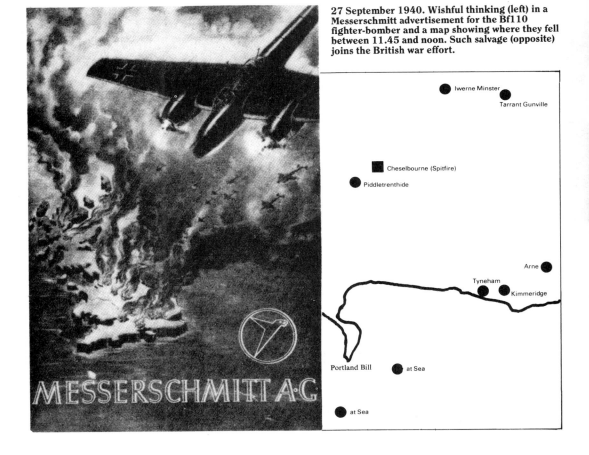

27 September 1940. Wishful thinking (left) in a Messerschmitt advertisement for the Bf110 fighter-bomber and a map showing where they fell between 11.45 and noon. Such salvage (opposite) joins the British war effort.

killed instantly. But the German pilot, Georg Jackstedt, was able to free himself and parachuted (minus his boots) into a field. He was given some lemonade and then taken off by police.

His dead comrade was treated with less respect: "Ralph Wightman recalled that when the body was removed from the wreckage it was left in full view for some hours before someone covered it with a sheet. Later a dispute arose over the burial, one report indicating that the local clergy refused to bury the body; apparently the dead airman was eventually buried beside the hedgerow where he fell." That was the boundary between Bellamy's and Dole's Ash Farm. The Spitfire came down to the east, nearer Cheselbourne. Miller was an Australian.

Another Bf110 (3U+IM) was exploding at about 11.45, at 1,000 feet over Salter's Wood, Middlebere, in Purbeck. It had been attacked by a Spitfire of 152 Squadron, Warmwell's second squadron. In the crashed plane were Arthur Niebuhr and Klaus Deissen. Both were killed.

Equally unfortunate, at 11.50, were the crew of another Bf110, between Tyneham and

Kimmeridge. It was almost certainly aircraft 3U+BD manned by Hans Carschel and Unteroffizier Klose. Luckier—five-minutes later and only a mile away—were the crew of 3U+DS. Fritz Schupp and Karl Nechwatal had been attacked by Spitfires and their port engine was hit and burning. But Schupp successfully brought his plane to a crash landing near Gaulter Gap. It had three 'kill' bars, which as Wakefield says, denoted "victories over RAF aircraft".

At noon, another Bf110 (S9+DU) made a belly landing. It received engine damage over Iwerne Minster and came down at The Beeches, beside the A350. The pilot was Friedrich Ebner, who was unhurt, but the gunner, Werner Zwick, was taken to Shaftesbury Hospital with major wounds.

Another noon crash was at Bussey Stool Farm, near Tarrant Gunville. It was S9+DH—the Bf110 of the attack's leader, Martin Lutz. It had been damaged at Bristol. The plane was travelling at speed but losing height and hit trees before ploughing into the ground. Both Lutz and his radio operator, Anton Schön, were killed. Lutz was aged 27, and had flown with the Condor Legion in the Spanish Civil War.

Two Bf110s were also shot down at mid-day into the sea off Dorset. One was S9+JH, the crew being Gerhard Schmidt and Gerhard Richeter, whose bodies were later recovered. The crew of the other plane, S9+GK (Wilhelm Rössiger and Hans Marx) were never found. They were brought down twenty-five miles south of Portland Bill.

The attacking Spitfire was flown by Noel le C. Agazarian, from Warmwell.

Footnote Agazarian was killed later in the war but he left one of the most evocative of all memorials. His plane, R6915, survived the war and is now suspended over the displays in the

1940. Pilot Officer Noel le C. Agazarian, of 609 Squadron from Warmwell and Middle Wallop. During August and September 1940 he shot down or helped destroy four German aircraft, and damaged another three. He would be posted to the Mediterranean and be killed in North Africa.

1989. Spitfire Mark 1A, R6915, outlived Agazarian and most of her other pilots, continuing to have a good war that was followed by honourable retirement at the Imperial War Museum.

Imperial War Museum, Lambeth Road, London SE1. It dominates the exhibits, as does Dorset's Roman mosaic of Christ in the British Museum.

28 September Armed trawler mined in Lyme Bay.

HMT *Recoil*, an armed trawler crewed by the Royal Navy, has hit a mine and sunk in Lyme Bay.

29 September Christchurch radar establishment hit.

01.07 hours. Six high explosive bombs and a number of incendiaries dropped on to the Ministry of Supply's Air Defence Experimental Establishment which makes radar components at Somerford, Christchurch. Damage, however, is slight. All the fires were put out by 02.48.

7 November 1940. Pilot Officer David Moore Crook, Distinguished Flying Cross, of Warmwell's 609 Squadron, in a pencil sketch by war artist Captain Cuthbert Orde.

30 September Morning and afternoon claims by Crook of Warmwell.

Scrambling at 11.00 hours from Warmwell Aerodrome, in Spitfire X4165, Pilot Officer David Moore Crook led Green Section of 609 Squadron as they swept in a line seawards across the Isle of Purbeck. Pilot Officer Mike Appleby quickly put a Messerschmitt into the sea, but

Crook's action was protracted.

He records the sortie in his log: "We intercepted some Me109s at 23,000 feet over Swanage. The fools tried to escape by diving and we all went down after them. I got up to about 600 mph and easily caught mine, gave it a burst and he crashed into the sea. I then chased another and put him into the sea about twenty-five miles from Cherbourg. It took me a long time to get back to the English coast . . . pleased to see the white cliffs."

Crook was airborne again in the afternoon, leading Green Section in combat against six Me109s, ten miles north of Poole: "I had a very enjoyable few minutes dog-fighting with one and though behind him all the time could not get sights properly on him. Finally he dived for cloud, but I chased him to Weymouth and then gave him a good burst. He turned over to his back and spun into cloud streaming glycol and smoke. I could not claim him as definite as I did not see him actually crash but he certainly never got back to France. This was my best day yet."

Footnote David Crook was awarded the Distinguished Flying Cross on 17 October 1940. His last operation with 609 Squadron, leading it in the Commanding Officer's absence, would be on 8 November 1940, also in Spitfire X4165. He became a flying instructor. Norman Franks records Crook's fate in the book *Wings of Freedom*. On 18 December 1944, at the age of thirty, he was lost over the North Sea, off Aberdeen, whilst flying Spitfire EN662 on a high-level photographic reconnaissance. He left a widow, Dorothy, and a four-year-old son, Nicholas.

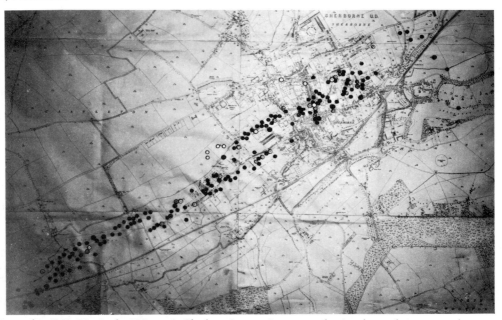

30 September 1940. Pins in the ARP map in Sherborne's operations room, showing the south-west to north-east pattern of bombing across the town. The bombers were flying into the wind. Contemporary claims, reproduced here, were of a total of 300 bombs but subsequent research has shown this was probably a considerable exaggeration. The actual figure may have been nearer one hundred. Counting the pins is of no assistance as the wardens said they ran out of them. For all that, the pictures that follow speak for themselves as to the scale of the devastation.

30 September **Sherborne's 300 bombs in three minutes.**

Yeovil's barrage balloons were raised a few minutes before four o'clock on a warm but cloudy afternoon. In Sherborne the air raid sirens wailed. Three hundred bombs would rain on it in three minutes as a disturbed grouping of fifty German bombers—they had been targeted on

1 October 1940. Sherborne. Looking west along Half Moon Street and showing the result of yesterday's bombing.

Bristol—followed the north side of the railway line into the ancient yellow-stone town of clustered terraces and scholastic and ecclesiastical roofs. In those moments the casualties were numerically less than the damage to the buildings: seventeen dead and thirty-two hospital cases, one of whom was to die. Fortunately the schools had just gone home.

1 October 1940. Sherborne. Phillips and Son's outfitting department (above, left) and the public bar of the Half Moon Hotel. Below is Foster's Infants School on the east side of Tinney's Lane, Newland.

Footnote This was to be just about Sherborne's only direct sacrifice for the duration of hostilities; only four others went to hospital as a result of the war in the period 1939–45. Despite the damage, in a line across the town from Lenthay Common to Coldharbour, it was of little architectural consequence. The Abbey, Sherborne School, the Almshouse, Sherborne Castle and even the older ruined castle survived with only flecks of superficial damage. For all that it was by far the worst air attack of the war on one of Dorset's inland towns.

There was a heroine amongst the debris. Miss Maud Steele, the supervisor of the telephone exchange which was blown apart by a direct hit, stayed calm and ensured that the town's initial calamity reports were sent out by road.

She was to be awarded the George Cross for her pluck; it had been instituted as the "Civilians VC" only a few days previously. The town had 766 damaged buildings, some ten per cent of them devastated, out of a total of 1,700. The sewers as well as the phones were out of action. Blankets had to be brought in by the Red Cross and a council appeal fund, competing with many others, raised £2,200 including contributions from Sherborne in Massachusetts.

For the victims there is a brass plate behind the cross that commemorates the Great War in Half Moon Street, in front of the Abbey precinct:

THOSE WHO DIED IN THE AIR RAID ON SHERBORNE
30 SEPTEMBER 1940

BUTLIN John
DAWE Leonard J.
GARTELL Albertina B.
GOULTER Percy H.D.
HUNT Douglas
IRELAND Henry
JEFFERY William C.
KNOBBS Edward D.
LEGG Horace G.

LE GALLAIS Albert I.E.
LINTERN Arthur J.
MARDEN Elizabeth A.
MORGAN William S.
REASON A.H.
TRASK Barry A.
WARREN Ronald K.
WARREN Robert G.
WARREN Patricia A.

1 October 1940. Sherborne. 'Homemead' on the west side of Acreman Street.

1 October 1940. Sherborne—the morning after. These were homes on Sherborne Urban District Council's estate in Lenthay Road. The first wave of bombs landed here. Nearby, others dropped in the town cemetery, but not that harmlessly as grief was caused by the uncovering of the recent dead. Eighteen other deaths were to follow from the raid. (These houses would be rebuilt to the same 'design'.)

1 October 1940. Sherborne. Crater and debris in the main commercial corner of the town, at the junction of lower Cheap Street with Half Moon Street. Charles Greenham, butcher, and Joseph Frisby, shoe store, are repairable, but only the props prevent the larger premises of Phillips and Son from following the rest of the building into the street.
(It would be rebuilt in stone to match the surviving corner frontage.)

1 October 1940. Sherborne. 'Stonegarth' (above) was Miss Margaret Billinger's home in Newland, at the south end of The Avenue. 'Sedber' (below, now known as 'Rathgar') is on the east side of The Avenue. Opposite is the centre of Cheap Street, with a crater outside T.E. Gillard's hairdressing salon. 'Have Faith In God' the sign reads above the clearance team.

1 October 1940. Sherborne. Cottages and terraced houses at the Knapp, Acreman Street, left in ruins by yesterday's bombs.

In 1984, for the story of the disaster and the town's resilience and recovery, I interviewed the District Air Raid Precautions Controller, Edward J. Freeman MBE who was also the Clerk to the Sherborne Urban District Council between 1936–74. The account was first published in Harold Osment's *Wartime Sherborne*. In it Mr Osment poignantly recalls that one of the dead was a school chum: "There came the cruel realisation, so cruel as to be almost beautiful, that we should never again see, let alone play with Bobby Warren." This is how Mr Freeman recalled the day and its aftermath, from his bungalow beside the fields at Rimpton, to the north of the town:

"The Sherborne raid is being forgotten. Last year I heard a guide at Sherborne Castle say in answer to a question, about whether any bombs had fallen at Sherborne during the war, that he thought there had been one dropped in the town. I interrupted to say that I had been the town's ARP Controller and there had been 300 bombs that fell in three minutes on 30 September 1940.

"At the time I was on the pavement in Yeovil standing in a queue to see a picture—it was one of the few days in the entire war when I was away from my desk. It was my birthday. The thud of the bombs in the east was followed by a pall of black smoke, which could only be from Sherborne, and I drove straight back. It took me twenty minutes to reach the council offices, picking my way through an unimaginable shambles.

"The theory is that the fifty German planes had been on their way to the Bristol Aeroplane Company at Filton" [seriously damaged by an attack five days earlier, on 25 September] "and were intercepted by a squadron of Hurricanes, two of which were brought down each side of Yeovil. The local people thought one of the pilots was a German as they saw his parachute open. The bombers came to us from the southwest, across Lenthay Common, and then they unloaded. We were underneath.

"There were no longer any services at all. No water, no telephones—the exchange had a direct hit—no gas, no electricity, and the sewers and all roads out of the town were blocked.

"One of the miracles was in Newland where Foster's Infants School received a direct hit and had to be pulled down afterwards. It was hit only a quarter of an hour after the children had left. One story I heard, though I cannot vouch for it, was that in The Avenue Miss Billinger climbed from her bath into the open air. Perhaps the strangest damage was in Horsecastles where bombs landed on both sides of the terrace and the outhouses imploded away from the main buildings, which was caused by a bellows effect. Six or eight delayed action bombs went off twelve hours later. One caught us out as it was hidden under debris. The strangest debris came from the midnight bakery next to the Picture Palace in Newland. They had hoarded silver coins which were thrown on to the cinema roof and retrieved by my ARP warden.

"As I plotted the bombs on to our ARP area map and the number climbed into the hundreds I ran out of red pins. It was quite extraordinary that there hadn't been more casualties.

"The worst thing was a direct hit in the cemetery. The coffin of a friend whom we had buried a week earlier was blown out of the ground. My gravediggers disappeared and we did the best we could to clear up with a firm of undertakers from Yeovil.

"Down Lenthay there was terrible damage and I sent the Billeting Officer down on his bike to see how many I had to rehouse and find accommodation for. Ten of our council houses were completely destroyed, and there was damage to all the remaining 108 of them, mainly on a serious scale. To my astonishment when he came back he said, 'No need to worry—people have come forward and offered shelter. Everyone has been given a home somewhere.' It was quite extraordinary what happened there, and it happened all over the town. If ever I have admired the people of Sherborne as a whole it was after the raid.

"I had told the schools they might have to put people up that night, but in the event it wasn't necessary. One little thing, after that raid there was no all-clear as we had no electricity. From then on we had to use rattles and a whistle for air raid sirens.

"The ministry men thought I was exaggerating and panicking when they heard from me on the only emergency phone line we had left, but when they came down they apologised to me. They had never seen such complete devastation in a small country town.

"I took the Regional Commissioner around in my car. Twelve hours later all my tyres were flat, punctured by the glass.

"Opposite Phillips and Son's store, outside the Westminster Bank, an unexploded bomb had fallen, leaving a hole that the bomb disposal team had covered with sandbags. An officer calmly sat down beside these on a lump of stone and lit a cigarette. I showed some concern that we were sitting down beside a bomb. 'If it goes off, we won't know anything about it,' he said.

"'It's a big one' he said, 'but I can't touch it for a fortnight. In the meantime you'll have to evacuate everyone around.' The police and army sealed off the area and we got the stretcher cases out as best we could.

"I had to arrange temporary rationing arrangements because we couldn't get into the butcher's shop.

"A fortnight later that officer came back to me laughing, saying: 'You'll never believe this, Mr Freeman, but it was only a small one. The big hole was because it had gone down a disused well shaft!'

"I was flooded with visits from people in London, Bristol, Reading and the cities, and had to explain how we got out of difficulties. It is surprising how the help came that we needed; there was a wonderful spirit everywhere.

"The ministry admitted there were certain things we had to do that might be outside the law, but they said go ahead anyway as legislation was on the way.

"I still wonder how the devil we coped with it all. Twenty or thirty evacuees would come down the day after a London raid and we would have to find homes for them. The evacuation was worked out on paper and by the train timetables, but we would have cases where 600 would come down from one school, bound for Sherborne, and some of ours would get off at Sidmouth. We had to sort that out, have the doctors inspect them, and give out 48-hours rations. You saw how people had been living in London. It was a trying time, particularly as my staff were being called up. We coped by making our minds up at a moment's notice.

"One night I had a red warning that there would be a raid, and suddenly the whole place was lit up by parachute flares, but then nothing happened. We had been told that if the flares dropped they would be followed by bombs. The lights ringed the town and someone phoned to say there was a landmine hanging out of his front door, but it was a flare that had caught in his chimney. He was so excited and frightened he said he couldn't get out of the house—I asked him what had happened to the back door!

"I kept on good terms with most of the town. The only time I upset the school was when I requisitioned its tuck shop as a British Restaurant.

"Later in the war, because of our experiences, we were chosen for bomb instruction exercises, and a special invasion exercise in Newland in May 1943. For that one they had a particularly realistic casualty, with his eye hanging by a thread, provided by the butcher. I think they went too far. One old lady in the crowd fainted.

"My biggest regret is that I didn't keep a diary, but I never had the time. A little regret is that there was a relic of the raid that could have been preserved, three pieces of bomb-case that were embedded out of harm's way in a school wall. I asked General Waller, the bursar, to leave them but he had them hooked out and the stone repaired."

1 October 1940. Sherborne. The German bomb that devastated 'Ashborne' yesterday, in Richmond Road, struck its balcony and ripped off the flat-roofed extension. Its rubble is strewn across the garden (left of the boy). The next-door house, 'Stonecroft' (right), suffered relatively minor damage.
(The houses survive but the flat-roofed extension was never rebuilt.)

30 September   **The boy who just made it back to Warmwell.**

The Heinkel 111s that jettisoned their bombs on Sherborne had been met by 152 Squadron as they flew at 21,000 feet over Portland. They had apparently been intending to raid Filton, at Bristol, or the Westland Aircraft factory at Yeovil which makes the Whirlwind, though with only a hundred produced this is set to turn into a failure. Anyway, the bombers were heading northward.

After his engagement with the formation that was to cause havoc in the abbey town of Sherborne, 19-year-old Eric 'Boy' Marrs (so called from his engagingly youthful looks) limped back to Warmwell in a crippled Spitfire and found that only one of his wheels would come down. It would not then retract, and to attempt a landing on one wheel is much more hazardous than a belly flop. He turned off the engine and glided in to land, touching down on the grass as gently as possible: "I began to slew round and counteracted as much as possible with the brake on the wheel which was down. I ended up going sideways on one wheel, a tail wheel and a wing tip. Luckily the good tyre held out and the only damage to the aeroplane, apart from that done by the bullets, is a wing tip which is easily replaceable.

"I hopped out and went to the MO to get a lot of metal splinters picked out of my leg and wrist. I felt jolly glad to be down on the ground without having caught fire."

Warmwell has, however, had a loss today. Sergeant D. Redington went down in the sea with a Spitfire of 152 Squadron.

56 Squadron, from Boscombe Down, has had half its Hurricanes put out of action over Dorset today, though without any casualties among the pilots. Hurricane P2866 crashed at East Knighton, near Wool, and N2434 was shot down over Okeford Fitzpaine. Both pilots parachuted safely. Pilot Officer Maxwell crash-landed Hurricane L1764 on the pebbles of the Chesil Beach across the water from Abbotsbury Swannery. Hurricanes P3870 and P2910

1 October 1940. Sherborne. 'Tanglin' was semi-detached and is now literally half a house. It stands on the east side of North Road, in the area immediately north of Newland that received a cluster of yesterday's bombs. (The left half, 'Green Bushes', would be rebuilt to match 'Tanglin'.)

force-landed, though without major damage, at Warmwell.

A Bf109 flown by Unteroffizier Alois Dollinger of 5/JG 2 Richthofen was shot down over Hundred Acre Farm, Sydling St Nicholas. Its pilot baled out but was found dead. His Black-2 had flown from Le Havre/Octeville.

Footnote   The crash site would later be farmed by escaped British prisoner of war and author George Millar, who wrote *Maquis* [1945], *Horned Pigeon* [1946] and *Through the Unicorn Gates* [1950]. This was the longest range of all the Me109 crashes of 1940.

For the month as a whole, September 1940, Warmwell's 609 Squadron claimed nineteen German aircraft for the loss of two Spitfires. Even allowing for overclaiming, the result was decisive. The confusion over claims was inevitable in that often several fighters had a part in accounting for the same bomber and it was frequently impossible to follow victims down to the ground. Station morale would have been depressed by continual inquests over dubious claims. What dropped on to the fields showed the trend, but the sea could anonymously accommodate any amount of further hopes.

Hawker Hurricane:
frequently joined with
the Warmwell Spitfires in
the dog-fights over the Dorset coast.
Hurricane squadrons operated from the sector base
aerodrome, Middle Wallop on the Hampshire Downs, at
nearby Chilbolton, and from Boscombe Down, Wiltshire.
Lyme Bay was shared with St Eval sector Hurricanes from Exeter.

30 September   **Hurricanes join the exhilarating coastal combat.**

Perhaps the most exhilarating flying of the day was enjoyed by 238 Squadron, flying Hurricanes from Middle Wallop. Flight Lieutenant Michael L. Robinson, in R4099 (VK-S), led the nine fighters south over Poole Bay and turned at Swanage to head towards Portland. They climbed into the cloud at 5,000 feet and rose to 15,000 feet above St Alban's Head, on a gyro-compass course westwards to get the advantage of the setting sun in Lyme Bay before wheeling into a dive on the German formations that were heading towards Portland.

They saw the enemy 3,000 feet below, to port, and swung into head-on attack. Robinson engaged an Me110 from 300 yards, ripping it to pieces and sending an aerial oil-slick across his cockpit, which cleared sufficiently to give him a view of the Messerschmitt splashing down some ten miles south of Portland Bill.

Still with a smeared windscreen, he then saw another Me110, which was at 7,000 feet and heading back to France. Robinson gave chase and came to within a hundred yards before opening up with three seconds of fire that pulled the port engine apart and moments later had the Messerschmitt explode. Its remains fell upside-down into the English Channel, fifteen miles south of Portland Bill.

Robinson then flew north, towards Portland, and climbed to 25,000 feet to join a line of what he thought were Spitfires, but which turned out to be Me109s. He still continued towards them and took on the closest, giving it a sustained six seconds of fire from 300 yards. Debris, smoke and white glycol streamed out as it flipped over and dropped seawards.

Mike Robinson switched to his gravity tank: "Landed at Exeter, no petrol." It was 16.30 hours; he heard that others in 238 Squadron also had something to celebrate, including Pilot Officer Bob Doe who had shot down a Heinkel.

Robinson and Doe joined the squadron only two days ago.

1940-41. Worth Matravers. Air Ministry Telecommunications Research Establishment, Renscombe Farm (left of centre). Seen from the south-west, from a reconnaissance aircraft above the Purbeck cliffs at Emmetts Hill. Four radio aerials can be seen and a variety of radar apparatus. Four separate compounds can be distinguished. 'Site A' is in the near distance on the left, and 'Site E' in the dark patch of the middle distance behind Renscombe Farm. 'Site B' is the large rectangular complex extending from the farmyard to beyond the right-hand edge of the picture. 'Site C' is the small circular-fenced installation crossed by the track in the near distance on the right.

September 'Beams' scientists dispersed to Langton Matravers.

The Telecommunications Research Establishment at Worth Matravers has requisitioned Leeson House and Durnford School in the nearby village of Langton Matravers. Further expansion of its hutted encampment beside Renscombe Farm, on the west side of Worth, had been considered inadvisable. The tall aerials of the coastal radar research station are attracting the attention of German bombers.

Scientists at Worth and Langton are deeply involved in what has become the "Battle of the Beams". The Luftwaffe is targeting inland English objectives by an intersection of radio pulses—one of synchronised dots and the other of dashes—transmitted from Kleve in central Europe and from Stolberg near the Danish border.

Dr Robert Cockburn has developed a Radio Counter Measure which is codenamed 'Aspirin'. This duplicates the continuous morse dashes, which are being transmitted on a frequency of 30 to 31.5 megacycles per second, and disorientates the German pilots by widening their direction beam.

A more ambitious plan was, in effect, to bend the beam by recording a sequence of synchronous German dots and re-transmitting the signal from a mast at Beacon Hill, near Salisbury. This scheme was thwarted, however, because the telephone land-line that Dr Cockburn was using, from Worth Matravers to Beacon Hill, was taken over by the military. The signal was recorded in the Isle of Purbeck but without the telephone link it could not be re-radiated from Beacon Hill.

Asynchronous signals are, however, having the desired effect without more sophisticated forms of interference being necessary.

1940. Langton Matravers. Leeson House has been requisitioned by the Air Ministry as an out-station for the scientists of the Worth Matravers based Telecommunications Research Establishment.

1 October   Plane crashes off Hengistbury Head.

An unidentified aeroplane fell into the sea off Hengistbury Head at 10.55 am. Machine gun fire had been heard. No one baled out.

7 October   Four die as bomb blasts Weymouth bus depot.

Four died and many were injured when the Southern National bus depot at Weymouth received a direct hit by a German bomb. Fourteen buses and coaches were badly damaged.

7 October   More Warmwell kills and losses.

609 and 152 Squadrons from Warmwell clashed with German aircraft on their doorstep, at times over the aerodrome itself, as an enemy force crossed the Channel at Portland to bomb the Westland Aircraft factory at Yeovil. Four kills were credited to 609 Squadron but for the loss of two Warmwell Spitfires and their pilots, Sergeant A.N. Feary and Pilot Officer H.J. Akroyd.

7 October 1940. Weymouth. 'Too low for Double-Deckers' — certainly the case now, with the Southern National bus depot having taken a direct hit from a Junkers Ju88 bomber. Four people have been killed.

Pilot Officer Eric 'Boy' Marrs, in Spitfire R6968, led Blue Section of 152 Squadron at 20,000 feet over the eastern Frome valley. They descended upon fifty German Junkers Ju88s and Me110s with Me109 escorts.

The enemy fighters were weaving defensive circles behind the bombers. Marrs waited for the final Me109 to pull out of a ring, in order to catch up with the bombers, and then struck at the last Me110 fighter-bomber in the exposed line. It belonged to II or III Gruppe of ZG 26 and had the nose section painted white.

'As glycol streamed from the Messerschmitt's starboard engine, Marrs switched his fire leftward across the fuselage: "Suddenly the back half of his cockpit flew off and out jumped two men. Their parachutes streamed and opened and they began drifting slowly earthwards. Their aeroplane, left to itself, dived vertically into the sea, making a most wonderful sight and an enormous splash . . . everything seemed to have cleared off, so I circled round the two Huns. They took an awful long time to come down on land and I watched the army rush up to capture them."

Footnote The two RAF officers are buried in the RAF plot at Warmwell churchyard. "One of the few," Feary's stone reads. He was twenty-eight.

7 October   **Close call for Spitfire R6915 and John Dundas.**

Engaging a defensive ring of fifteen Me110s, above Cheselbourne and Dewlish at 16.30 hours, Flight Lieutenant John Dundas, leading Blue Flight of 609 Squadron, flew guns-blazing over the top of the Messerschmitts. Then as he climbed away from the circle of fighter-bombers he came across a lone Me110 at 16,000 feet.

Approaching its tail he gave a sustained twelve seconds of fire from his eight guns. Both engines belched smoke and white ethylene glycol coolant.

As Dundas closed again on his crippled target its gunner hit back with a shell that splintered his leg and sent Spitfire R6915 reeling into a spin. Pilot and aircraft both recovered sufficiently to level out and glide into Warmwell Aerodrome.

The burning Me110 was spotted crossing the coast at Weymouth, at 14,000 feet, and is presumed to have crashed in the English Channel, though Dundas will only have credit for a probable kill.

Footnote Spitfire R6915 is the machine that now hangs from the ceiling of the Imperial War Museum as its main Battle of Britain exhibit. It has already been mentioned, on 30 September 1940, when its flier was Noel le C. Agazarian. As for John Dundas, he was back in the air next day, and awarded the Distinguished Flying Cross on 10 October. He reappears in the story.

7 October   **German aircraft shot down at Lulworth and Owermoigne.**

15.45 hours: a formation of German aircraft, estimated in excess of sixty, are approaching the coast at Lulworth.

15.50: the attackers are engaged by the anti-aircraft gunners at Lulworth Camp and by Warmwell's Spitfires which are intercepting them as they cross the Frome valley.

15.55: meeting heavy opposition the German aircraft have turned back towards the sea.

16.37: the air raid sirens have given the All Clear at Lulworth where an Me110 was seen to fall into the sea about 2,000 yards off the Arish Mell Gap. Another German aeroplane is understood to have crashed close to Owermoigne.

8 October   **Bomb wrecks Moreton church.**

21.00 hours. Moreton's eighteenth century parish church has been completely wrecked by a German bomb that fell beside the north wall. This has collapsed and the glass is blown out and fittings destroyed. The building is a ruin.

Footnote The building was restored and re-dedicated, in May 1950, and since 1958 has been enriched by the finest set of modern engraved glass windows in Britain—the creation of Laurence Whistler.

10 October   **Hurricane pilot killed at Wareham.**

Czechoslovakian flier Sergeant Jaroslav Hlaváč of 56 Squadron, from Boscombe Down, was killed at 12.20 this afternoon when Hurricane P3421 was shot down at Manor Farm, Worgret, to the west of Wareham. He was twenty-six and had been intercepting a flight of Bf109s. The body is being taken to Warmwell churchyard for burial in the RAF plot.

Hurricane P3984 of 238 Squadron, from Chilbolton, crashed at 13.00 hours below Corfe Castle—missing the famous ruin by only two hundred yards and plummeting into a roadside quarry just north of the Castle Hill. It came down close to the viaduct that carries the railway across the Studland road.

This time the pilot, though wounded, was able to bale out. Pilot Officer Bob Doe landed on Brownsea Island and has been taken to Cornelia Hospital at Poole. He is twenty years old and was recently awarded the Distinguished Flying Cross.

The lunchtime problem for the Hurricanes seems to have been the dense cloud-base which extended up to 16,000 feet. As British fighters came up through it they were visible to the enemy formations in the clear sky above—but for those last fatal moments the visibility for the RAF pilots was still obscured by water droplets.

9 October 1940. Moreton church, the morning after, in a snapshot taken by E.W. Pride that was confiscated by the military.

11 October   **Poole boy killed by bomb.**

Stanley Ricketts, an 11-year-old Poole boy, was fatally injured this evening by a German bomb as he walked home at Kingsbere Road. Incendiaries also landed in the Constitution Hill area and other parts of the town, including the Cornelia Hospital where Stanley died.

14 October   **Lyme minefield claims another Navy trawler.**

The British armed trawler HMT *Lord Stamp* has sunk after striking a mine in Lyme Bay.

15 October   **609 Squadron get an Me110 over Bournemouth.**

Leading Blue Flight of 609 Squadron from Warmwell Aerodrome, in Spitfire P9503, Flight Lieutenant John Dundas flew through the gunfire of three Me109 fighters at 14,000 feet over Christchurch. One Spitfire reported a bullet hole, but no apparent damage, though the squadron's flight pattern was thrown into disarray.

Dundas failed to regroup his flight and soared alone to 18,000 feet where he found some fifteen Me110 fighter-bombers. He made two runs at them, giving bursts of fire from only a hundred yards, but then broke away as Me109s came on the Spitfire from above.

An Me110 has reportedly crashed near Bournemouth as a result of the engagement. It is the squadron's ninety-ninth accepted claim.

16 October   **Bovington and Poole air raids.**

Cryptanalysts at Bletchley Park, deciphering the German 'Enigma' radio traffic, gave warning of today's bombing raid on east Dorset, which hit Bovington and Poole. The intercepted signal was "Target No. 1 for Y".

Target No. 1 is known to be the Armoured Fighting Vehicles School at Bovington, and 'Y' indicates that Y-beam radio direction signals were being used.

17 October   **Further Navy trawler goes down.**

The Royal Navy's losses of armed trawlers to the German minefield off west Dorset continued today when HMT *Kingston Cairngorm* blew up off Portland Bill.

17 October The 'false invasion'.

An intended raid on the Dorset and Devon coast to cover the infiltration of fifth columnists, mostly Irish Republicans, has been thwarted by the Royal Navy. Submarine L27, an ex-Danish boat, has shadowed the attack on the German convoy and many of the enemy have drowned, including SS agents. It has been the day of the false invasion.

The German force included the 5th T-boat Flotilla, 1,300 ton vessels the size of a light destroyer, and the destroyers *Karl Galster, Friedrich Ihrs, Hans Lody* and *Erich Steinbrinck.* They are having a running fight to escape from a mixed Allied force of two British cruisers supported by two Free French destroyers, two Norwegian destroyers, and one each from the Dutch and Danish navies.

19 October Bournemouth firemen go to London.

Bournemouth firemen, who were the first provincial reinforcements to arrive in the capital at the beginning of the Blitz in September, among the fifty pumps at Millwall Docks, have now instigated an exchange scheme with London firemen. Forty members of the Auxiliary Fire Service, from Bournemouth—divisional area 16C of No.6 Region—will today swap duties for a week with some of the City's exhausted heroes.

Deputy Chief Officer Ken Devereux is leading the Bournemouth team and it is expected that they will gain valuable experience in tackling major bomb damage.

Footnote Ted Hughes, who dealt with the administration at the Bournemouth Fire Service headquarters, records that 625 of his men attended city blitzes in 1940, in Southampton, Portsmouth, Bristol, Exeter and Plymouth as well as London, and that on eighty-three occasions they drove their pumps to the action. Usually that was at night, with only much diminished cowled slit-lights, along roads without any direction signs.

19 October Two 12-inch guns en route for Dorset.

Two 12-inch Mark II railway mounted howitzers, dating from the Great War, have been released to Southern Command from the Ordnance Depot at Chilwell, Nottingham. They have arrived at Ringwood where they will remain in a siding until they can be deployed in the Isle of Purbeck.

22 October Portland minefield sinks the 'Hickory'.

The *Hickory*, a diesel-powered civilian vessel, is the latest victim of the German minefield off Portland.

October Dorset's Somaliland hero returns from the dead to a VC.

Captain Eric Wilson of Long Crichel, who was seconded to the Somaliland Camel Corps, has been gazetted posthumously for the Victoria Cross as a result of his part in the heroic defence of the British colony in the Horn of Africa during the Italian invasion of 4–19 August. He commanded a series of Bren gun positions that were blown to pieces in a sustained attack over four days and he held out until the end.

The award was cited in the London Gazette but the story does not end there as three days later news reached the British that Captain Wilson had survived and was prisoner-of-war.

Footnote Neither would the story end there. As the war turned against the Italians he was liberated and fought with the Long Range Desert Group. Lieutenant-Colonel Wilson retired from the Army in 1949 and became an administrator in Tanganyika, until 1961, before returning to a West Country cottage, at Stowell near Sherborne.

October   **Winterbourne Abbas loses last church band.**

The last church band in England is now a memory as William Dunford, its sole surviving player, has taken his bass-viol home from Winterbourne Abbas parish church.

26 October   **Bournemouth's Carlton Hotel becomes a rations office.**

The prestigious Carlton Hotel on the East Cliff at Bournemouth has been requisitioned by the Board of Trade for use as a ration-coupon issuing office for the documents that are now needed for the restricted allowances of petrol and clothes.

In recent months it has only had five residents, since visitors were banned from the Defence Area, and one of these, Mrs Myers, has been fined 10 shillings with £1 12s 6d costs for an infringement of the blackout. The hotel felt obliged to pay.

October   **Bournemouth's Home Guard totals 8,000.**

Recruitment of civilian volunteers into the Hampshire Regiment (Home Guard) units under the control of the Officer Commanding Troops, Bournemouth—whose area includes the other two towns in the conurbation, Poole and Christchurch—is set to reach eight thousand men. The detachments and their approximate manpower on call are:

> 3rd (Poole) Battalion—2,500 men
> 6th (Bournemouth) Battalion—2,300 men
> 7th (Boscombe) Battalion—2,500 men
> 22nd (Post Office) Battalion—400 men
> B Company (Southern Railway) Battalion—300 men

October   **City pets evacuated to Shaftesbury.**

The animal shelter opened by Nina, Duchess of Hamilton, on her estate at Ferne to the east of Shaftesbury has become a refuge for hundreds of city pets, made homeless by the bombings and the general upheavals of war. As far as possible they are being cared for as if they were still at home, with freedom and exercise, rather than being permanently impounded in cages. Larger animals, such as horses, ponies and goats, are also being given refuge.

In reply to criticism that it is a waste of resources to care for animals in wartime, the Duchess quotes a Regional Commissioner of the Ministry of Home Security: "Experience shows that effective arrangements for dealing with animal casualties and for caring for the domestic pets of homeless people plays an important part in the maintaining of public morale after air raids."

Footnote   Nina was the wife of the thirteenth Duke of Hamilton who died on 16 March 1940. Three of their four sons—Lord Douglas Douglas-Hamilton, Lord G.N. Douglas-Hamilton and Lord Malcolm Douglas-Hamilton—were serving with the RAF at the outbreak of war. The first, the fourteenth Duke, had been chief pilot of the Mount Everest flight expedition in 1933. Ferne Animal Sanctuary survives, but is now at Wambrook, Somerset.

1 November   **Rail-guns brought to Purbeck.**

Two 12-inch Mark II railway mounted howitzers are now in the Isle of Purbeck where the first gun-spur has been made ready near Furzebrook by the 14th Super Heavy Battery of 5th Corps the Royal Artillery. The gunners came down from Catterick, Yorkshire, on 15 October and have now been united with their weapons.

The guns are being pulled by a Drummond K10 class mixed traffic locomotive, a 4-4-0, number 393.

1 November   **Anti-Aircraft Co-operation Unit at Christchurch.**

'H' Flight of the No.1 Anti-Aircraft Co-operation Unit has arrived at Christchurch Aerodrome from Gosport. Its varied assortment of the older types of aeroplane, including Avro Ansons, Tiger Moths, a Fairey Battle, Miles Magister and a Bristol Blenheim, will be at the disposal of research scientists, who are working on countermeasures against the German bombers, at the Air Defence Experimental Establishment at Christchurch.

    Footnote   The trials, which also involved Westland Lysanders, lasted until the end of July 1941.

3 November   **Motor-cycles leave Blandford.**

The Blandford Camp Reconnaissance Battalion, the 4th Battalion of the Royal Northumberland Fusiliers, are leaving Dorset today for Amesbury Abbey, Wiltshire.

6 November   **Heinkel lands at Bridport—thinking it France.**

In the early morning a Heinkel 111 of Kampf Gruppe 100, the élite two per cent of German bombers operating from Vannes, Brittany, and acting as pathfinders for the attacking formations, suffered a compass failure. It was confused by the British masking of German radio beacons into thinking it was back over France when in fact it was running out of fuel above Dorset.

    The pilot landed on the shingle beach at West Bay, Bridport, and three out of the four crew survived—though they soon had their illusions shattered regarding France and found themselves in captivity.

    Soldiers guarded the aircraft and had some difference of opinion with a naval detachment that came to drag the plane up the beach. The soldiers followed orders not to let anyone touch the bomber and it was engulfed by the tide.

    The aircraft has three vertical aerials and related radio equipment. This apparatus is to be salvaged for inspection by the Air Ministry boffins.

6 November 1940. The Heinkel awash at West Bay—see 21 November for the sequel.

8 November   **Both rail-guns now operational in Purbeck.**

Another gun-spur has been completed at Furzebrook, on the heath north-west of Corfe Castle, for the second railway mounted 12-inch howitzer. It is positioned three hundred yards from the gun that was emplaced on 1 November — but this time after some difficulty as it was brought down the branch line facing the wrong way.

Last night the gun had to be taken to Swanage to go round the turntable there so that it now points towards the coast. Both guns can fire 750 lb. of high explosives at three minute intervals and are controlled by observation posts on Ballard Down to the east, East Man to the south-east and Tyneham Cap to the south-west.

They have a range of eight miles and are targeted on prospective invasion beaches. To protect them from air attack they have been draped with 4,200 yards of Cullacort netting, suspended between the pines on 3,456 feet of scaffolding and 10,400 yards of wire.

14 November   **Junkers explodes on a Poole cobbler's shed.**

This morning No. 10 Group Fighter Command, at its headquarters near Bath, plotted a single German reconnaissance aircraft crossing into the Middle Wallop sector from France. Pilot Officer Eric 'Boy' Marrs, flying Spitfire R6968 with 152 Squadron, and Sergeant Bill Kearsey, in Spitfire P9427, were scrambled from Warmwell to investigate.

Kearsey spotted the intruder, on a course for Yeovil or Bristol, between Blandford and Sturminster Newton. Both Spitfires attacked and the Junkers Ju88 turned for the Channel. The German was at 24,000 feet.

Marrs engaged it first, coming up from underneath to 150 yards and giving a burst that "started a fire under the port engine, an ominous red glow being clearly visible". Not that Marrs could take any further part in the action: "Unfortunately the rear gunner of the 88 landed one plumb in the middle of my windscreen, splintering it in all directions and making it quite opaque."

Kearsey was still "going hard at it" and the Ju88 dropped to 5,000 feet. The Warmwell pilots caught up with it over Poole where the smoking German aircraft, via its determined rear gunner and the pilot's last struggle with the controls, desperately attempted to effect a different ending.

Marrs had withdrawn, forced to become an observer by his shattered windscreen, and Kearsey found himself out of ammunition. By this time the Junkers was becoming a fireball. One of the four crewmen dropped out but his parachute failed to open and his body fell through the roof of Kinson Potteries.

The pilot, Oblt A. von Kugelgen, may have been making some last attempt to level the plane but it hit the ground near the corner of Ringwood Road and Herbert Avenue, exploding fifty feet from a cobbler's shed. Mr Stainer and his family had narrow escapes, as did their neighbours. One night-time fire watcher was trapped in his bed by roof debris. Part of the fuselage ended up in the roof of Moore's Garage.

15 November   **Coventry bombers pass over Christchurch.**

Last night a massed formation of 499 German planes flew across the Channel on a directional radio beam from the Cherbourg peninsula and crossed the coast at Christchurch and New Milton. They then headed up the Avon valley and passed two miles to the east of Salisbury.

Their code name for the operation was "Moonlight Sonata" and they were aiming for Target 53, which turned out to be Coventry. The city was devastated by 1,500 bombs [503 tons] leaving 554 dead and many more injured, and the cathedral and a third of the factories destroyed. The total number of damaged houses is estimated at 60,000.

15 November **Escape flight from Belgium to Dorchester.**

Two officers have escaped from Belgium in a light aeroplane which they took from an airfield near Dinant. They flew down the English Channel and landed in the Dorset countryside near Dorchester. One of the men is Belgian and the other French.

16 November **Four killed in Poole blast.**

Sidney Sherwood and his sons, Fred, Henry and Robert, were killed when a parachute mine landed on their home in Fancy Road, Poole, early this morning.

There were other blasts in Haskell's Road and Cynthia Road, causing serious injuries. Though she was able to protect her daughter, Molly, Mrs Lillian Kitkat was badly lacerated by flying debris and lost an eye.

16 November **Fifty-three died in Bournemouth raid.**

German bombers attacked Bournemouth last night and left major destruction in three suburbs. At about 03.30 hours today six parachute mines floated down on Westbourne, Malmesbury Park Road, St Leonards Road, Turbary Common, and Alma Road Schools. High explosive bombs and incendiaries have fallen at Gervis Road East, Meyrick Road, Knyveton Road, Groveley Manor, Terrace Road, Leven Avenue, Montague Road and Southern Avenue. Fifty-three people have been killed and 2,321 properties damaged.

Footnote This was by far the worst of Bournemouth's five November raids. In total that month, in addition to the six parachute mines, the town received a total of twenty-four high explosive bombs and a number of incendiary devices. Sixty-two people were killed, 132 injured, and 2,829 properties damaged.

16 November **R.L. Stevenson's house is bombed.**

Last night's Bournemouth air raid badly damaged Skerryvore, Robert Louis Stevenson's home at Westbourne—near the head of Alum Chine—where he lived from 1885 until he left for the Pacific in 1887. Two poems about the house appeared that year in *Underwood*.

Footnote Pleas for its restoration were ignored and the remains of the house were demolished in 1941. In 1954 the site became a municipal garden, with the footings of the house being marked in concrete and a model erected of the Skerryvore lighthouse. Perhaps it would have been saved if he had written *Treasure Island* there; probably not.

17 November **Parachute mine devastates Chapelhay, Weymouth.**

At 21.00 hours, when the Jack Buchanan programme had finished on the wireless, a German raider glided over Weymouth—he is said to have cut his engine—and dropped a parachute mine.

This caused the town's worst explosion of the war, destroying seventy-seven of the tightly packed terraced houses at Chapelhay and inflicting damage on another 879 properties. Twelve died, including children.

The device had been intended for the harbour—investigation of its remnants showed it was a sea mine.

November 1940 arrival, photographed on 17 May 1941. Opposite. Furzebrook, north-west of Corfe Castle. One of the two 12-inch rail-mounted howitzers, which fire shells weighing a third of a ton.

The photographs show the arming of the shell, moving it on a trolley, then manhandling it into a hoist cradle. This crane arm is part of the massive gun carriage.

1. Arming.

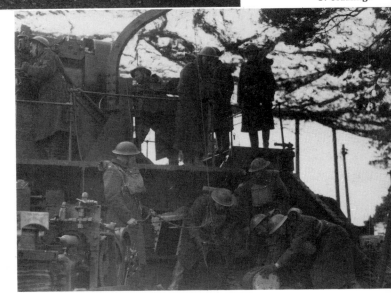

2. Trolleying.

3. Cradling.

1940-41. Furzebrook, near Corfe Castle. The full sequence of loading the twelve-inch railway mounted howitzer, carried out by 5th Corps on 26 February 1941 for the benefit of Mr Malindine, the visiting photographer sent by Southern Command. 'One of Britain's teeth', the captions would read—omitting that the fillings tended to fall out. When used the guns jammed. Not that it mattered; by that time Hitler had decided to go to Moscow.

The top photograph shows the shell, weighing a third of a ton, being hoisted on the loading cradle. This was followed by ramming it into the breech. A shot from behind shows the breech block about to be swung closed. The loaded gun was then elevated.

4. Hoisting.

5. Loading.

6. Elevating.

1940. The graceful and reassuring lines of the commonest aircraft in the Dorset skies. Spitfires from Warmwell had most of their dog-fights along the coast, particularly around Portland, but they were also a daily sight over the Stour valley and Cranborne Chase as 609 Squadron flew a daily shuttle to and from Middle Wallop, between Stockbridge and Andover, where they spent the night and were maintained. That practice came to an end in December 1940 and then 609 Squadron and 152 Squadron shared Warmwell Aerodrome as their home base.

18 November   **Poole houses evacuated.**

Houses in Newtown, at Poole, were evacuated last night after an unexploded bomb had created a large crater in Gwynne Road. Not that it was anything like as large as the hole left by the bomb that did explode in Grove Road—you could put a house in that one!

21 November   **West Bay bomber could have foiled Coventry raid.**

Scientists at the Royal Aircraft Establishment, Farnborough, have reassembled radio beam-flying equipment removed from the Heinkel He111 bomber of the Luftwaffe's pathfinding Kampf Gruppe 100 which crash-landed at West Bay on 6 November. The aircraft had three vertical aerials and an intact X-Gerät radio receiver, also known as Wotan I, which is used for precision bombing by enabling the aircraft to follow a radio direction beam emanating from the Cherbourg peninsula.

What has surprised the Air Ministry boffins is that the apparatus is tuned to 2000 cycles per second (approximating to the 'C' which is two octaves above standard-pitch middle 'C'), whereas British jamming countermeasures had assumed a note of 1500 cycles (approximating to the 'G' below this upper 'C').

They are less than pleased that the vital equipment was corroded and full of sand, this avoidable damage to the delicate light alloy components being due to the crass folly of the Dorset soldiers who prevented sailors from pulling the aircraft up the beach to safety. It became awash with the rising tide.

Particular anger has been expressed that the secret could have been cracked in time to foil the Coventry raid, which took place a week ago: "Someone in Dorset should be shot!"

Footnote   The significance of the discovery, and the frustrations it unleashed, are outlined by Dr Reg Jones, who was head of scientific intelligence at the Air Ministry, in his *Most*

Secret War:

"So the filter could distinguish between the true beam and our jamming, even though we had got the radio frequencies correct. It was one of those instances where enormous trouble is taken to get the difficult parts right and then a slip-up occurs because of the lack of attention to a seemingly trivial detail."

This revelation came too late to prevent the Coventry raid but it did ensure that radio countermeasures were perfected in time to save the vital Rolls-Royce aero engine plant at Derby. On the night of 8 May 1941, in moonlit conditions similar to those of the Coventry raid, Derby's bombs fell on Nottingham—and those intended for Nottingham fell into open fields.

27 November   **Spitfire follows a Junkers to France.**

Though denied permission to intercept a Junkers Ju88 that was heading south-west from Southampton, Flight Lieutenant John Dundas was allowed to take up his section of 609 Squadron on a "practice flight" instead. The two Spitfires climbed rapidly and found the German bomber at 22,000 feet, flying into the sun. Throttling to 2,600 revolutions the fighters' Merlin engines gave 280 miles per hour as the Spitfires closed on their target in its descent towards the Cherbourg peninsula. Dundas put Spitfire X4586 into an attacking glide at 14,000 feet, firing with five-second bursts at 400, 300 and then 200 yards.

Flames shot out of the Ju88's port engine and it lurched out of control as they crossed the French coast. There being a German aerodrome below, the Spitfires did not follow their quarry any further towards the ground, but turned north-west for the eighty mile return flight to RAF Warmwell.

28 November   **609 Squadron loses two for a Luftwaffe ace.**

"I've finished an Me109—whoopee!" These were the last words received by radio from Flight Lieutenant John Dundas, flying Spitfire X4586 with 609 Squadron which operates a daily shuttle from Middle Wallop to Warmwell Aerodrome.

Dundas had scrambled at 15.50 hours. Missing also is Pilot Officer P.A. Baillon in Spitfire R6631. Both were over the sea off the Isle of Wight.

Tonight German radio announced that the Luftwaffe had lost one of its ace fighter pilots, Major Helmut Wick, who had 57 white kill-bars painted on the rudder of his Me109E. He was leading Jagdgeschwader 2.

28 November   **Warmwell's 152 Squadron also loses two Spitfires.**

Having quietly congratulated itself on an "unusually quiet most of November" the month has been marred for 152 Squadron at Warmwell Aerodrome by the loss of two pilots today. Sergeant Z. Klein's Spitfire fell into the sea and Pilot Officer A.R. Watson, flying Spitfire R6597, crashed near Wareham, as a result of dog-fights with Me109s over Poole Bay and off the Needles, Isle of Wight.

The Polish sergeant "just disappeared" but Watson "bungled his baling out and tore his parachute" which "streamed out behind him but owing to the tears did not open".

Watson's death was avenged almost immediately by Pilot Officer Eric 'Boy' Marrs in Spitfire R6968. He crept up slowly on the culprit Me109, staying in his blindest spot, until he was within a hundred yards.

Marrs fired for just a second, unleashing 55 rounds of .303 ammunition from each of his eight guns—"the easiest victory I've had". There was an instant result:

"Black smoke belched forth and oil spattered over my windscreen. He half rolled and dived away. I followed in a steep spiral to see what was going to happen but my speed became so great I pulled away and my wing hid him for a bit.

"When I looked again there was a large number of flaming fragments waffling down to the sea. One large black lump, which was not on fire, trailed a white plume which snapped open and became a parachute. This was the pilot, and he must have baled out just before the petrol tank blew up. However, he landed in the sea and might just as well have blown up, for he was never found."

29 November 1940. Where a Spitfire fell: the shattered stump at Field Grove, Durweston Forest. It had a plaque, placed on the tree by Captain Gerald Portman: 'In grateful and respectful memory of Pilot Officer John Frederick Woodward Allen aged 19 years, who gave his life for his country on this spot 29 November 1940.' In 1978 the stump was removed and replaced by a much less evocative granite memorial.

29 November **Spitfire plunges into Field Grove, near Durweston.**

15.14 hours. A flight from 152 Squadron, including Spitfire R6907 flown by Pilot Officer John Woodward Allen, was scrambled because of a suspected enemy fighter sweep. They were instructed to patrol Warmwell at 25,000 feet.

Allen sent a radio message but it was unintelligible and nothing further was heard from him. His Spitfire was then seen to break away and dive shallowly, though under control. Suddenly it plummeted vertically into the ground and completely disintegrated on impact. The severity of the crash precluded any mechanical examination. It is thought the pilot fainted because of loss of oxygen. He had been flying Spitfires for three weeks. The fighter crashed at Field Grove, a wood half a mile west of Travellers' Rest, on the downs two miles south-west of Durweston.

Footnote The crash site was marked by a plaque, replaced in 1978 by a granite memorial. Ernest Day of Okeford Fitzpaine recalled seeing the plane in difficulties: "It was late afternoon, the day that a sixpence fell from the sky, hit my right shoulder and fell in the main road at Thornicombe. The fighter was climbing. Then I saw, very high in the sky, three German bombers returning from Bristol. The fighter made one attack on the bombers, then slowly descended towards me for a while, then it came straight down towards the ground with the throttle open.

"I stood thinking it was going straight into the ground, nose first, about fifty yards from me. Then what seemed like seconds before hitting the ground the throttle closed and the fighter turned out of the dive very sharply, just missing the ground by inches.

"It proceeded on a course towards Blandford, very unsteadily, just missing the telegraph poles on Thornicombe Hill, but slowly gaining height. When it reached Gipsy's Corner it turned left, then it flew over Fairmile where it slowly descended and went out of my view. A few hours later a friend told me that the fighter crashed near Travellers' Rest."

30 November **Bf109 belly-lands on Purbeck spy mission.**

Unteroffizier Paul Wacker of JG 27, who was flying a Bf109 from the fighter-bomber unit 4/ LG 2, suffered engine failure whilst on a weather reconnaissance over Swanage this afternoon. He was fortunate to belly-land on fields at Woodyhyde Farm, beside the railway between Swanage and Corfe Castle, in heavily wooded countryside.

Footnote The tail section of his machine survives. It was used to repair the captured test-flown Bf109 that is now in the Royal Air Force Museum at Hendon.

1 December **Bournemouth AA gunners claim two planes.**

This evening and last night there was bombing at Southampton and the enemy aircraft were harassed by Hurricanes and anti-aircraft fire as they flew over Poole Bay and Bournemouth.

Six German aircraft were shot down—two of them being claimed by anti-aircraft gunners. One of the planes dropped into the sea off Hengistbury Head.

3 December **Hurn Aerodrome bombed.**

The aerodrome being built at Hurn, to the north of Bournemouth, had its first raid today. Five high explosive bombs and a number of incendiaries fell at 18.50 hours.

Footnote The site had previously been recommended by Sir Alan Cobham to Bournemouth Corporation for a municipal aerodrome, but in the event—a war—it was the Air Ministry that took the initiative, on behalf of the Royal Air Force.

Bournemouth's previous airfield, Ensbury Park Aerodrome and Racecourse, became a housing estate in 1932. Its first scheduled commercial flight, in a Handley Page bomber, was flown by William Sholto Douglas in 1919. By 1940 he would be Deputy Chief of the Air

Staff, then Air Officer Commanding-in-Chief of Fighter Command in the midst of the conflicts of 1940-42, finishing the war as Marshal of the Royal Air Force and retiring in 1948 as first Baron Douglas of Kirtleside.

13 December **Christchurch families evacuated just in time.**

Families between Freda Road and Kings Avenue, Christchurch, were evacuated from their homes just in time this evening. A crater with an unexploded bomb, outside 1 Kings Avenue, had been reported at 09.25 hours but the decision to clear the area was not taken until 17.25. A bomb disposal team had then taken a look and decided to leave the bomb for 96 hours.

At 18.55, however, it went off—damaging three houses and rupturing gas and water pipes.

December **Spitfires now spend the night at Warmwell.**

The daily two-way shuttle of Spitfires from Warmwell to Middle Wallop, where the planes were dispersed at night, has ceased. 609 Squadron is now stationed solely at Warmwell.

20 December **Alexander and Montgomery see Studland Bay set ablaze.**

General Harold Alexander, Commander of the 1st Division, and Major-General Bernard Montgomery of 5th Corps, today stood on the clifftop between Redend Point and Old Harry Rocks, Studland, to watch the sea on fire. Pipes have been laid from the beach in Project Fougasse to release oil in a series of slicks to form a continuous strip that is then ignited. It has been a calm day and the water was burning; waves would disperse the slick, though on the other hand the enemy is likely to choose a day when landing conditions are favourable.

Footnote The intention had been to repeat the exercise in the night, because British intelligence suggested that the German troops feared a conflagration on the beaches, but this was a disappointment due to waves lashed up by a cold on-shore wind.

20 December 1940. Opposite. The sea is to burn—VIPs watch the oil slicks emerging from underwater pipes between Old Harry Rocks and Redend Point (top left) at Studland. General Harold Alexander (left) turns towards the camera.

Below—the sands of Studland are ignited in another Project Fougasse experiment. Turn the page.

24 December **E-boats sink two ships off Dorset.**

Convoy FN 366, sailing between Portland and the Isle of Wight last night, was attacked by the German 1st Schnellboot Flotilla (of six E-boats, S26, S28, S29, S34, S56 and S59). The enemy torpedo boats sank a Dutch ship, the *Maastricht*, and a Royal Navy armed trawler, HMT *Pelton*.

25 December **Mobile radar goes into the field at Sopley.**

A mobile ground-to-air radar antenna, developed by the Telecommunications Research Establishment at Worth Matravers and built at Somerford, Christchurch, by the Air Defence Experimental Establishment, is being tested for the first time today in the countryside. Known as Type 15 the unit has been placed on a flat part of Lord Manners's estate at Sopley, between the River Avon and the New Forest.

20 December 1940. Opposite. Project Fougasse. The sea burns off Redend Point (towards the top left) at Studland for the benefit of General Harold Alexander and Major-General Bernard Montgomery—and to remind any German invaders that they will receive a warm welcome.

25 December 1940. Christmas cheer: the Type 15 ground to air mobile radar antenna that was devised at Worth Matravers, built at Christchurch, and installed at Sopley.

December   **Blandford's Battle Training Camp.**

Blandford Camp is now designated a Battle Training Camp and provides a variety of intensive assault courses to simulate combat conditions.

1940. The year of retreat and anti-invasion precautions—a tommy-gunner in a cliff exercise at Bournemouth.

1940. Bournemouth. Slit trenches are a normal sight along the invasion coast, though with its protected access and the infantry, this is a scene reminiscent of the Western Front.

1940. Bournemouth. Gas, the terror weapon of the Great War, is part of the practice preparations, though so far it has not been used operationally in the current conflict.

Airspeed Oxford:
made at Christchurch.

4 January   Night-flying Hurricane ices-up over Portland and crash-lands.

Pilot Officer Bob Doe DFC, flying a Hurricane of 238 Squadron from Chilbolton, found his engine cooling system icing up last night as he flew over the sea off Portland Bill. His radio control at Middle Wallop sector headquarters talked him inland towards Warmwell Aerodrome but the engine of V6758 was overheating badly and cut-out as he approached the snow-covered airstrip.

He avoided its hangars but found himself landing among a stack of oil-drums. These ripped the light-weight fighter apart but the pilot was brought out of the wreckage alive. He was given emergency treatment in the station sick-bay and then taken to Bovington Military Hospital where fragments of glass were successfully removed from his eye.

Footnote   Leslie Dawson records, in the revised edition of *Wings Over Dorset*, the comforting words that Doe remembered hearing from the nurse as he regained consciousness at Bovington: "Lawrence of Arabia died in this bed!" The pilot would continue his career into post-war jet fighters and retired as Wing Commander R.T.F. Doe DSO, DFC and bar.

4 January   Warmwell intruder shot down off Portland.

Pilot Officer Eric 'Boy' Marrs led Green Section of 152 Squadron, in Spitfire R6968, from Warmwell Aerodrome at 13.00 hours today in a sortie to find a German aircraft that was reportedly entering the Middle Wallop sector.

Marrs became separated from his accompanying Spitfire in cloud and returned to Warmwell. As he prepared to land he was told to stay airborne as the intruder was flying towards the aerodrome, from the sea, at about 5,000 feet. Marrs was just under the cloud layer at 4,000 feet.

He swept over the chalk cliffs at White Nothe and across Weymouth Bay as a Dornier Do17 lumbered above Ringstead Bay: "I approached from the sea and opened fire at about 400 yards from the port rear quarter. He then turned south and dived like stink for the clouds. I turned in behind him, and closing to about 250 yards, fired at the fuselage and two engines in turn. Black and white smoke came from the engines and all return fire from the gunners ceased. I was overshooting and just before he reached the clouds I had to break away."

The Dornier was spotted from the ground at Lulworth Cove, as it came out of the cloud, trailing smoke and losing height. Its attempted return to France ended in the English Channel, five miles south-east of Portland Bill. No one survived.

10 January   Two Poole men blown up as they leave shelter.

Leaving their garden air raid shelter last night after an incendiary attack, Frank and Henry James of Canford Cliffs Road were blown up by the following wave of German bombers. The town was well alight for a time from numerous incendiaries and there was even a fire at the Fire Station. 248 houses are damaged though only one, a Lilliput bungalow, was completely gutted.

Henry James died yesterday evening and Frank, an auxiliary coastguard, died today in the Cornelia Hospital, Poole.

13 January   Observer Corps post machine gunned.

00.38: a Heinkel 111 passed about a hundred yards from the Poundbury Camp observation post, Dorchester, at about 300 feet. 02.45: the post was machine gunned by an enemy aircraft. There was no casualty.

25 January   More mines laid off Dorset.

Over the past three days the German destroyer *Richard Britzen*, operating with two T-boats, the *Iltis* and *Seeadler* of about 1,300 tons displacement, have been laying mines off the Dorset coast.

27 January   Dorchester burglary ends in murder.

01.30 hours. Private David Jennings, aged twenty, has been charged with the murder last night of Dorchester tailor Albert Farley of The Grove.
   What started as a burglary had turned horribly wrong. Jennings was breaking into what he thought was an empty licensed club and did so in the style of the American films. He shot the lock off the door. Unknown to Jennings the building was still occupied and Farley was about to unlock the door from the other side. The tailor was shot dead.

Footnote   Jennings was to hang at Dorchester.
   Such homicides ceased to be murder under the Homicide Act 1957 and Criminal Justice Act 1967, in that the jury can now decide whether the accused intended or foresaw the results of his action. Clearly here he did not as the object was theft from a building he considered to be locked-up and unoccupied. The present definition would be manslaughter, not that the surviving jurymen have much patience with such niceties. One told me: "We didn't think of things like that, we were at war."

January   Airspeed moves to Christchurch Aerodrome.

Christchurch Aerodrome has been selected as a shadow-factory for an aviation company. Airspeed (1934) Limited will move to the grass pre-war club flying ground at Somerford near Christchurch Harbour. The company is best known for the Envoy and the Oxford.

Footnote   550 of the twin-engined Oxfords would be made at Christchurch, mainly for use as trainers.

January   Worth scientist takes over Alexandra Palace tv transmitter.

In the last week of this month, Dr Robert Cockburn of the Telecommunications Research Establishment, Worth Matravers, has commandeered the BBC's pre-war television transmitter at Alexandra Palace. The powerful aerial, on Muswell Hill in north London, was brought back into action on the very night that the Luftwaffe refined its blind-flying system of following radio beams to English targets.
   The bombers had changed to a frequency of 42.5 megacycles per second and this was jammed by Cockburn in countermeasure 'Domino'. The German signal is being re-radiated back to the attacking aircraft, from Alexandra Palace, at 46.9 megacycles per second.

Footnote   A second transmitting station, constructed on Beacon Hill near Salisbury, extended Cockburn's jamming across the whole of southern England.

1 February   First Catalina flying boat lands on Poole Harbour.

The first of the long-range American-built Consolidated Catalina flying boats descended on to Dorset waters today. *Guba* (G-AGBJ) was the graceful visitor from Hythe, on South-ampton Water, and she will use the extended series of water-runways, the 'Trots', on Poole Harbour for the BOAC service to Lisbon in neutral Portugal.

She also brought a new sound. Hers are the Twin Wasp engines of Pratt and Whitney which are louder than the familiar Bristol Pegasus turbines of the Sunderlands.

2 February Fougasse breaks the blackout.

For a time last night there was no blackout over Bournemouth. You could read a newspaper in the Square. The cause was the ignition of the anti-invasion oil slicks of Project Fougasse on the beaches of Studland. It was a test; to remind the enemy that we are ready.

12 February Coast batteries fire on E-boats.

The two six-inch guns at Hengistbury Head coast battery opened fire at 06.50 hours on E-boats in the Channel.

24 February 609 Squadron leaves Warmwell.

The Spitfires of 609 Squadron have lifted off from Warmwell's turf for the last time. They are now stationed at Biggin Hill, Kent. Their replacements at Warmwell are the Spitfires of 234 Squadron. With 609 went their two odd-job planes, a Puss Moth and a Magister.

24 February German radar signal picked up at Worth Matravers.

Derek Garrard, a scientist from the Air Ministry seconded to the Telecommunications Research Establishment at Worth Matravers, has succeeded in picking up transmissions on a VHF receiver at the 2.5 metre wavelength. Having failed with the official equipment he put a radio set in his car and drove off to St Alban's Head to point it towards the Cherbourg peninsula; for which activity he was arrested as a Fifth Columnist in a 'Defended Area'.

He returned to London today with bearings that suggest a source in the area of Auderville, where coincidentally two square-mesh aerials in a field were photographed by Flight Officer W.K. Manifould two days ago. The twenty-foot turntable apparatus is the 'Freya' unit to which the Germans credited the sinking, off Portland, of HMS *Delight* on 29 July 1940.

Air Marshal Sir Philip Joubert has called a meeting for this afternoon with one item on the agenda: "To discuss the existence of 'German radar."

Footnote More than fifty Freya units would be located by a combination of listening, intercepted messages and reconnaissance, by the end of 1941.

4 March Sopley radar claims first kill.

The Type 15 mobile radar unit established in a field at Sopley, four miles north of Christchurch, on Christmas Day is fully operational and today celebrates the first kill to result from one of the aerial interceptions that it has stage-managed.

The unit provides combat guidance to 604 Squadron which operates from Middle Wallop.

9 March Another burn-up of the Studland beaches.

Last night the Studland 'Sea Flame' experiment was repeated for the benefit of General Harold Alexander, Commander 1st Division, as the pipes of Project Fougasse ignited the sea with burning oil. A landing craft was towed through the flames to show the effect of the scorching.

Footnote The Petroleum Warfare Department were authorised to instal fifty miles of such barrages but shortages of steel piping would restrict 'Sea Flame' to Deal, Dover and Rye in the prime invasion area of Caesar's coast and Porthcurno at the landfall of the transatlantic cables.

12 March **Bombs shatter Winton houses.**

Eight houses were destroyed by German bombs at Portland Road and Morley Road, Winton, at 22.09 hours. Bournemouth rescue squads are digging people out of the wreckage.

12 March **Poole flying boat 'Clio' fitted with gun turrets.**

The Poole 'Empire' flying boat *Clio* has today been returned to service after a refit at Belfast to equip her with armour plating, bomb-racks on the wings, four machine guns in each of two Boulton-Paul turrets in the dorsal and tail, and radar, for her new Coastal Command role. She has logged over four thousand miles of civilian flights. Her new number is AX 659 and she will serve with 201 Squadron covering the Iceland Gap from northern Scotland.

Footnote She would be lost on 22 August 1941.

12 March **Royal Blue depot hit at Bournemouth.**

A bomb has damaged the Royal Blue's coach depot in Bournemouth.

14 March **Re-equipped squadron's first combat.**

Improved Mark II Spitfires issued to 152 Squadron at Warmwell, replacing their Mark I planes, were scrambled today for their first combat patrol. They intercepted a Junkers 88 reconnaissance plane which was hit but escaped back across the Channel.

21 March **'Bournemouth II Crest' is the town's Spitfire.**

54 Squadron at Hornchurch, Essex, has taken delivery today of the Mark Va Spitfire that will be known as 'Bournemouth II Crest'. It has been paid for by public collections and war-weapons events in the town.

Footnote 'Bournemouth II Crest' would have a good war. It passed to 403 Squadron, and on to 332 Squadron and then 164 Squadron in 1942. The next users were 602 Squadron, and then it was seconded to the 82nd Fighter Group of the United States Army Air Force, on 8 November 1941. Then it went to 349 Squadron before being passed between a couple of operational training units, and finally, as 5586M, being handed on by a succession of maintenance units. Finally it would cross the Channel and the RAF relinquished 'Bournemouth II Crest' to the post-war French Air Force.

21 March **'Glamour Puffer' is shell-shocked.**

The 'Glamour Puffer' as she is known—a works train for the Royal Naval Cordite Factory on Holton Heath that brings young ladies from Christchurch, Bournemouth and Poole—attracted the attention of a German raider as it steamed home this evening. It pulled out of Holton Heath station at 17.19 hours.

Just as it crossed Rocklea Bridge towards Hamworthy Junction a stick of six bombs straddled the embankment and blew out all the windows of the ancient non-corridor "birdcage" stock. It kept going to the semi-protected cutting and waited but he plane did not turn back. The train

1941. Blenheim bomber over someone's shipping loss in the Channel—till now it would have been British but by the end of the year the German lake will have open fishing rights.

then drew into the platform.

None of the ladies was found to have anything worse than minor cuts; apart that is from quite a fright.

26 March Four bombs hit Warmwell Aerodrome.

A solitary Junkers 88 came across the Channel today and dropped four bombs on the RAF station at Warmwell. There were no casualties and the damage was limited to holes in the grass.

The station did, however, lose a flier today; Pilot Officer L.D. Sandes who held the Distinguished Flying Cross. He was aged twenty-eight.

27 March 1941. The wreckage of the canteen at Branksome Gas Works, in which 34 have been killed by a lunchtime German bomber.

27 March Thirty-four killed by Branksome Gas Works bomb.

The air raid siren has sounded at Branksome almost every day this month, and sometimes more than once, but today has been different. Despite the alarm business continued as usual at Branksome Gas Works and the staff were gathering in the canteen at noon for lunch. Then a single enemy aircraft dived out of the clouds towards the Bourne Valley viaducts.

Two bombs fell short and landed on the gas works. The first blew up the stores and the second smashed through an upper storey and wedged for a few seconds protruding from the canteen ceiling to the horror of those beneath. There was no time to evacuate the crowded tables before the not-much-delayed fuse activated the bomb with deadly effect. The explosion devastated the hall, killing thirty-four men, including Home Guard members Leonard Bartlett, Archibald Cherrett and Herbert Williams, and injuring twenty-three.

Anxious wives soon thronged the gates as Royal Artillerymen helped the survivors to drag out their dead and wounded colleagues.

27 March Unexploded bomb at Winton.

In Bournemouth a high explosive bomb that fell at Lowther Road, Winton, failed to go off.

27 March   Lyme Regis pilot lost in action.

Wing Commander Edward Collis de Virac Lart, who was born in Lyme Regis in 1902 and has served as an RAF pilot since he was twenty-three, has failed to return to his base. He was one of Britain's most experienced fliers. In the 1920s he flew with 60 (Bombing) Squadron in India.

28 March   Bournemouth's army of part-time firemen.

"Bournemouth has over 17,000 civilian fire-fighters," the Bournemouth Times boasts. Since a mass-meeting on 15 February 1941 the town has implemented the Fire Precautions (Business Premises) Order which requires all healthy men between sixteen and sixty, who are not otherwise involved in the war effort, to register for up to forty-eight hours duty a month as part-time firemen.

Stirrup pumps and whistles are being widely distributed and steel helmets will be ordered. Six-inch diameter steel piping is being laid on the pavements along the main roads in the centre of the town to ensure a ready and repairable water supply. Underground mains pipes are much more liable to fracture and usually impossible to repair during a night-time air raid. Fire, the Government believes, is the most devastating aspect of air attack.

March   Canford Cliffs bomb for the bouncy Air Marshal.

One of the bombs that dropped on Canford Cliffs this month hit the home of Air Marshal Sir Philip Joubert, nominally the commanding officer of Combined Operations which is being set-up at Poole. In fact that job is a blind; since 14 June last year he has been running the RAF's radar and signals intelligence system, right through the Battle of the Beams, and in effect he controls the Telecommunications Research Establishment at Worth Matravers.

It all couldn't have happened to a nicer chap—he must be the bounciest Air Marshal the RAF has yet appointed.

March   Wareham family has five sons in RAF.

Aspiring to some sort of record, Mr and Mrs R.J. Brennan of the bakery at Worgret, near Wareham, have written to a local newspaper saying that all their five sons have enlisted in the RAF. They are Samuel, Eric, Peter, Archibald and Edwin and their ages range from twenty to thirty-three.

The other two Brennan children are girls.

1 April   German bombers kill ten at Warmwell.

Three Heinkel 111s slipped low across the Dorset coast from Lyme Bay and followed the railway east from Dorchester to the aerodrome at Warmwell. They had not been picked up by radar or spotted by the Observer Corps and the station had no warning of the attack. Ten were killed by the bombs, shortly after noon, and twenty injured.

Among the dead is Sergeant Fawcett, one of the Spitfire pilots of 152 Squadron. He was killed by a machine gun bullet as he sat eating lunch.

A bomb crashed through the room of Eric 'Boy' Marrs but the pilot was elsewhere—having the Distinguished Flying Cross, which was awarded last December, pinned on his uniform in Buckingham Palace by King George VI.

Similarly honoured, and also from 152 Squadron, was Pilot Officer Dudley Williams. Pilot Officer Marrs had a shock at the weekend, hearing of the death of his best friend, Flying Officer Charles Davis DFC of 238 Squadron from Middle Wallop. His Hurricane flew into a hill near Winchester, which was obscured by low cloud, on 26 March.

5 April   **Heinkel crash-lands on the Dorset ridgeway.**

A Heinkel He111 bomber is lying on its belly beside the coastal ridgeway to the east of Weymouth. Pilots from Warmwell Aerodrome have inspected the stranded aeroplane which had been attacking shipping off Portland. It is fitted with a curved tube which projects forward from the nose and extends from the tip of one wing to the tip of the other. This refinement is to push barrage balloon cables aside and prevent them fouling the wings and engines.

The aeroplane came into this predicament through navigational error. Its crew survived and have become prisoners. The sheep also had a fright.

10 April   **Poole buildings destroyed by fire.**

This evening's raid on Canford Cliffs and Parkstone has left incendiaries blazing in a number of buildings, including the Canford Cliffs Hotel, Tennyson Buildings and Pinewood Laundry. The Tennyson Buildings are in a main shopping street, Ashley Road, and the laundry stands beside the Pottery Junction. Paintings have been removed from the blazing hotel but otherwise the inferno will be left to itself as there is no longer any water coming out of the mains.

Footnote   Canford Cliffs came out of it lightly as far as its residents were concerned; the Royal Engineers bomb disposal unit found and defused eight unexploded bombs in Haven Road the next morning.

11 April   **Sleeping Bournemouth poet killed by German bomb.**

Cumberland Clark, a familiar figure in central Bournemouth with white hair and walrus moustache, was killed in his sleep last night when a German bomb destroyed his flat in St Stephen's Road at three minutes to midnight. He was a prolific author with sixty-seven books to his credit, many of them poetry, and his *War Songs of the Allies* have proved a tonic for the town's morale:

> Down in our Air Raid Shelter
> There's no cause for alarm,
> It is so sure and strongly built
> We cannot come to harm.
>
> Let the bombs bounce round above us,
> And the shells come whizzing by,
> Down in our Air Raid Shelter
> We'll be cosy, you and I!

The same plane dropped an incendiary on Woolworths, in the Square, which burned fiercely for some time. The fire was brought under control at 02.20 hours and the all-clear sounded at 04.10 hours.

Seven women had also died in the attack which destroyed several flats at Hampshire Court and in St Stephen's Road. A bomb that was dropped in Bodorgan Road failed to explode.

Footnote   Boots now stands on the site of the burnt-out Woolworths.

12 April   **Bombs fall on Upton.**

Six high explosive bombs and a quantity of incendiaries fell on Upton shortly after midnight.

15 April   Warmwell's Roland Beamont to test-fly Typhoon.

Battle of Britain pilot Roland Prosper Beamont, who flew a Dorset Spitfire with Warmwell's 152 Squadron, is being attached to Hawker Aircraft Limited and will test-fly its latest aircraft. This machine, the Hawker Typhoon, is expected to be at the forefront of the next generation of dual-function fighter-bombers.

Beamont enlisted with the Royal Air Force on 1 October 1939, at the age of nineteen, and flew with the British Expeditionary Force in France. He was mentioned in despatches during the air war over the Dorset coast through the summer of 1940. His new career as a test pilot is being restricted to what he terms "rest periods".

Footnote   Those working holidays would extend to the trials of the Hawker Tempest. Wing Commander Roland Beamont finished the war DSO and bar, DFC and bar, and United States DFC, and was now the experimental test pilot for Gloster Aircraft Company. He went on to become Britain's most famous post-war aviator. In 1948 he was the first Briton to fly at the speed of sound. In 1954 he was the first Briton to fly at twice the speed of sound. As English Electric's chief test pilot he was the first to take up Britain's first jet bomber. That was the Canberra and he put her into a climb of fighter-like steepness for a breathtaking display of manoeuvrability at the Farnborough Air Show of 1949. In 1954 he made the first flight in Britain's first supersonic fighter, the P1.

16 April   Poole flying boat 'Cordelia' is armed.

Another Poole 'Empire' flying boat, *Cordelia*, has been armed with gun turrets and bomb-racks and provided with radar at a major overhaul in Belfast. From today she is AX 660 and will carry out depth charge trials with 119 Squadron.

Footnote   She returned to BOAC's Poole fleet in September 1941 and survived the war, being scrapped at Hythe on 6 March 1947.

28 April   Hurricane mishap at Christchurch.

Hurricane L1592, one of three that are stationed at Christchurch Aerodrome to protect the Special Duty Flight which operates from there, crashed at 12.20 this afternoon when its port undercarriage failed to lock upon touch-down. The fighter spun across the grass but was not seriously damaged. The pilot was unhurt.

Footnote   L1552, L1562 and L1592 were the Christchurch Hurricanes. The latter, the one of the mishap, was an unusually lucky aircraft. It survived this accident and the war to become part of the National Aeronautical Collection that is displayed by the Science Museum in London.

28 April   Fairey Battle crashes off Hengistbury Head.

A Fairey Battle fighter-bomber (K9230), with a crew of two, crashed into the sea off Hengistbury Head, Bournemouth, at 15.45 hours today. The pilot baled out and Second Lieutenant Andrew Page of the Lancashire Fusiliers swam to his aid but the airman was entangled in his sodden parachute. The soldier could not prevent the pilot from drowning and nearly lost his own life from exhaustion and the intense cold of the water. Two of his comrades dragged him back on to the beach.

Footnote   In July Andrew Page would be awarded the George Medal for his heroism. As for the Fairey Battle, it was disliked by the RAF, Sergeant Fitter Bob Chacksfield recalls: "Useless aircraft, they shouldn't have been allowed in the war. Shameful aircraft—every time we started it, the thing began to catch light. It was totally underpowered."

29 April   **Two Frenchmen fly to Christchurch in stolen Nazi plane.**

Two young Frenchmen, former members of the Armée de l' Air, today landed at Christchurch Aerodrome in a German biplane, a Bücker Jungmann, they had stolen from an airfield near Caen.

They landed at 12.30 hours, after a flight of seventy-five minutes, and were spared some rounds of Bofors fire through the quick thinking of Second Lieutenant H.G. Graham and Sergeant Gill of 229 Battery of the Royal Artillery who saw the swastikas on the plane but realised there was something unusual in a short-range aeroplane coming this distance. Monsieurs Denys Boudard and Jean Hebert will be debriefed by Free French Forces.

Footnote   Hebert was lost over the sea in 1943 but Boudard was still flourishing in the 1980s.

April   **Commando unit formed at Poole.**

Under the command of Captain Gustavus March-Phillips, an operational guerrilla unit of commandos known as the Small Scale Raiding Force has been formed at Poole, with its headquarters in the High Street, in the Antelope Hotel.

Their rôle, in Winston Churchill's words, will be to create "a reign of terror down the enemy coasts".

29 April 1941. Christchurch Aerodrome. Fliers, Free French as of this moment.
Denys Boudard (left) and Jean Hebert (right) with Flight Sergeant Pritchard
of the Royal Air Force, after their daring escape from the Nazis.

29 April 1941. Christchurch Aerodrome at lunchtime. Opposite.
Centre of attention, replete with black cross and swastikas, was a biplane belonging
to the Luftwaffe's Luftdienst training section — newly arrived from Normandy.

1 May Bailey Bridge tested at Christchurch.

The Experimental Bridging Establishment of the Royal Engineers, formerly known as the Bridge Company, has spanned the River Stour at Christchurch with a prefabricated steel bridge. It took shape almost instantly, taking a total of thirty-six minutes from commencement to the first lorry driving across.

This seventy feet structure was designed in 1939 by Donald Coleman Bailey. The bridge-building sappers took over the former horse barracks beside the river at Barrack Road.

Footnote   Bailey Bridges were taken to war in Tunisia and Italy and in the Normandy campaign of 18-21 July 1944 they enabled British armoured divisions to cross the River Orne at five points to the north of Caen.

The length of the bridges grew to meet the size of the obstacle, such as 1,200 feet to cross the Chindwin in Burma and a record 4,000 feet plus at Genneps in the Netherlands.

Donald Bailey would be knighted in 1946. He retired to 14 Viking Close, Southbourne, Bournemouth.

4 May   Junkers 88 crashes on Winfrith Heath decoy.

The decoy-airfield at Winfrith Heath, which is rigged with flares and moving lights to draw air attack from Warmwell Aerodrome, today claimed a German bomber to add to the craters it has successfully attracted. The victim was a Junkers 88 that had apparently been hit by anti-aircraft fire.

The crew had been able to bale out and are now prisoners of war.

7 May   German bomber crashes at Oborne.

A German bomber crashed into the hillside below Oborne Wood, to the east of Sherborne, in the early hours of the morning. The pilot baled out and gave himself up but the remainder of the crew, Feldwebel E. Ebert, Feldwebel H. Ottlick, and Unteroffizier T. Kowallik, died in the wreckage.

Footnote Their bodies were buried the following day at 10 am in the north-west corner of Oborne churchyard. Prayers were given. In 1963 the Volksbund removed the remains to the German war cemetery, Cannock Chase, Stafford.

9 May   All clear at Weymouth then six die.

After the all clear sounded at Weymouth earlier this morning, Mrs Lilian Adnam and her daughters Dorothy, Margaret, Mary, Violet and Vivian left their shelter and returned to bed. At 04.30 hours a single German bomber slipped over the town and dropped five bombs. The house received a direct hit and all six were killed. Two other daughters escaped with injuries.

10 May   Christchurch Aerodrome bombed.

Christchurch Aerodrome and the buildings of Airspeed Limited, at Somerford, were bombed and machine gunned early this morning, between 00.40 and 01.09 hours. Several bombs failed to explode.

10 May   Bridport's Spitfire is 'The Brit'.

The Spitfire appeal in west Dorset, which raised nearly £6,000, has paid for Spitfire R7062 which was today handed over to 308 Squadron. It is being named 'The Brit' after Bridport's river.

Footnote   The fighter was transferred to 403 Squadron, on 28 May 1941, and later to a training unit near Chester. It was lost in a flying accident on 21 December 1941.

12 May   Heinkel and flying boat sink in Poole Harbour.

A Heinkel He 111 of the German 8th Staffel attacked the seaplanes on Poole Harbour in the moonlit early hours this morning and sank *Maia*, a BOAC 'Empire' flying boat, killing its watchman, off Salterns Pier.

The low-level attacker (G1+ES) was brought down with machine gun fire from the ships in the harbour and land-based light anti-aircraft fire from Bofors Mark II guns firing 40 mm shells. It plunged into the harbour off Patchin's Point, Arne.

Unteroffiziers Karl Scheuringer and Karl Rohl survived but the pilot, Willer Wimmer, and his other crewman are missing. Scheuringer, the flight engineer, received a punch in the mouth that sent him reeling back into the sea during the course of his rescue-cum-capture.

Maia, recently converted to a C-class flying boat, had been a pioneering composite aircraft as the mother craft, having a cradle between her wings, for a Mercury mail-carrying seaplane.

12 May 1941. The flying boat 'Maia'—sunk in Poole Harbour. She was no longer in tandem with the smaller 'Mercury' float-plane but this is how she will be remembered.

12 May   Bomb blasts Ashley level crossing.

03.25 hours. The railway line from Ringwood to Wimborne has been blocked by a bomb crater at Ashley Heath level crossing. Twenty houses are damaged and the phone wires down.

12 May   Kennels and cafe hit by Somerford bombs.

A raid on Christchurch Aerodrome at 02.18 hours hit nearby civilian buildings, wrecking the bungalow at Somerford Kennels and smashing Bert's Café. There are four craters opposite the café and the Somerford Road is strewn with debris for a hundred yards. The family at the kennels are safe and have returned to look after their horses.

14 May   Swanage bomb hits Wesley's Cottage.

16.30 hours. Wesley's Cottage, a picturesque stone-roofed dwelling in the High Street at Swanage, where John Wesley stayed on a preaching trip, has been badly damaged by a German bomb. It has been the town's 315th air raid alert.

Footnote   The ruined cottage would be demolished.

22 May   Christchurch loses war trophy to London's War Weapons Week.

The German Bücker Jungmann biplane in which two patriotic Frenchmen escaped from Caen to Christchurch on 29 April has been dismantled and taken to London for display in the War Weapons Week.

27 May 1941. HMS 'Dorsetshire'. She has finished off the 'Bismarck', in the South Western Approaches.

27 May 'Dorsetshire' sinks the 'Bismarck'.

The county of Dorset will take special pride in the fact that today the cruiser HMS *Dorsetshire* delivered the coup de grâce to the battleship *Bismarck* at 10.36 hours this morning.

The *Bismarck* had been pounded by Royal Naval gunfire and was ablaze from stem to stern, rolling in a heavy sea, as Captain Martin of the *Dorsetshire* received the order to finish her off—with two torpedoes into the starboard side from 2,400 yards. The cruiser then steamed around the battleship's bows to fire another torpedo into the port side, sending the great grey ship lurching and exposing her red-painted hull as she rolled over to sink within fifteen seconds.

For a time the *Dorsetshire* stopped amongst the clusters of some four hundred survivors but many were too weak to climb the rope ladders and a British midshipman jumped in fully clothed to help. He was nearly left behind when a hundred and ten of the Germans had been dragged aboard and a submarine alert was received. Many of the exhausted sailors fell from the ropes into the sea as the cruiser gathered speed and left the area.

So ended an epic of naval warfare in less than heroic fashion. This chase across the North Atlantic and into the South Western Approaches has been an expensive victory for the British—three days ago the Admiralty announced the loss of the battle cruiser HMS *Hood* without being able to offer any prospect of survivors.

Footnote   Admiral Sir John Cronyn Tovey, Commander-in-Chief of the Home Fleet and key participant in the action, retired to Swanage after the war.

May The wealthy hoard gold and butter.

Some of the best-heeled residents in the county have passed through the courts in the past few months to face accusations of ignoring wartime restrictions. Sir John Sherlock of West Wings, Clarence Road, Dorchester, was fined £4,000 with £100 costs for concealing 3,647 sovereigns, 4,590 half sovereigns and £499 in other gold. He was forced to sell his hoard to the Treasury.

Eyebrows were also raised when the county's premier political households, the Wimborne St Giles dynasty of the ninth Earl of Shaftesbury, the Lord Lieutenant of Dorset, and their neighbours at Cranborne Manor, represented by Viscount Cranborne, MP for South Dorset, were charged with buying black-market butter.

At the other end of the social spectrum, Albert Bulley of the Bungalow at Owermoigne had the distinction of being the first in the county to be convicted for refusing to take in evacuee lodgers. He was fined £5.

May **Minefield laid off Brownsea Island.**

An electrically triggered anti E-boat minefield has been laid beside the passages between the scaffolding obstructions at the entrance to Poole Harbour. It is controlled from an observation post on Brownsea Island, manned by a unit who have taken over the derelict Rose Cottage.

6 June **Convoy-hit Bf109 crash-lands at Worth.**

Hit by flak from an escort vessel, Oblt. Werner Machold, the Staffel Kapitan of 7/JG 2 Richthofen, today turned his stricken Bf109 inland from the Channel convoy and crash-landed the White 15 among the stone workings of Worth Matravers.

Machold is among the most famous of the Nazi fliers. He was credited with JG 2's one hundredth victory over France and personally congratulated by Field Marshal Hermann Göring. When his comrades were upgraded to the 109F he insisted on sticking with his old Bf109E but he had it improvised with a special Z-gear to feed nitrous oxide to boost the engine power.

For this reason the crashed plane has been impounded on behalf of the Royal Aircraft Establishment, Farnborough.

9 June **'Dagmar' sinks off Swanage.**

The steamship *Dagmar* was today sunk by a German bomber off Durlston Head, Swanage. One of the convoy escorts, the Free French Navy's gunboat *Chasseur 43*, picked up survivors and took them to Poole Quay. Many were admitted to hospital.

12 June **Poole family wake up to a bomb in the kitchen.**

A family in Bournemouth Road, Branksome, came downstairs to breakfast this morning to find an unexploded bomb in their kitchen. They had heard the explosions from a stick of bombs that were dropped across Layton Road but ignored their own lighter thud. A bomb disposal unit pronounced it a dud.

14 June **Warmwell Whirlwinds strafe Cherbourg airfields.**

Four Westland Whirlwind fighter-bombers took off from Warmwell Aerodrome at 05.05 hours on their first cross-Channel expedition. The aircraft were escorted by Spitfires of 234 Squadron and strafed two airfields on the Cherbourg peninsula. The operation was accomplished successfully and all the fighters returned.

22 June **Bournemouth buys a second Spitfire.**

Paid for by the town's Spitfire Week fund raising, the second of the town's Spitfires, the Mark-1 'Bournemouth', was today handed over to 457 Squadron at Baginton, Coventry.

Footnote   457 Squadron flew to the Isle of Man in August and 'Bournemouth' left them in October to join a training unit at Grangemouth. It was lost in a flying accident on 16 March 1942.

22 June **Poole's Spitfire is 'Villae de Poole'.**

Street collections and fund raising events in Poole have paid for Spitfire 'Villae de Poole' which was handed over today to 411 (Royal Canadian Air Force) Squadron.

Footnote   Sergeant S.W. Bradshaw was killed on 7 December 1941 when 'Villae de Poole' crashed at Chester during a blizzard.

1941. Heathland tank training. The furze and heather of Purbeck and Bovington was to become increasingly churned as the war developed. This tank is an A13. It was a cruiser tank, a long-range vehicle, and the first British chassis to use Christie suspension. The idea for this was developed in the United States and smuggled to Britain in 1936 as tractor parts and in cases labelled 'grapefruit'.

1941. Gatemerston and Brooms Plantation, south of Lulworth Park—an area now known as the Bindon Range. Cruiser tanks of the Gunnery Wing of the Armoured Fighting Vehicles School, Lulworth Camp, line up and prepare to fire seawards at Bindon Hill, the western line of the Purbeck Hills.

June **Dorset supports 'Dig for Victory'.**

Helping to take the message of "Dig for Victory" to the people is the Dorset County Produce Association which has been sponsored by the Ministry of Agriculture to help promote the vital cause of restocking the nation's larder. Similar associations are being set up in other counties.

Each will in turn establish branch associations in the villages and towns to give technical advice and encouragement. More families must start keeping rabbits and hens in their gardens and be persuaded to turn over their lawns and flower beds to the growing of vegetables.

June **Lyme's £25 a head for a warship.**

Lyme Regis has contributed no less than £69,222 "towards sending another ship to fight in His Majesty's Navy for the freedom of mankind from the Nazi thrall". This is £25·10s per head from the 2,700 inhabitants.

Champion town crier Walter Abbott made the announcement of "this Empire's determination to guard our rightful place on the good earth".

Footnote The town's special warship would be the *Bangor* class minesweeper HMS *Lyme Regis*, a 650 ton vessel launched from Alexander Stephens and Sons yard on the Clyde, 19 March 1942.

1941. The newly introduced Churchill tank coming over a ridge on the Lulworth tank gunnery ranges.

June **Bere Regis boy, Fred, clambers into the first Churchill.**

Fred Pitfield, aged ten, of Bere Regis has enjoyed one of the privileges that extreme youth can sometimes bestow. He has been allowed by armed guards to momentarily ignore the security restrictions and climb into the brand new interior of one of the first three Churchill tanks that are en route to the Armoured Fighting Vehicles School at Bovington and Lulworth. The Driving and Maintenance Wing is at Bovington Camp and the Gunnery Wing is based at Lulworth Camp, with a coastal firing range on Bindon Hill and in the Arish Mell valley.

This tank is a winner; it has to be with a name like Churchill. Fred and his friends are used to all the tanks that Bovington can field but when these pulled on to the verge at Court Green they realised that here was the shape of things to come.

The thirty-nine ton Churchill has evolved from specification A20 into A22, the Mark IV Infantry Tank, and is produced by Vauxhall Motors with ten centimetre frontal armour and a two pounder gun.

Footnote Three would also get as far as El Alamein for their testing. They were then armed with six pounder guns, the Bovington crews having dismissed the two pounder as a peashooter.

2 July   234 Squadron re-equips with ungainly Spitfires.

The sleek lines of Dorset's Spitfires look somewhat compromised from today. 234 Squadron, flying from Warmwell Aerodrome, have changed to Mark II machines; each has an unjettisonable fuel drop-tank added to centre of the left wing.

This is to extend their flying range so that the fighters can go on escort duties for offensive operations against the Brest peninsula.

Pilots are unimpressed. The superb aerodynamics have been disturbed and will require delicate teasing of the rudder to compensate. There is also the danger that when it has an empty tank the fighter can spin out of control on tight turns.

10 July   Warmwell Spitfires escort Blenheims to bomb Cherbourg docks.

The Spitfires of 152 Squadron joined with those of 234 Squadron and flew from Warmwell Aerodrome today to link up with a flight of twelve Blenheim bombers that were heading across the English Channel. The fighters provided an escort for the bombers in a low-level raid on the harbour at Cherbourg. As it went into attack each Blenheim had a Spitfire to its left and right flanks and another following its tail.

Me109s engaged the British formation and Mindy Blake, the officer commanding 234 Squadron, shot down two. He was then found to be missing, however, on the return journey.

The final sweep of the day came home with the report that Blake had been sighted, by Sergeant Fox, alive and well and cheerfully paddling his dinghy in the general direction of the Isle of Wight.

17 July   Bomb dropped on boy saying his prayers.

The funeral took place today in Melcombe Regis cemetery of a ten-year-old Weymouth boy, Kenneth Polden, who was killed when a German bomb dropped on his house. His mother had said to him a minute earlier: "Go to bed. Say your prayers and ask God to keep us safe."

The rescue squad found Kenneth beside his wrecked bed with his hands clasped in prayer.

17 July   Blenheim lost in strange encounter.

A Blenheim of the Special Duty Flight, from Christchurch Aerodrome, descended to take a closer look at a silvery shape they had spotted floating in the English Channel thirty-three miles south from St Alban's Head. The Blenheim, P4832, was on a calibration flight.

Its pilot, Flight Lieutenant Douglas L. Rayment, was monitored by radio from the mainland. He was heard telling his wireless operator and gunner, Sergeant R.Sadler, that the mystery object seemed to be a weather balloon. Rayment's last words were: "There you are, have a go. You can't miss!"

Two bursts of machine-gun fire followed. The aircraft's wireless then went dead.

25 July   Warmwell's hero killed over Brest.

Pilot Officer Eric 'Boy' Marrs of 152 Squadron from Warmwell was shot down today over the French coast on one of the first offensive missions undertaken by the station, which was the backbone of Dorset's defences in last year's Battle of Britain. They flew to Brest.

Marrs's Spitfire was hit by chance flak, bringing true a station prophecy that no German fighter pilot was going to take the 'Boy'. In December he had been awarded the Distinguished Flying Cross. A week ago, on 10 July, he celebrated his twentieth birthday.

Footnote   His body was recovered and is in the military cemetery at Brest.

July Purbeck's howitzers withdrawn.

The 14th Super Heavy Battery, which has been stationed at Furzebrook in the heart of the Isle of Purbeck since 1 August 1940, is experiencing troubles with its two rail-mounted 12-inch howitzers. They are being taken to the Royal Artillery's main depot at Bulford on Salisbury Plain for trials. Though only fired a few times for practice shots the recoil system has failed and shattered the mountings.

Meanwhile, for their return, the Royal Engineers and Southern Railway are building two new sidings for railway-mounted guns: one half a mile on the Wareham side of Furzebrook and the other on Norden Heath, Corfe Castle.

Footnote The project was abandoned and no more rail guns were brought into Purbeck. The battery's locomotive, number 393, rejoined the Southern Railway on 9 August.

July Shirburnian hits back at American presumptions.

An ex-Sherborne schoolboy, A.N. Whitehead, has reminded Americans that "as a training in political imagination, the Harvard School of Politics and Government cannot hold a candle to the old-fashioned English classical education of half-a-century ago."

July Cinemas show selected US newsreels.

The *March of Time* is the most active United States newsreel propagandising for American aid and munitions for Britain. It is widely shown here, with the emphasis on Roosevelt's speeches— "We must be the great arsenal of democracy" is their theme—but never are there any clips from the speeches of his opponents. Neither is any mention made of the price exacted for United States aid; throughout the war nothing is going to be said about the realisation of British dollar assets as the price for lend-lease.

1 August Hurn Aerodrome handed over to the RAF.

RAF Hurn, a new aerodrome with hardened concrete runways, has been completed on the flat ground between the Stour meadows and the heathland to the north of Bournemouth. It has three runways. The longest is 5,200 feet and the others 4,800 and 3,400 feet. Seven large and ten small blister hangars have been provided for under-cover maintenance. The aerodrome was today handed over by the contractors to the Air Ministry, which passed it to 11 Group Fighter Command.

It was received on Air Ministry's behalf by Wing Commander G.K. Horner of the Special Duty Flight, from Christchurch Aerodrome, who handed over interim control of RAF Hurn to Flight Lieutenant Theobald.

6 August Shot-up Whirlwind force-lands at Hurn.

A shell-damaged Westland Whirlwind, with one engine out of action and the other leaking glycol, force-landed at RAF Hurn at 17.40 hours. Flight Sergeant H.G. Brackley brought P6983 down on an obstructed runway and hit both wings in the process but was able to walk clear of the wreckage.

He claimed two Me109s in a dog-fight off the Cherbourg peninsula when four Whirlwinds from the Filton-based 263 Squadron had been attacked by a formation of twenty enemy fighters.

13 August Telecommunications Flying Unit formed at Hurn.

Aircraft of the Fighter Establishment from Middle Wallop have landed today at RAF Hurn where they will re-group as the Development Section of the Air Ministry's newly formed Telecommunications Flying Unit. Another technical research team, the Blind-Landing Detachment from the Royal Aircraft Establishment at Farnborough, is also moving to Hurn to become part of the new unit.

Group Captain P.J.R. King will take charge of RAF Hurn from Flight Lieutenant Theobald on the 19th.

18 August National Fire Service formed.

The local fire brigades which were organised by town councils are from today part of the National Fire Service. Number 16 District covers Hampshire and Dorset, with the two Dorset divisions being based in Bournemouth and Weymouth.

9 September Warmwell Pole is killed.

T.W. Pytlak, serving at RAF Warmwell with 30 Squadron, has been killed. He was twenty-two.

13 September Poole commandos killed in Normandy.

A raid by No 62 Commando from Poole was last night foiled by the Germans as it attempted an attack on the defences of the Atlantic Wall West. Though the commandos had killed the seven-man German patrol that had come across them and retreated to their wooden boat it was then hit by a shell.

Three of the men were taken prisoner and one escaped; the others, including their commander, Major Gustavus March-Phillips, are dead.

25 September Wavell's Dorset partridges for Tehran.

The Daily Telegraph reports the following anecdote about General Sir Archibald Wavell. He had been shooting partridge in Dorset on a Friday and was departing on the Saturday with a couple of brace of the birds.

As he was leaving the country the following day his hosts asked the Commander-in-Chief India what he was going to do with the birds. "Eat them myself, of course," he replied, "in Tehran on Tuesday."

21 October Focke-Wulf 190 crashes at Lulworth.

There was a huge explosion at Lulworth today when a Focke-Wulf 190 flew in low from the sea and crashed into the side of Bindon Hill. The pilot was killed instantly. He had apparently misjudged his position and course.

21 October Churchill on behalf of Turing: 'Action this day.'

Twenty-nine-year-old mathematical genius Alan Turing, as dishevelled now as in the days when he was at Sherborne School, is using his "Turing Bombe" to crack the cipher codes of the polyalphabetic German 'Enigma' cryptographic teleprinter-enciphering machines which scramble their military radio commands and responses.

His work at the Government Code and Cipher School, Bletchley Park, Buckinghamshire, is providing what Winston Churchill calls the "golden eggs" from geese who never cackle. Having shown Churchill how cryptanalysts function, Turing today sent the Prime Minister a personal memo of demands that he sees as vital if full efficiency is to be achieved.

Churchill responds instantly, writing on the list of complaints: "Action this day. Make sure they have all they want on extreme priority and report to me that this has been done."

Footnote   Alan Turing designed the first programmed electronic digital computer in the world. His personal behaviour would also prove to be ahead of his time, a conviction in 1952 for gross indecency with another male causing him to take his life with a cyanide-dipped apple, in 1954. Sherborne School, however, partly acknowledges its greatest pupil, with the Alan Turing Laboratories. As the tonnage of 'Enigma' decrypts are reappraised—thousands were produced at Bletchley each day—it has become clear that Alan Turing was the factor, as much as radar, that enabled victory in the Battle of Britain in 1940 and would turn the tide of the Battle of the Atlantic in 1942, at a time when the German U-boats were sinking ships faster than America could build them.

23 October   King and Queen visit Bournemouth.

King George VI and Queen Elizabeth are in Bournemouth today to inspect Dominion airmen assembled at the Pavilion.

October   Leslie Howard in Christchurch to make 'The First of the Few'.

Leslie Howard, the actor and film-maker, is staying at the King's Arms Hotel, Christchurch, to work on a motion picture, *The First of the Few*. This will dramatise the legend of the Spitfire from its creation by Reggie Mitchell whose inspired designs first took to the air from Eastleigh Aerodrome, Southampton, on 6 March 1936. The eight-gun Supermarine monoplane K 5054 was at the hands of Mutt Summers who was watched throughout by an already ailing and constantly stressful Mitchell.

A grass aerodrome is in keeping with the story and Warmwell was selected but Howard, who

**2 November 1941. Weymouth. Adelaide Hotel, Abbotsbury Road.
The town's mayor, John Goddard, lay trapped in the rubble.**

is also the director, has decided upon the new concrete runways at Ibsley, two miles north of Ringwood. Not only has this suddenly become the look of modern aviation but it has advantages for the film-makers in providing smoother footage, rather than having to track the fighters as they bounce up and down across the grass.

The film will also star Rosamund John and Major David Niven.

2 November Mayor trapped by rubble as three die in Weymouth.

Three died and eleven were injured yesterday at about 23.20 hours, when four high explosive bombs dropped around Abbotsbury Road, Weymouth. Among the 171 damaged buildings was the Adelaide Arms, at 182 Abbotsbury Road, which received a direct hit.

Publican John Goddard had a lucky escape from death but was trapped under the rubble until after midnight. He is the Mayor of Weymouth. His rescue was effected by mayoral mace-bearer Bill Docksey, who also managed to save the first citizen's chain of office and Great War medals.

10 November Special Duty Flight joins TFU at Hurn.

The Special Duty Flight has moved from Christchurch Aerodrome to RAF Hurn where it is now the Research Section of the recently formed Telecommunications Flying Unit. Christchurch is now a satellite station to Hurn.

A wide variety of ancient and modern aircraft types are among the twenty-three single engined machines and thirty-three twin engined aeroplanes which the unit possesses. It also has two communications aircraft. Among their functions are the provision of aerial guinea pigs for the radar scientists of the Telecommunications Research Establishment.

11 November Crashing Hurricane kills pilot and two Warmwell soldiers.

Two members of the Dorsetshire Regiment, on guard duty at Warmwell Aerodrome, were killed today when a Hurricane of 32 Squadron came down out of control and crashed into the ammunition dump. The pilot also died in the explosions that followed.

17 November Buses and paper in short supply.

There are further restrictions on the omnibus services which will mean even longer crowds for the last ones. In fact the Regional Transport Officer is trying to discourage any idea of having a night out using public transport because in future no bus may leave after 21.30 hours. Fuel shortages are to blame.

Paper controls are also being tightened. There will be no Christmas cards this year and it is now illegal to use paper for advertising leaflets, posters, or the production of paper handkerchiefs. Efforts to recycle materials, particularly waste paper, scrap iron and pig-bin collections, are being intensified as the shortages become felt.

November Boffins in a Blenheim find that radar can map Bournemouth.

There was elation this month among radar scientists at the Telecommunications Research Establishment in Worth Matravers and Langton Matravers following a discovery made from a Blenheim bomber of the Telecommunications Flying Unit. It had taken off from Christchurch Aerodrome to test a theory—that it is possible to devise an airborne radar system that can map the ground.

An AI (Airborne Interception) Mark VII radar set was installed in the aircraft and its centimetric beam tilted towards the ground. The Blenheim climbed to 8,000 feet and the aerial

1941. Pilot Officer David Glaser's Spitfire of 234 Squadron at the edge of Warmwell Aerodrome and his co-pilot (below, left), Blackie. Right: actor Leslie Howard—in Christchurch to film the Spitfire's story, 'First of the Few'.

was then spun at thirty revolutions per minute.

As had been predicted, the apparatus acted as an effective "Town Finder" for bomber navigation and returned varying signals from the streets and roofs of Bournemouth and its adjacent landscape of pinewoods, heath and cliffs.

November   RAF Hurn operational.

RAF Hurn, which is already being used by 1425 Communications Flight and is due to receive 170, 296 and 297 (Army Co-Operation) Squadrons, is now an operational aerodrome for No.11 Group of Fighter Command.

23 December   Air Minister backs Dorset 'Blind Navigation' tests.

Upon hearing a report of last month's flight in which a Blenheim bomber had flown from Christchurch Aerodrome, and used a down-turned radar set to map the ground, the Secretary of State for Air, Sir Archibald Sinclair, today ordered a further six such flights. These are to "determine whether the signals obtained . . . could be definitely associated with ground objects".

The experiments are to be co-ordinated by Bernard Lovell, a young scientist in Professor Philip Dee's section at the Telecommunications Research Establishment in the Isle of Purbeck.

The ramifications of the discovery are considerable. BN (Blind Navigation) would enable bombers to find distant targets in poor weather and at night. Bomber Command experiences extreme difficulty in finding the general area of German cities let alone in delivering a significant proportion of the bomb load to any specific location.

December   RAF fighter shot down British bomber at Manston.

Investigations have shown that it was an RAF night-fighter, apparently a Beaufighter from Middle Wallop, that shot down a British Whitley bomber over the River Stour earlier in 1941. It crashed half a mile east of Manston church, midway between the village and the hamlet of Fontmell Parva, two miles from Sturminster Newton.

Pilot Officer M.E. Sharp was able to parachute to safety. It was the second time he had baled out this year, the earlier escape being from an aircraft returning after a Bomber Command raid over Bremen in February.

1941-42. RAF Sopley, the ground to air radar system near Christchurch which acts as an air traffic control to guide British fighters, particularly night-fighters, in their interceptions of enemy aeroplanes. The Type 15 antenna is seen, and its tented Operations Room. The station is known as 'Starlight'.

S(S) EXP BEAUFIGHTER
OF FUSELAGE NOSE
(PERSPEX)

1940-42. Worth Matravers and Langton Matravers developed, at the Telecommunications Research Establishment, is AI (Air Interception) radar. It is seen fitted in the perspex nose-cone of a Bristol Beaufighter, now operational in the night-skies.

1941-42. RAF Sopley, codenamed 'Starlight' for its night-time direction of fighters against enemy intruders. This is its first lorry-mounted mobile control room. The radar was turned by pedal power, using bicycle parts, by two airmen assigned to 'Aircraft Hand General Duties'. They became known as 'Binders' from their consequent level of complaining.

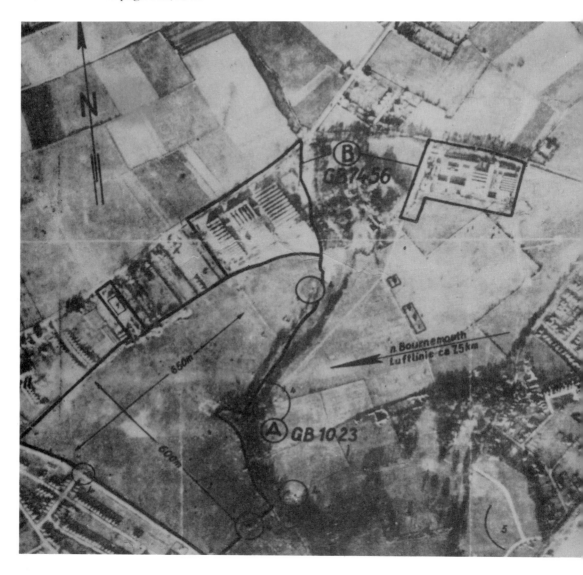

1941. German air reconnaissance photograph of Christchurch Aerodrome, taken before the building of the main runway. 'A' signifies 'Christchurch Flugplatz'—'Christchurch Flying landing-ground.' 'B' shows two 'Flugzeugzellen reparaturwerk'—'Aeroplane repair works'. Here the Germans underestimated the importance of the Somerford factories: for Airspeed was manufacturing aircraft and the Air Defence Research and Development Establishment of the Ministry of Supply (known in the town as the Air Defence Experimental Establishment) was one of the country's major producers of radar components. It made apparatus pictured on the previous pages, working in conjunction with scientists of the Air Ministry's Telecommunications Research Establishment at Worth Matravers.

The arrowed 'Bournemouth Luftlinie' shows the flightline for Bournemouth. North is at the top, and the ringed positions show 'Kleinkampfanlagen' (light machine guns). '5' at the bottom right locates 'Scheinwerferstellung' (searchlight positions).

Short Sunderland:
landing on Poole Harbour.

13 January   **Tizard inspects Hurn and Christchurch.**

A naval experimental party demonstrated a Walrus seaplane today to Sir Henry Tizard, the scientist on the advisory council of the Ministry of Aircraft Production, who visited the Telecommunications Flying Unit at RAF Hurn and its satellite station at Christchurch Aerodrome.

18 January   **Hurn despatch-point for Middle East Liberators.**

1425 Communications Flight, which delivers long-range aircraft from the factories to overseas operational bases, is to ferry out Liberators from RAF Hurn. The aircraft are being flown via Gibraltar and across the Sahara Desert to the Middle East.

The first Liberator landed at Hurn today and several are expected over the next few weeks. A detachment of 1425 Communications Flight will start ferrying operations from Hurn next month.

Footnote   The Liberator was the RAF version of the bulky high-wing American Consolidated B-24 bomber which was powered by Pratt and Whitney 1,200 horsepower Twin Wasp engines. Five Liberators left Hurn for the Middle East in February-March 1942.

January   **The Yanks arrive, bringing good food.**

The first American contingents have arrived to the tune of *Lilli Burlero*, the Ulster Protestant march. The American soldiers have found it is a shilling a meal in the British Restaurants, but for what? They are much better fed in camp and for free.

The tendency to contrast the public menu with their own is being counteracted with a special US forces newsreel: "The best food in England is GI, but don't keep rubbing in how good your food is."

The commentator then added: "And don't say you've come over to win the war!" Which, of course, they have.

Footnote   The Japanese attack on Pearl Harbor on the Hawaiian island of Oahu began at 07.50 hours Honolulu time, 7 December 1941—"a date that will live in infamy," in Roosevelt's words to Congress. There had been no declaration of war and isolationist sentiment in America ceased to exist; the Japanese had stung a sleeping tiger. The United States declared war on Japan on 8 December. The question of US neutrality in the European war was conveniently settled by the Axis powers themselves, when Germany and Italy declared war on the United States on 10 December.

February   **Hurn unit prepares for airborne landings.**

Part of Hurn Aerodrome has been set aside for Number 3 Overseas Aircraft Despatch Unit. They will modify Halifax, Whitley and Stirling bombers into tow-craft and muster a fleet of gliders for airborne landings.

Footnote   In 1943 the Whitleys were replaced by Albemarles. The unit would remain at Hurn until D-Day. One Sunday evening four of its gliders crash-landed into the lane, immediately west of the aerodrome, that led to the East Parley mission church.

18 February 1942. The Channel Dash: German battleships Scharnhorst (right), Gneisenau and Prinz Eugen escape from Brest to Kiel.

18 February **The Channel Dash.**

Three of the capital ships of the German fleet escaped today up the Channel from Brest to Kiel. They were the battleships *Scharnhorst* and *Gneisenau* and the battle-cruiser *Prinz Eugen*. The Times is anguished: "Nothing more mortifying to the pride of sea-power has happened in home waters since the seventeenth century."

The Admiralty assumed that the break-out would start in daytime and pass southern England during darkness. In fact the reverse has happened. Admiral Ciliax left last night and sailed up the Channel in daylight, despite the efforts of Commander Esmonde and his Swordfish torpedo-dropping biplanes.

February 1942. Weymouth Bay. Rescue flotilla rehearses the retrieval of the Bruneval raiders.

27 February **Bruneval raiders bring Worth a German radar.**

Having practised for the operation off Redcliff Point, Osmington, 'C' Company of the Second Battalion of the Parachute Regiment has sailed from Portland to Bruneval on the Cherbourg coast to bring back a German Würzburg radar apparatus. The raiding party is led by Major J.D. Frost with technical expertise being provided by Flight Sergeant C.H. Cox.

They jumped from twelve Whitley bombers and landed on top of the 400 feet cliff in deep snow to take their objective with complete surprise and dismantle the equipment for removal by landing craft from the beach below. Its components will be examined by the Telecommunications Research Establishment at Worth Matravers. Only one important piece had to be left behind, despite only ten minutes being available for the technical side of the operation.

Würzburg operates on 53 centimetres (between 558 and 560 mHz) and is a coast defence radar apparatus with a range of about forty kilometres. Its parabolic aerial had shown on air reconnaissance photographs of a clifftop at Cap d'Antifer. The Biting Plan for the seizure of its aerial, receiver and cathode-ray tube was organised by Combined Operations headquarters under Acting Admiral Louis Mountbatten.

February 1942. 'C' Company of '2 Para', the Bruneval raiders, rehearsing their pick-up from the Cherbourg peninsula. The setting is Redcliff Point, Osmington, looking towards Ringstead Bay.

February 1942. Redcliff Point, Osmington. The rehearsal for the pick-up of '2 Para' at the end of the cross-Channel Bruneval raid—which is to bring home a German Würzburg radar for the Telecommunications Research Establishment to study at Worth Matravers. Things will go better on the night. Here, however, the men descend from Redcliff Point (above) to a landing craft that the tide leaves behind (below). Eventually (opposite) they are taken off and join the rescue flotilla.

15 March 1942. HMS 'Vortigern' is sunk off Dorset. She is seen on a better day, in peacetime up the Avon Gorge.

5 March **Change-over of 'Hurri-bombers' at Warmwell.**

Hurricanes of 175 Squadron have been flying into Warmwell Aerodrome today. They are taking over from 402 (Royal Canadian Air Force) Squadron which departed yesterday. The Canadians had been at the station since November 1941 and also flew the 'Hurri-bomber' variant of the Hurricane fighter.

This has been adapted into a ground-attack aircraft for cross-Channel offensive sweeps over Normandy and Brittany.

8 March **Woman machine-gunned as she reads at Christchurch Quay.**

At 18.00 hours two Me109s machine gunned Christchurch Quay, hitting a woman who was sitting reading on a riverside bench. Josephine O'Reilly, of Iford Bridge Hotel, has been admitted to Fairmile House with a shoulder wound. Her condition is described as fair.

14 March **German raider escapes into Atlantic.**

There was naval activity off Dorset last night as the destroyer HMS *Walpole* and the New Zealand destroyer *Ferine* tried with twenty-one motor torpedo boats and four of the larger motor gun boats to block the passage of the Nazi raider Schiff 28 *Michel*. She slipped through, however, towards the Atlantic, with the aid of the 1,300 ton light destroyers of the 5th T-boat Flotilla, *Falke, Jaguar, Kondor, Iltis* and *Seeadler*, and nine minesweepers.

15 March **British destroyer sunk off Dorset.**

HMS *Vortigern*, a destroyer, was sunk last night in the English Channel by a Schnellboot, S104, though the Germans also suffered an own-goal when another E-boat, S53, was blown up by one of their own mines. S111 was also lost, following an attack by British motorgunboats (MGB87, MGB88, MGB91); she was captured but sank under tow.

22 March **New bomber arrives at Hurn for radar-map tests.**

A new Halifax bomber — the type went into operational service only on 11 March — has been delivered to the Telecommunications Flying Unit at RAF Hurn. V9977 has been adapted by Handley Page Limited to the requirements of the Telecommunications Research Establishment, at Worth Matravers, and has a perspex cupola covering the space which would normally house the nose gun-turret.

Here the scientists will install the magnetron section of a Mark VII AI (Airborne Interception) radar, adapted into the first prototype of a version codenamed H2S which is being developed for ground-mapping.

March **Royal Fusiliers guard Christchurch radar establishment.**

The 12th Battalion of the Royal Fusiliers have been sent to Christchurch to guard the top-secret Air Defence Research and Development Establishment, at Somerford and Friars Cliff, against the possibility of the Germans staging a retaliatory Bruneval-style commando raid. The Establishment, known locally as the Air Defence Experimental Establishment, works in conjunction with the Telecommunications Research Establishment at Worth Matravers and specialises in radar and radio counter-measures.

1 April **King reviews 2nd Dorsets en route for Bombay.**

The 2nd Battalion of the Dorsetshire Regiment were today lined up along the Oxford Road at Banbury for an inspection by the King. 'A' Company then went through a jungle assault course high in the trees above the officers' mess. The battalion is under orders to move to Liverpool from where it will sail to Bombay.

1 April 1942. King George VI's farewell to the 2nd Battalion of the Dorsetshire Regiment, bound for India and the war against Japan. He is seen with Lieutenant-Colonel G.N. Wood, inspecting 'A' Company.

2 April **Twenty killed and Weymouth's newspaper blitzed.**

21.00 hours. Twenty people are dead and fifty-six injured after Nazi dive-bombers indiscriminately swept across Weymouth. Only one of the bombs hit the central area of the town but it has devastated the Dorset Daily Echo's offices and works. A few hours earlier new foundry equipment was being installed and the current edition of the paper distributed for this Maundy Thursday.

The staff are gathering to salvage what's left. Just one item of standing type has been found and that, ironically, carries the headline: "Hitler's Nightmare!"

Footnote The eight-page paper could miss Good Friday but it appeared again on Saturday, 4 April, with 12,730 copies printed at Bournemouth. The Richmond Hill plant had already taken on the Southern Daily Echo, bombed out from its works in Southampton.

2 April 1942. Weymouth. The Dorset Daily Echo's offices and works were destroyed by the single German bomb that landed in the centre of the town.

6 April **Churchill inspects Churchills at Lulworth.**

Ranks of Churchill tanks, the first to go into service, received their namesake's approval today in the Arish Mell valley on the Dorset coast. Prime Minister Winston Churchill had a full tour of the Gunnery Wing of the Armoured Fighting Vehicles School at Lulworth Camp. Some of the Churchill tanks have been refitted with six-pounder guns to give them much increased fire-power. The first production versions carry two-pounders.

6 April 1942. Halcombe Vale, East Lulworth (above Sea Vale Farm). Wearing that bulldog look, Prime Minister Churchill inspects the new British tanks that bear his name.

6 April 1942. Bindon Range, East Lulworth. Winston Churchill watches the mass formation of his tanks, the newly introduced Churchill, roll by below the north-eastern slope of Bindon Hill, at the western end of the Purbeck Hills.

12 April   Sinking of HMS 'Dorsetshire'.

Japanese dive-bombers, coming out of the sun at 13.40 hours this Easter Sunday in waves of seven, sank the cruisers HMS *Dorsetshire* and HMS *Cornwall* in the Indian Ocean. The warships were hunting for surface raiders about three hundred miles west of Colombo.

Footnote   The 1,100 survivors floated in clusters around two leaky whalers in which the worst of the wounded were tended. They were told by the *Dorsetshire's* captain, Commodore A.W.S. Agar VC, to conserve their strength by making as little noise as possible and cover their heads against the equitorial sun. Rescue did not come for thirty-three hours, after they were sighted by a Fleet Air Arm 'Stringbag', a Swordfish torpedo-reconnaissance biplane.

13 April 1942. Survivors from the cruiser HMS 'Dorsetshire'—yesterday the sinkers of the 'Bismarck' got the same treatment themselves. The myth of British naval supremacy went down off Ceylon as the Japanese showed once again what airpower can achieve. Some of these men will have been in the water 33 hours. The first Royal Navy destroyer had arrived on the scene but its rescue boats did not complete their task until after midnight.

17 April   'Blind' Halifax spots Bournemouth from six miles.

The first version of an H2S town-finding radar set, intended for use in long distance bombers, today succeeded in giving scientists a convincing signal that was Bournemouth from six miles, seen from a height of 8,000 feet. Halifax V9977 carries the set behind a perspex dome. This morning's flight, undertaken by the Telecommunications Flying Unit for the scientists of the Purbeck-based Telecommunications Research Establishment, then used the equipment to distinguish between the outlines and land-forms of the adjoining towns of Poole and Christchurch.

Progress on several types of airborne radar apparatus has gathered pace since the start of 1942. Five important versions are now in production or being perfected—AI (Airborne Interception; for night fighters), ASV (Air to Surface Vessel; for Coastal Command, to detect submarines surfacing to charge their batteries), Gee (renamed TR to indicate Transmitter/Receiver, which it is not; instead it forms a grid-lattice map from synchronised pulses on a cathode-ray tube in a colour coded pattern that shows the aircraft's location when superimposed on a chart); Oboe (navigation beam to aid target marking for Pathfinders, as they became known); and H2S (ground-mapping; for Bomber Command to bomb blind, straight through the clouds).

The latter prototype would have been tested on a similar flight with the Halifax that took place last night—but the operator failed to find a concealed switch and the radar was not turned on. Scientists spotted the switch after the bomber had landed back at Hurn.

April   **Weymouth scholarship boys meet again in Libya.**

The war has brought about a surprise reunion for two of the brightest pupils of recent times from Weymouth Grammar School, A.E. Walkling and R.R. Head, who have had a brief encounter in the Western Desert. From 1928–37 they had competed at Weymouth for honours and both had gained scholarships and gone to Oxford.

Lieutenant Alec Walkling has written to Norman Windust in Weymouth: "You will be amazed when I tell you who I ran into the other day. About a month after the campaign started, I was wandering the desert in a truck looking for Jerries.

"I spotted a large column early one morning and crept up on it as stealthily as an army truck will allow. It was a friendly column, and out of the nearest vehicle popped a long thin figure with glasses. It was Head. I don't know which of us had the biggest surprise. It seems strange to me, but there was both of us, with more than our fair share of brains, yet we had nothing better to do than chase our fellow men around the desert."

Footnote It would be their last meeting; Head's parents, at Queen's Street, Weymouth, were to hear that their son had been reported missing. As for Walkling, he survived the war; to become Major-General, and Colonel Commandant of the Royal Artillery in 1974.

14 May Charmouth radar station slips down cliff.

A radio location [radar] station on the Dorset coast was lost at 08.00 hours today through natural causes when three hundred feet of clifftop subsided in a landslip at Cain's Folly, to the east of Charmouth.

Footnote The concrete building lies partly submerged in the lias clays in the undercliff, 150 feet below the edge, and was half visible in 1985 with its seaward side tilting upwards.

19 May Germans lose two T-boats.

Two of the 1,300 ton craft of the German 5th T-boat Flotilla, *Iltis* and *Seeadler*, have been sunk off Dorset in recent days. They were intercepted by Portsmouth-based motor torpedo boats. MTB220 was lost during the action.

23 May Luftwaffe ace Langar killed at Shaftesbury.

Luftwaffe ace Hauptmann Langar, the officer commanding the elite Kampf Gruppe 100, was killed today when his Heinkel He111 plunged into a hillside in low cloud. He had been intercepted by Squadron Leader John 'Cat's Eyes' Cunningham whose Beaufighter had been scrambled from Middle Wallop on the Hampshire Downs.

Cloud cover was dense and carried heavy rain. Langar dived in an attempt to evade the Beaufighter and then crashed into the hills. No shot had been fired.

The intruder had been detected by the Type 15 radar antenna in the field near Christchurch that is RAF Sopley. Its tented Operations Room directed the Beaufighter, of 604 Squadron, and brought about the interception. Sopley radar station is enabling fighters to operate in total darkness, as well as dense cloud, and has been given the codename 'Starlight'.

25 May Brownsea decoy draws bombs from Poole.

The western end of Brownsea Island rocked to countless explosions in the early hours of this Whit Monday morning. Pathfinder bombers had dropped incendiaries nearly on target for the new Coastal Command base, RAF Hamworthy, and these landed with some high explosives in Rockley Road, Coles Avenue and Hinchcliffe Road. Many bungalows were destroyed and five civilians killed, including firewatcher Cecil Cowley, but fortunately for Poole the fires were extinguished in time for the newly completed 'Starfish' apparatus of the Major Strategic Night Decoy to come to light across the water on Brownsea Island.

The combination of wood, coal, paraffin and flushes of water produce white-hot flashes just like those of bursting bombs and lured the fifty-five enemy planes to unload 150 tons of high explosive harmlessly on to the island.

Only one bomb found a military target—a stray made a direct hit on Poole Home Guard's company headquarters in Lindsay Road, causing the unit's first death from enemy action with the loss of Private W.J. Griffiths.

The bombers had come from the Pas de Calais and been tracked by radar to St Catherine's Point, Isle of Wight, from where they turned north-westwards.

Footnote The Brownsea decoy was to save Poole and Bournemouth from a total of a thousand tons of German bombs.

25 May   **Worth radar establishment evacuated.**

The Telecommunications Research Establishment is being evacuated from Worth Matravers and Langton Matravers to Malvern College, Worcestershire, because of fears that the Germans might attempt their own Bruneval-style raid on the Dorset coast.

In order to emphasise the danger, Reginald Jones and Hugh Smith arrived on the Dorset coast from Air Ministry Scientific Intelligence in London with revolvers ostentatiously strapped to their belts, when they came to inspect the enemy radar apparatus captured at Bruneval.

25 May   **Telecommunications Flying Unit exits from Hurn.**

As a result of the departure from the Purbeck coast of the Air Ministry's Telecommunications Research Establishment, because of fears of a German raid, its support team and their unusual collection of some fifty assorted aircraft were today flying from RAF Hurn. The Telecommunications Flying Unit is on its way to Defford, near Worcester.

1 June   **RAF Hurn taken over by Army Co-Operation Command.**

RAF Hurn was transferred today from 11 Group Fighter Command to 38 Wing Army Co-Operation Command. The Air Officer Commanding, Air Marshal Sir A.S. Barratt, inspected the aerodrome which is under the command of Group Captain H.J.G.E. Proud.

1 June   **Fleet Air Arm aerodrome for Charlton Horethorne.**

An airstrip to the north of Sherborne, at Sigwells Farm, Charlton Horethorne, which has been used as an emergency landing ground, is to become a satellite aerodrome for the Fleet Air Arm station at Yeovilton. Flight Lieutenant H.C.V. Jolleff was today on the 600 feet high limestone plateau to the north of the farm to meet an advance party from Exeter.

4 June   **Arne decoy blaze saves Holton Heath.**

The Royal Naval Cordite Factory on Holton Heath was saved from a potentially devastating major raid last night by the swift ignition of half a ton of waste shell propellant at its dummy factory on the other side of the Wareham Channel. Inspection of the Arne decoy site today revealed 206 craters and it is estimated that fifty or more bombs also fell into the harbour.

4 June   **Germans nearly set Hamworthy ablaze.**

A German raid on Hamworthy and Poole, by fifty bombers in the early hours this morning, was partly thwarted by heath fires started by the incendiaries of the pathfinder bombers in the gorse and heather at Rocklea. This drew many of the bombers westwards from the urban area but it nearly created a disaster.

One of the bombs that exploded on Ham Common ruptured a giant tank of 100-octane aviation fuel concealed in the old claypits at Doulting's Pier. A million gallons flowed into lakes across the wasteland and fire teams could only pray that no one dropped a match let alone a bomb as the whole area began to reek with fumes.

Some of the bombs did find the urban areas of Hamworthy and the densely-packed Georgian buildings of the Old Town. A grocer's shop opposite the parish church was hit, as was Yeatman's Mill on Poole Quay. Bolson's store at their Wessex Wharf shipyard in Ferry Road, Hamworthy, was gutted. The yard manufactures twin-screw harbour defence motor launches, HDMLs, which are vessels of 72 feet. There a firewatcher, 55-year-old Louis Pittwood, was fatally injured. He died today in the Cornelia Hospital, Longfleet Road. Twenty-three others are having their injuries tended.

Mrs Florence Diffy of Green Road and a six-year-old boy who was staying at Hamworthy, Victor Park, have also died in the Cornelia Hospital from injuries received in the raid.

The Royal Navy's headquarters ship for the port, HMS *Sona* which is berthed beside Poole Quay, was sunk by a bomb which dropped through the funnel and buried itself in the mud beneath the hull. It did not explode and the sailors were able to scramble up the quayside.

5 June   Whitleys arrive at Hurn for Resistance 'Special Duties'.

297 (Army Co-Operation) Squadron has flown into RAF Hurn from Netheravon. Its Tiger Moth biplanes have been replaced by twin-engined Whitleys.

Their flights include Special Duties across the Channel to drop agents for the Special Operations Executive and supplies for resistance groups.

6 June   Bournemouth is bombed.

High explosive bombs have damaged a total of 454 properties in Bournemouth. One landed on a railway siding at Southcote Road. Others dropped near St Peter's church, on the Anglo-Swiss Hotel, and at Hill House in Parsonage Road.

7 June 1942. Poole. HMS 'Sona' is no longer the Royal Navy's headquarters ship.

7 June   Delayed bomb destroys Navy's Poole headquarters.

00.52 hours. The bomb which sank the Royal Navy's headquarters ship at Poole Quay, HMS *Sona*, but failed to explode, has now detonated itself and completely destroyed what was left of the vessel and the frontages of several quayside buildings. The area had been roped off and there were no casualties.

15 June   Mustangs arrive at Hurn.

Mustangs of 170 (Army Co-Operation) Squadron have flown in to RAF Hurn from Weston Zoyland, Somerset. They are to provide fast forward reconnaissance in an army-support rôle and are both manoeuvrable and toughly armed.

More Whitleys are arriving from Netheravon with the redeployment to Hurn of 296 (Army Co-Operation) Squadron. Routine exercises for this and the existing Hurn-based 297 Squadron include paratroop drops over Salisbury Plain.

18 June   Royal Navy puts into Bournemouth for repairs.

The Royal Navy's coastal forces have anchored and tied up around the remnants of Bournemouth Pier—broken at the centre in 1940 to prevent it being used in a German invasion—for running repairs. They are leaving for Portland.

The damage to HMS *Albrighton* and SGB6 and SGB8 was sustained whilst trying to stop an Axis convoy of four German, Italian and Finnish ships that were being escorted by the 1st Schnellboot Flotilla. One of the four enemy transports was sunk but the Royal Navy lost SGB7.

June   Campaign to replace the 'Dorsetshire'.

The HMS *Dorsetshire* Replacement Campaign, launched by the Earl of Shaftesbury, aims to double the level of war savings in the county and raise £2,750,000 in six months to the end of the year.

9 July   The Battle of Lyme Bay.

This has been the battle of Lyme Bay, carried out by the German 1st Schnellboot Flotilla (S48, S50, S63, S67, S70, S104, S109) against Allied Coast Convoy E/P 91. 12,192 tons of shipping has gone down; the tanker SS *Pomella* and four freighters. One of the British escorts has also been lost, an armed trawler HMT *Manor*.

22 July   Germans put more mines into the Channel.

The central part of the English Channel has been heavily mined by the Germans over the past three days through the efforts of Operation Rhein and Operation Stein. The 3rd T-boat Flotilla (T4, T10, T13, T14) have been depositing the mines through their torpedo tubes.

29 July   HMS 'Poole' adopted by the town.

HMS *Poole*, a new Bangor-class minesweeper, has been adopted by the town, at a civic reception held on the edge of the harbour at Poole Park.

July   Americans fly into RAF Warmwell.

British-made Spitfires returned to Warmwell Aerodrome this month but are being flown by a detachment of the 31st Fighter Group of the Eighth United States Army Air Force.

July Hurn Aerodrome to have Churchill's Liberator.

A VIP hangar is being constructed at RAF Hurn to house the Prime Minister's personal Liberator and other special aircraft. This hangar will have blast-walls but be open at each end to avoid containing any explosion.

Footnote The hangar survives, plus doors but no longer with blast-walls, and handles millions of kilos of air freight each year.

2 August And more German mines.

Once again the 3rd T-boat Flotilla (this time using T10, T13, T14) has been sowing German mines in the Channel sea-lanes, in Operation Masuren.

5 August Plane explodes off Bournemouth.

An aeroplane approached Bournemouth from the sea shortly before 03.00 hours with its navigation lights on. It then blew up with a tremendous flash.

6 August Portland radar test plays on German nerves.

A test off Portland today that amplified the enemy's radar echo from a formation of eight Defiant fighters caused the Luftwaffe to scramble thirty fighters from airfields in the Cherbourg peninsula to intercept the phantom force.

12 August Tarrant Hinton flier shot down over Malta convoy.

Michael Hankey, a young fighter pilot in the Fleet Air Arm, was killed in combat today whilst trying to protect a Malta convoy. He was the son of the rector of Tarrant Hinton, Rev Basil Hankey, and grew up in the village in the 1930s.

17 August First crash for Charlton Horethorne aerodrome.

The first squadron at the new Fleet Air Arm aerodrome at Charlton Horethorne, 887 Squadron, have left for St Merryn, Cornwall, and been replaced by 790 Squadron and the Sea Hurricanes of 891 Squadron.

A Hurricane of 891 Squadron crashed on landing. This was the first crash at this aerodrome. Only slight damage was done to the aircraft and the pilot was uninjured.

24 August Poole and Weymouth boats at Dieppe.

Boats from Poole and Weymouth have since 18 August been operating as support vessels for the Operation Jubilee reconnaissance to test the strength of the German West Wall at Dieppe. The Dieppe Raid returnees have brought back stories of amazing escapes and days of contrast which started with the Frenchmen uncorking wine in the belief that they had been liberated and ended with the Canadians setting up machine guns on parapets comprised of their own dead.

31 August Australians fly into Hamworthy.

Nine Sunderland flying boats of 461 (Royal Australian Air Force) Squadron today landed in Poole Harbour from Mount Batten, Plymouth. Squadron Leader R.C. Lovelock heads a complement of 132 men. The new base at Hamworthy was established as RAF Poole at the start of the month and renamed RAF Hamworthy a week later.

Squadron headquarters are being established on the north-eastern shore of Poole Harbour in the Harbour Yacht Club buildings at Lilliput.

The Australians are flying anti-submarine patrols in the South Western Approaches and the Bay of Biscay where U-boats have been caught napping by airborne radar and are now under orders to surface only for the recharging of their batteries.

August **Bovington's remaining Great War tanks rescued for a film.**

The old tanks from the Great War that were used as pill-boxes around Bovington in the anti-invasion defences of 1940 have come back to life for the making of a film, *Victory*. It has realistic scenes, shot on the Dorsetshire heaths at Turners Puddle and Gallows Hill, of British light tanks advancing under heavy enemy artillery bombardment in the war of 1914–18.

1942. Bovington. The Royal Tank Corps' historic collection of the world's first tanks was scrapped in 1940. Those machines that had not been broken up, and were merely lying around as pill-boxes near the Armoured Fighting Vehicles School, came back to life for an admiring audience in 1942: 'A realistic scene from the British film "Victory" which was filmed in Dorsetshire. British light tanks are seen advancing under heavy artillery bombardment from the enemy in the war of 1914-18.'

3 September **Poole Commandos raid the Channel Islands.**

No 62 Commando of Combined Operations, based at Anderson Manor near Bere Regis and operating out of Poole Harbour, last night raided a German U-boat signalling station in the Casquets Lighthouse in the Channel Islands. Code books have been captured and seven German wireless operators, who were taken completely by surprise, found themselves in Poole at 04.00 hours this morning and prisoners of war.

Footnote The leader of the Small Scale Raiding Force, Geoffrey Appleyard, was promoted to Major and awarded the Distinguished Service Order.

3 September **Prayers for the third anniversary.**

Today, the third anniversary of the outbreak of war, churches have been packed for the national day of prayer. Services have also been held at places of work, including the Bournemouth department stores of Allens and Beales.

1942. Poole Harbour. The 'Trots'. These are the straight pecked lines across the centre of the map. They are the water-runways used by RAF Coastal Command and British Overseas Airways Corporation flying boats in landing and taking off. No.1 Trot is off the Lake area of Hamworthy; No.2 Trot is off Lower Hamworthy; No.3 Trot off Parkstone Bay and Lilliput; No.4 Trot between Brownsea Island and Sandbanks.

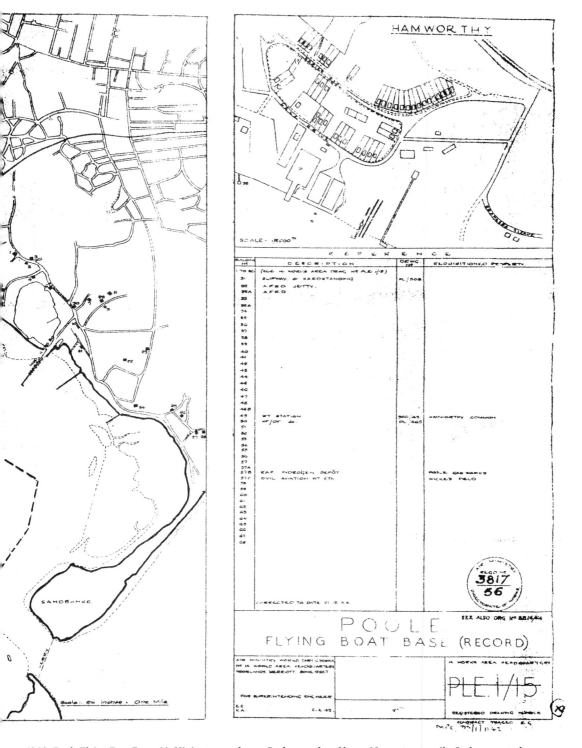

1942. Poole Flying Boat Base. Air Ministry record map. Scale, as reduced here, 40mm. to one mile. It shows—at a larger scale top right in detail, and on the main map inside a rectangle—the slipway, jetty and hardstanding that comprise RAF Hamworthy.

1942. Lulworth Camp. Tests at the Gunnery Wing of the Armoured Fighting Vehicles School for an American General Grant tank (below) and a British Valentine (above) which has been armed with a six pounder anti-tank gun, replacing its standard two pounder.

9 September **Squadrons change at Charlton Horethorne.**

891 Squadron today left Charlton Horethorne for St Merryn, Cornwall, and are being replaced by 893 Squadron. The aerodrome is being used for working-up training, with Sea Hurricanes practising on target-towing Martinets.

11 September **Poole raider kills five.**

A single German bomber ignored the Bofors guns at Canford Cliffs today to come in from the bay and drop a single bomb that has killed five people in Poole. The dead are Rev William Russell and his son Frank at 11 Marlborough Road, Mrs Winifred Phillips and her 11-year-old daughter June at 'Woodgrove' in Bournemouth Road, and Mrs Annie Watts at 12 Earlham Drive.

14 September **Twenty-one killed on Poole flying boat.**

The Poole flying boat *Clare*, outward bound for Bathurst, West Africa, with thirteen passengers and six crew has crashed in flames into the English Channel. She radioed soon after takeoff to report engine trouble and half an hour later to say she was on fire.

Footnote Nothing more was heard or found.

17 September **Piddletrenthide man found shot dead.**

In the early hours this morning the body of farm worker Louis Aubrey Stickland, aged 42, was found lying beside Chapel Lane, Piddletrenthide. He had a single gunshot wound in the chest.

Stickland enlisted with the Home Guard two months ago. Last evening he went to the Golden Grain Bakery for cigarettes but did not return. His wife was unconcerned because she thought he was having a long chat with the baker, Frederick Davis.

Mrs Stickland did not report her husband missing until 00.30 hours today. The body was found by the local magistrate, Henry Levi Green. Locals know the spot as Darkie Lane but it is called Chapel Lane on the map.

Footnote The story is set to continue, with November and December entries.

September **Coastal Command aerodrome at Holmsley.**

RAF Holmsley South, an aerodrome with concrete runways for Wellingtons of Coastal Command on anti-submarine patrols, has been constructed across the flat expanse of heather and gorse at Plain Heath on the south-western edge of the New Forest.

Footnote In 1943 they would be joined by four-engined Halifax bombers, the tugs for troop-carrying gliders.

September **Aerodrome being constructed at Tarrant Rushton.**

Work is in progress on the construction of a major aerodrome for the RAF, with hardened runways, on the sheep downs between Badbury Rings and Tarrant Rushton valley about five miles east of Blandford.

September **Poole baker raises £3,600 for Russia.**

Joe Bright, the Mayor of Poole and the man voted "Best Baker in Britain", has raised £3,600 in aid of Uncle Joe. To help Stalin's heroic struggle and relieve some of the appalling suffering on the Eastern Front he has been working tirelessly for the Medical Aid to Russia and China Fund which he founded. Bright's shop is at 117 High Street, Poole.

1 October   **Sherborne postman loses his arm in a propeller.**

Levelling off runways and the rolling of relaid turf has led to some changes in the usual pattern of aircraft movements at the Fleet Air Arm station near Charlton Horethorne.

At 09.00 hours a Fulmar of 790 Squadron, being moved by Lieutenant Commander Hodgson, was involved in a taxying accident with a postman from Sherborne Post Office, Mr W.J. John. The latter was riding a combination motor cycle and hit the propeller of the Fulmar, severing his right arm at the shoulder. He was taken to the Royal Naval Hospital at Sherborne and is expected to recover.

7 October   **Hamworthy becomes a landing craft base.**

The Admiralty today commissioned the Lake camp-site at Hamworthy, along with Hamworthy Common and the Round Island two miles away near the opposite side of Poole Harbour, as shore-based HMS *Turtle*. It will be concerned with training British, American and Canadian crews in the handling of landing craft at sea and their use in beach assaults.

14 October   **Losses on both sides in major Channel battle.**

Last night a Coastal Command reconnaissance aircraft from Calshot spotted the German auxiliary cruiser Schiff 45 *Komet* attempting to break out from Le Harve, westwards into the Atlantic. She was being escorted by the 3rd Schnellboot Flotilla and German minesweepers.

In an attack by a Royal Navy flotilla of Hunt class destroyers (HMS *Cottesmore, Esdale, Glassdale, Quorn*) and motor torpedo boats (MTB55, MTB84, MTB95, MTB229, MTB236) plus another destroyer, HMS *Albrighton*, the *Komet* was sunk with the loss of all her crew by two torpedoes. They had been fired by MTB236.

From Portland a supporting force set sail comprising HMS *Brocklesby* and *Tynedale* with the Danish ship *Fernie* and the Polish *Krakowiak*. There were a large number of casualties aboard the *Brocklesby* though she survived the action.

In a separate incident the armed trawler HMT *Jasper*, making for Portland from Dover, was sunk by a German Schnellboot, S81.

17 October   **Fuel shortages stop Royal Blue expresses.**

Royal Blue express services to London finally ceased operation today, after months of steadily slimmer timetables, as a result of the gravity of the national fuel shortages. Half of the familiar dark-blue fleet is anyway reserved for manoeuvres and other military uses.

A few of the coaches will still be seen with civilian passengers, however, as the following services have been licensed to run seven days a week. The Ministry of Transport concession has been granted because it is accepted that alternative ordinary bus services and rail facilities are less than adequate in many parts of Dorset:

Service 400, Bournemouth to Southampton. Four journeys each way of 88 minutes.

Service 402, Bournemouth to Dorchester, Bridport and Exeter. Two journeys each way of 250 minutes. Re-booking will be necessary at Dorchester as through tickets cannot be issued; the licence is for the run in two separate stages, Bournemouth to Dorchester and Dorchester to Exeter.

Service 403, Bournemouth to Blandford, Sherborne and Yeovil. One journey each way of 136 minutes.

Service 404, Honiton along the A30 to Shaftesbury. One journey each way of 167 minutes.

Service 405, Bournemouth to Blandford, Shaftesbury and Trowbridge. Two journeys each way of 215 minutes.

Footnote The coach express service to London did not resume until 15 April 1946.

25 October   **Army Co-Operation Squadrons leave Hurn.**

The Mustangs of 170 (Army Co-Operation) Squadron and the Whitleys of 297 (Army Co-Operation) Squadron have departed from RAF Hurn for Thruxton on the Hampshire Downs. The other Hurn Whitleys, those of 296 (Army Co-Operation) Squadron, have left for Andover.

Hurn has been evacuated so that it can be used as the springboard for a major overseas operation.

31 October   **Eisenhower and staff fly into Hurn.**

Six Boeing B-17 Flying Fortress bombers of the 97th Bombardment Group of the United States Army Air Command touched down at RAF Hurn today with a large contingent of top-ranking American officers.

They are led by Lieutenant-General Dwight D. Eisenhower who is the Commander of Allied Forces North-West Africa.

October   **Weymouth's famous aviator killed in Middle East.**

The latest casualties in the Middle East include George Stainforth, an old boy of Weymouth College who rose to fame in 1929–31 when he took the world airspeed record in Schneider trophy flights. He pushed the speed to 246 miles per hour and then averaged 379 mph. Other records included flying upside down for a duration of eleven minutes seven seconds and the title of RAF revolver champion.

As a Wing Commander in the Middle East he was the oldest fighter pilot serving in that theatre. He was shot down in night fighting, his particular forte.

3 November   **VIP Fortresses leave Hurn for Gibraltar.**

Lieutenant-General Dwight D. Eisenhower, the Commander of Allied Forces North-West Africa, has flown out from Hurn today with his staff officers and a British contingent for a conference in Gibraltar to discuss Montgomery's break-out into the Western Desert from El Alamein and the advance towards Algiers. They are aboard five Flying Fortresses; a sixth had to abort its take-off when the undercarriage hydraulics failed.

The top-brass include General Kenneth Anderson, the Commander of the British 1st

31 October to
3-4 November 1942.
Hurn, visitors.
Brigadier-General
Jimmy Doolittle (far left)
and Lieutenant-General
Dwight D. Eisenhower.

Army; Major-General Mark Wayne Clark, the co-ordinator of the secret moves to see whether the Vichy French will defend North Africa; and Brigadier Lyman Lemnitzer. Their transit to Gibraltar is being code-named Operation Cackle.

Footnote Eisenhower's pilot, Major Paul Tibbets, would fly the B-29 *Enola Gay* to drop the first atomic bomb, on Hiroshima.

4 November Sixth Fortress flies from Hurn.

Brigadier-General Jimmy Doolittle, the aviator who set the world air-speed record in 1932, flew from Hurn today to Gibraltar aboard the Flying Fortress that experienced wheel-jamming yesterday. Doolittle is Commander of the United States air forces in North Africa.

The news today from General Bernard Montgomery, the desert Commander of the British 8th Army, is that everywhere Erwin Rommel's Afrika Korps is in full retreat. El Alamein is only seventy miles from Alexandria and Rommel had been poised to attack Egypt.

Troop-carrying American C-47 Dakota transports will be leaving for Gibraltar via RAF Hurn. Thirty-nine Dakotas of 51 Wing Troop Carrier Group of the United States 12th Army Air Force assembled at Hurn today in connection with the planned landings in North Africa. More are to follow.

7 November Churchill orders church bells to ring.

Hearing that the 8th Army has taken 30,000 prisoners after the Battle of Alamein, Winston Churchill tells the nation to celebrate by ringing church bells—the first time they have been heard since the outbreak of war.

The prisoners include nine generals. Only the rains of the past two days have saved the enemy from utter annihilation.

General Montgomery is to be knighted. The victorious church bells will ring out across Britain next Sunday morning, 15 November.

31 October
to 4 November 1942.
El Alamein.
The Eighth Army
has achieved its
'Break-out'and
the war in the
Western Desert
has turned.

Footnote There was still a psychological factor, that of Rommel's reputation, inhibiting what should have been a British stampede across the desert. For there was now literally nothing that could have stopped them; on 9 November 1942 the Afrika Korps was down to ten tanks and had insufficent petrol to field even this number in combat.

8 November 1942. Planned at Hurn—ashore this morning, in Morocco, to a welcome amid the palms. Not that Eisenhower's 'United Nations' forces, as they are styled, have enjoyed a universal walk-over. Lyautey and other colonial French garrisons are putting up stout resistance.

8 November **Eisenhower takes over North Africa and Dakotas return to Hurn.**

A combined British and American force involving a total of 107,000 men has landed in French North Africa at Casablanca, Oran and Algiers. Operation Torch is under the overall command of Lieutenant-General Dwight D. Eisenhower and has five hundred transport craft being shepherded by three hundred and fifty naval vessels.

Back home, fifty-one C-47 Dakota troop transports have returned empty to RAF Hurn, where debriefings were attended by Major-General Frederick Browning, the General Officer Commanding the 1st British Airborne Division. A total of 180 transport aircraft passed through Hurn in the build-up for the operation. They included sixty-one Boeing B-17F Flying Fortress bombers.

Operation Cackle, the Hurn-Gibraltar air ferry service, has been completed without a single casualty.

13 November **Accused man's wife exhumed at Piddletrenthide.**

Following the charging of Frederick Davis with the murder of another Piddletrenthide villager, Louis Stickland, on the night of 16 September, police today exhumed the remains of the accused man's 32-year-old wife, Freda Davis. She died in August, with an illness described as ulcerative colitis.

The coffin was removed to the County Hospital for the body to be given an autopsy by Sir Bernard Spilsbury, the chief Home Office pathologist. At the graveside the accused man watched as soil samples were removed.

Footnote No evidence of foul play was found.

25 November **Weymouth grenade accident.**

Major-General A.A. Dowler of Southern Command reports that during an NCO battle practice by the 5th Dorset (Weymouth) Battalion of the Home Guard a member accidentally burst a No 76 (S.I.P.) grenade over himself. He would probably have been burnt to death but for the prompt action of QMS W. Marsh and Sergeant W. Andrew in removing his burning clothing.

November **Cannon-fire is the Creekmoor sound.**

Aircraft cannon-fire is now heard incessantly on the heathland north of Poole, around Fleet's Corner, but the noise comes from the ground. The Creekmoor munitions factory in Soper's Lane makes Oerlikon machine guns which are fitted to the latest versions of the Spitfire and other fighters. Production continues around the clock and test-firing is carried out daily.

3 December **HMS 'Penylan' sunk off Bournemouth.**

The German 5th Schnellboot Flotilla (S81, S82, S115, S116) today attacked two British convoys in the Channel, in the area off Bournemouth and the Isle of Wight, sinking the escort destroyer HMS *Penylan* and a freighter.

4 December **Barnes Wallis bomb fails to bounce on The Fleet lagoon.**

Barnes Neville Wallis, the assistant chief designer at the aviation section of Vickers-Armstrongs Limited, flew today from their Weybridge works to the Chesil Beach bombing range. He was in Wellington BJ895/G, an aeroplane he designed, and acted as the bomb aimer when the pilot, Captain J. 'Mutt' Summers, came in low over the flat waters of The Fleet lagoon which lies between the offshore pebble bank and the inshore coast of Langton Herring and Abbotsbury.

Captain R.C. Handasyde acted as the observer. Two steel spheres were dropped, with the hope that they might bounce along the surface of the water, but both burst upon impact. Neither carried explosives.

10 December **Poole, the port, gets Seamen's Mission.**

Admiral Sir Reginald Aylmer Ranfurly Plunkett-Ernle-Erle-Drax of Charborough Park, who fought in HMS *Lion* at the Battle of Jutland and headed the diplomatic mission to Moscow in 1939, has today opened the Mansion House in Thames Street, Poole, as a Mission to Seamen. It is a mark of Poole's restored status as a port that it should have a Seamen's Mission.

13 December **The sea engulfs a hundred Portland houses.**

Shortly after 11.00 this Sunday morning the sea started to seep through the pebbles of the Chesil Beach at Portland. By noon the first waves were splashing over the top. Within a short time a shallow layer of water across Victoria Square surged to over five feet. It almost covered the letter box and the mail floated out on the tide.

More than a hundred houses in Chiswell were inundated and all road and rail communications between Portland and the mainland are dislocated. The stout stone wall beside the beach road is reduced to rubble at many points and the railway line breached for several yards; sleepers were swept away and rails buckled.

The water put the island's gasworks out of action and has left a trail of mud, clay, shingle and boulders across the low-lying part of Chiswell. Many are homeless and have been told that their ruined cottages will have to be demolished.

Portland Women's Voluntary Service was soon in action with hot dinners, bedding and clothes—at least help comes fast when there is a war on—and this evening the extensive damage caused by the chest-deep waters to the Cove House Inn had been cleared sufficiently for it to open punctually at seven o'clock.

England's motto is business as usual. In Portland that defiance has been extended to an older enemy—the sea.

14 December   **Tank Workshop strafed at Lulworth.**

The Workshop of the Gunnery Wing of the Armoured Fighting Vehicles School at Lulworth Camp was devastated today in a surprise attack by two German fighter-bombers. The first one passed over the camp without incident but the second dropped a 1,800 kilogram high explosive bomb which landed at the road junction at the edge of the camp. It embedded itself in the concrete, leaving several feet of the casing and fins sticking up into the air, but did not explode.

Then the second aircraft returned low across the camp and raked the Workshop with 20mm cannon fire. The welder, Sergeant Jack Stevens, was fatally wounded in the head, and three other soldiers were injured. The building is an utter shambles.

The aircraft had come from the east, across the Tank Park, and then turned south-west, disappearing over Lulworth Cove and out to sea.

15 December   **Further bouncing-bomb test is a failure.**

Wellington BJ895/G put down at Warmwell Aerodrome en route for further testings of the bouncing-bomb designed by scientist Barnes Wallis of Vickers-Armstrongs. As with the first test, on 4 December, both drops failed.

It is decided to try again after Christmas.

16 December   **Lunchtime bombs kill four at Poole.**

A Dornier 217 bomber swept low over Poole Quay at lunchtime today and dropped a stick of five bombs. They have fatally injured 14-year-old William Matthews and a Home Guard member, George Davis, who was working at Poole Iron Foundry, Thames Street.

There were casualties from other blasts, at the Gasworks, in Barbers Piles, and at Newman's Shipyard. A worker died as a result of the latter blast.

The other explosion sank a Royal Navy harbour patrol vessel, killing the only rating aboard.

17 December   **Airman's farewell to Came Woods.**

Sergeant-Pilot Marcel Fussell of Monmouth Road, Dorchester, has been killed in action. Shortly before he died he wrote about Came Woods—autobiographically, though presented in the third person—appreciating it "for the last time, for tomorrow he was to leave his native life, his home, the fields and woods, where he had spent his life as a boy . . . to join the Air Force and serve his country."

At the top of the paper he had written one word:
"Farewell."

21 December   **French gunboat sinks off Swanage.**

The sea was the villain today in its age-old war against those who take it for granted. The Free French Navy's gunboat *Chasseur* underestimated the tide-flow and rough waters off Durlston Head, Swanage, and sank after capsizing.

25 December   **Bells are enjoyed once again.**

To celebrate El Alamein, and now this Christmas Day, we have enjoyed a rare sound. The bells of Christchurch Priory have echoed in joyful celebration. It is an unusual treat, not that their silence over the past three years has been in any way unwelcome; had they tolled it would have been to warn of invasion.

31 December Poole machine gunner brings down a Dornier.

New Year's Day at Poole will belong to Sergeant William Hanbury who was manning a Poole searchlight post. He illuminated a Dornier 217 bomber coming at low level across the sea and sprayed it with his Lewis machine gun. The pilot veered away but struck a gasometer and crashed into Poole Harbour.

Another raider was more successful and has destroyed Bradford's store on Poole Quay which had just been completely rebuilt after being hit on Whit Sunday.

December Piddletrenthide baker acquitted of murder.

Summing up after the trial for murder of Piddletrenthide baker Frederick Davis, Mr Justice MacNaughton said that in his opinion there was a matter of real doubt for the jury to consider: that the defendant's story might be true. He had said that he was examining a gun with Louis Stickland when it fired:

"When I found I had killed my best friend I was frightened. I was afraid of being found in the house with a dead man. On the impulse of the moment I moved the body."

After being out only forty-five minutes the jury returned to the Assize Court at Winchester with their verdict—not guilty.

December Swordfish fly from Hurn in search of E-boats.

Torpedo-carrying Swordfish biplanes of 811 and 816 (Fleet Air Arm) Squadrons, from Thorney Island, have been flying from RAF Hurn to widen their patrols against German E-boats. Six aircraft are involved in this attempt to counter the growing menace from these fast attack vessels.

Hurn has also hosted the Halifax bombers of 138 and 161 (Special Duty) Squadrons, usually based at Tempsford in Buckinghamshire, which runs flights deep into occupied Europe for the Special Operations Executive.

The Mustangs of 239 Squadron arrived from Odiham, Hampshire, on 7 December; one of their aeroplanes was involved in a collision with a Lancaster bomber.

1498 Gunnery Flight was formed at Hurn on 10 December. Its Lysander and Martinet light aircraft will provide realistic bursts of air-firing to accompany glider-towing exercises. Ventura and Boston light bombers came to Hurn on 11 December to provide the smoke-screen for a practice landing in Studland Bay.

Later on 11 December, the twin-engined Whitleys of 297 (Army Co-Operation) Squadron returned from Andover with almost all their personnel and equipment following in tow in seven Horsa gliders. They had been ousted from Hurn to provide space for the massive Operation Cackle.

December No 5 Commando billeted in Boscombe.

Back from Madagascar, which they helped recapture on behalf of Free French Forces, the men of No 5 Commando, Combined Operations, are being billeted in Boscombe and Bournemouth. Their base is at Boscombe, in the Broughty Ferry Hotel.

Footnote They were amalgamated with No 1 Commando and 42 and 44 Companies, Royal Marines, and became the 3rd Special Services Brigade.

December Spies for France fly from Christchurch.

Christchurch Aerodrome has been used by the Westland Lysanders of the Special Operations Executive for several cross-Channel missions to land and recover agents in occupied France.

Handley Page Halifax: tug-plane for glider troops, operating from Tarrant Rushton and Holmsley South.

1943

9 January   **Third bouncing-bomb test also a failure.**

Two more steel spheres were dropped today by Wellington BJ895/G, from the Vickers-Armstrongs Weybridge works, on the Chesil Beach bombing range. The tests were once again a failure. The aim of aircraft designer Barnes Wallis is to devise a bomb that can bounce across the water and have a dam-breaking capability.

So far, of the six dummy bombs that have been dropped, five have fragmented on touching The Fleet lagoon and the other was incorrectly released and hit the land.

10 January   **At last, Barnes Wallis bounces a bomb!**

Vickers-Armstrongs scientist Barnes Wallis last night carried out modifications to one of his prototype bouncing-bombs at Warmwell Aerodrome. Wellington BJ895/G lifted off with it today for another low-level drop over The Fleet lagoon at Chesil Beach bombing range.

The boffin and his crew are jubilant! For the first time their bomb, which had been strengthened, skimmed the surface of the water. It spun for fifty feet and then shattered — but the principle had been proved.

13 January   **Dorchester anxiety at ploughing of public paths.**

The Rights of Way Committee of Dorchester Rural District Council has expressed anxiety that public paths are being lost in the ploughing of grasslands for grain production. "With regard to the temporary ploughing up and diversion of rights of way consequent upon the service of directions under the Cultivation of Lands Order, the committee were extremely anxious that, during hositilities, the existence of rights of way should not be lost, and their chief anxiety was lest at the cessation of hostilities the formerly existing rights be not restored to the public."

January 1943. Warmwell Aerodrome. Four Burmese pilots flew with 257 Squadron. They had been training in India when the Japanese invaded Burma. Left to right are Pilot Officers M.H. Yi of Pegu, H.Y. Lau and S.J. Khin of Rangoon, and T. Clift from Shan States.

15 January   HMS 'Dorsetshire' appeal reaches £3,057,703.

Dorset's savings campaign to raise the money, through the war loan scheme, to buy the Royal Navy a cruiser to replace HMS *Dorsetshire*, is well ahead of its original £2,750,000 target. This has been exceeded by £307,703 and stands at £3,057,703.

23 January   Barnes Wallis bomb bounces thirteen times.

Wellington BJ895/G today dropped a wooden version of the bouncing-bomb devised by Vickers-Armstrongs designer Barnes Wallis. It achieved thirteen bounces on the inshore lagoon of The Fleet to the east of Langton Hive Point, Langton Herring, on the RAF's Chesil Beach bombing range.

24 January   Bouncing-bomb jumps a boom at Langton Herring.

Twenty bounces were recorded this morning by scientist Barnes Wallis as his revolutionary bomb zipped across The Fleet lagoon at Langton Herring. Once again it had been dropped from Wellington bomber BJ895/G which then flew back to Warmwell Aerodrome.

The team from the Vickers-Armstrongs Weybridge works then prepared a boom across the shallow waters. This is intended to simulate the wall of a dam.

The evening saw another successful trial when the Wellington returned to the Chesil Beach bombing range. It again turned over the sea and came in across the lake-like waters of The Fleet. The bomb was dropped, and bounced, and proceeded to jump the boom.

24 January   Halifax bomber crashes at Kingston Lacy.

A four-engined Halifax bomber from RAF Holmsley South [Plain Heath Airfield] at the south-west edge of the New Forest faltered today shortly after its 13.30 take-off. It made two circuits of the aerodrome and was fifteen minutes into a transit flight to Talbenny, Haverfordwest, when it lost height over parkland near Wimborne.

The bomber crashed to the north-west of Kingston Lacy House, the seat of Ralph Bankes, and all the crew were killed. A terrified stag jumped through one of the ground floor dining room windows of the house. The aeroplane, DT684, belonged to 58 Squadron.

The dead are Flying Officer M.A. Legg of the Royal New Zealand Air Force (aged 32), Flying Officer G.R. Pringle, a Royal Canadian Air Force air observer (29), and Warrant Officers L.E. Gilpin (21) and S.J. Prince (25) of the Royal Canadian Air Force, who were wireless operators and gunners.

Footnote   They are buried in Bransgore churchyard.

31 January   H2S works—thanks to Worth, Christchurch, Hurn and West Howe.

Bomber Command last night operationally used H2S airborne radar sets for the first time, over Hamburg, and enabled Pathfinder flares to be dropped on their target. The need for this apparatus has been apparent since the night of 9 March 1942 when Bomber Command, in its Chief's words, "attacked Hamborn in mistake for Essen". Sir Arthur Harris, Commander-in-Chief Bomber Command, has enthusiastically backed the development of H2S—promised for last autumn—which takes its name from the chemical formula for the obnoxious gas hydrogen sulphide, because Churchill's chief scientific adviser, Professor Frederick Lindemann, had commented about the excuses he heard from the Telecommunications Research Establishment at Worth Matravers: "It stinks!"

The invention was the product of Group 8, working from a Nissen hut in the grounds of the Establishment's eastern out-station, Leeson House at Langton Matravers.

31 January 1943. Invented by Group 8 of the Telecommunications Research Establishment, at their out-station Leeson House, Langton Matravers, in 1941. H2S airborne radar-mapping module on the belly of a Lancaster of Bomber Command, used last night operationally for the first time, over Hamburg, to allow Pathfinders to drop their target flares with precision. No longer the original unaesthetic appendage it has become almost sexual in appearance, with the perspex casing moulded into what resembles the cloaca of a newt.

"TF" was its earlier code but that was reckoned to be a give-away [try for yourself, the answer is in the footnote] and it came into being after J.T. Randall and H.A.H. Boot invented the centimetric valve which was put into the new Beaufighter. Giving power on a low wavelength it provided an image on a screen that showed features of the ground below.

This was tested by a Blenheim bomber at eight thousand feet above the Air Defence Experimental Establishment beside Christchurch Aerodrome.

Six more flights were made and then a Halifax bomber was drafted to the new aerodrome at RAF Hurn for fitting with the first specially designed unit shielded in a protruding cupola from the belly which made the aeroplane seem ungainly and pregnant. The casing is perspex.

Then Air Commodore Donald 'Pathfinder' Bennett tried the apparatus with the result that Winston Churchill agreed it should be in production by the end of 1942. The Prototype Research Unit is making the sets—which have been perfected by Philip Dee and Bernard Lovell at Worth Matravers—in a factory beside the Northbourne Golf Links at West Howe, Bournemouth.

Footnote "TF", as you probably guessed, stood for "Town Finder".

The factory at West Howe that produced H2S now makes Max Factor cosmetics.

In practice, H2S was to create its own disaster. Not only could it be jammed but German technology advanced to exploit the signals and home in upon them. This again accelerated the rate of losses to the stage where on 30 March 1944 ninety-four bombers were shot down on a raid upon Nuremburg and seventy-one of those that made it home were damaged.

1942-43. Acting Admiral Louis Mountbatten, Commander of Combined Operations which has its headquarters at Anderson Manor, north-east of Bere Regis, and trains commando squads in Poole Harbour and at the rifle-range on Canford Heath.

11 February 1943. Brigadier Harold Woodhouse, Commandant of Blandford Camp, has died from a heart attack triggered by German bombs. His peacetime job was managing the family brewery.

January **BOAC's land-based operations now at Hurn.**

Hurn Aerodrome has become a multi-tasked airfield since the transfer of the British Over-seas Airways Corporation's dry-land flights—as distinct from the Poole flying boats—from Lyneham in Wiltshire.

January **Spitfire pilot rescued from Poole Bay.**

The Poole Air-Sea Rescue launch *Commodore* has picked up a Spitfire pilot whose plane ditched in Poole Bay.

5 February **Bombs bounce 4,000 feet across The Fleet.**

The trials of wooden prototypes of Barnes Wallis's bouncing-bomb resumed on The Fleet today. They were dropped from Wellington BJ895/G, coming from Weybridge and operating for the day out of Warmwell Aerodrome. The bomber is now making faster approach runs.

It swept in across the Chesil Beach bombing range at 300 miles per hour and succeeded in sending bombs jumping across the sheltered and wave-less inshore water for distances around 4,000 feet.

11 February **Blandford Commandant dies in raid.**

The Commandant of the Battle Training Camp at Blandford, Brigadier Harold Woodhouse of the local brewing family, has died from a heart attack caused by the exertion and excitement induced by a stick of German bombs. A single bomber attacked the camp and one of the cookhouses suffered blast damage.

29 February **Germans sink four ships off Dorset.**

In the past four days the 5th Schnellboot Flotilla has been harrying a Channel convoy in Lyme Bay and between Portland and the Isle of Wight. Two of the escorts protecting Convoy CHA 172, the armed trawlers HMT *Harstad* and HMT *Lord Hailsham*, have been sunk. The freighter *Modavia* (4,858 tons) has also gone down, together with a new 658-ton tank landing craft, LCT381.

February **Evelyn Waugh oversees Special Services at Canford.**

Rifle-range shooting by the 2nd Special Services Brigade is being carried out at Canford Heath. It is being overseen by Evelyn Waugh, the author—who last year published *Put Out More Flags*.

He is Staff Officer to the Acting Admiral Louis Mountbatten, Commander of Combined Operations which has its country house headquarters at Anderson Manor, near Bere Regis.

The Brigade is also training with landing craft in assaults on Brownsea Island and at Shell Bay and Studland beach which have now been cleared of their anti-invasion scaffolding and mines.

February **Five rescued from bomber off Christchurch.**

The five-man crew of a RAF Whitley bomber were plucked from the eastern side of Poole Bay, five miles south of Christchurch, after they had crashed into the sea. The rescue was carried out by the Poole launch *Commodore*.

1 March **Cattistock man jumped out of a safe job.**

Sergeant-Navigator Robert Paull of Cattistock has been reported missing after a bombing raid. He previously had a safe reserved occupation as an inspector of 'Predictor' work in an aircraft factory but insisted upon volunteering for the RAF.

1 March **'The Advance Post' on the Wessex front-line.**

Such is the growing sophistication of this Second World War that the present major military game, Exercise Spartan, has been marked by the appearance of the "first daily newspaper of its kind to be printed specially for the purpose of a military exercise in this country".

The hypothetical cause had been the invasion of southern England by the British Expeditionary Force; but for southern England one should read northern France for the war is moving ahead. "On to Eastland," as the headline puts it. "We are not on the defensive; we are

1 March 1943. Southland, the Wessex frontline. Opposite. 'Army field newspapers are not unknown but The Advance Post is the first daily newspaper of its kind to be printed specially for the purpose of a military exercise in this country.'

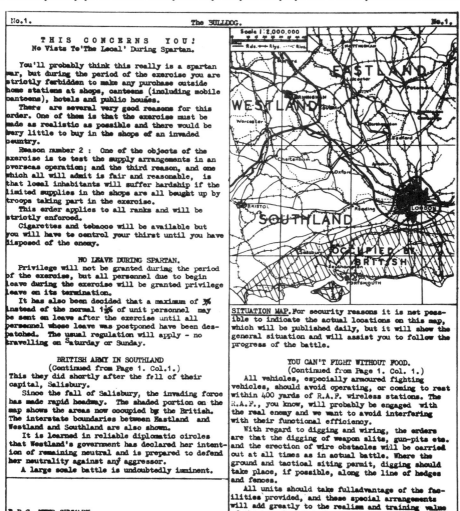

No.1.   The BULLDOG.   No.1.

THIS CONCERNS YOU!
No Visits To 'The Local' During Spartan.

You'll probably think this really is a spartan war, but during the period of the exercise you are strictly forbidden to make any purchase outside home stations at shops, canteens (including mobile canteens), hotels and public houses.

There are several very good reasons for this order. One of them is that the exercise must be made as realistic as possible and there would be very little to buy in the shops of an invaded country.

Reason number 2 : One of the objects of the exercise is to test the supply arrangements in an overseas operation; and the third reason, and one which all will admit is fair and reasonable, is that local inhabitants will suffer hardship if the limited supplies in the shops are all bought up by troops taking part in the exercise.

This order applies to all ranks and will be strictly enforced.

Cigarettes and tobacco will be available but you will have to control your thirst until you have disposed of the enemy.

NO LEAVE DURING SPARTAN.

Privilege will not be granted during the period of the exercise, but all personnel due to begin leave during the exercise will be granted privilege leave on its termination.

It has also been decided that a maximum of 3% instead of the normal 1½% of unit personnel may be sent on leave after the exercise until all personnel whose leave was postponed have been despatched. The usual regulation will apply - no travelling on Saturday or Sunday.

BRITISH ARMY IN SOUTHLAND
(Continued from Page 1. Col.1.)

This they did shortly after the fall of their capital, Salisbury.

Since the fall of Salisbury, the invading force has made rapid headway. The shaded portion on the map shows the areas now occupied by the British. The interstate boundaries between Eastland and Westland and Southland are also shown.

It is learned in reliable diplomatic circles that Westland's government has declared her intention of remaining neutral and is prepared to defend her neutrality against any aggressor.

A large scale battle is undoubtedly imminent.

B.B.C. NEWS SUMMARY

There is no official news from Central and Northern Tunisia to-day (1300 hrs Sunday).

In the South the 8th Army is continuing its probing of the Mareth Defences.

The Russians are still meeting strong German counter-attacks at the Western end of the Donetz Basin.

Scale 1:2,000,000

SITUATION MAP. For security reasons it is not possible to indicate the actual locations on this map, which will be published daily, but it will show the general situation and will assist you to follow the progress of the battle.

YOU CAN'T FIGHT WITHOUT FOOD.
(Continued from Page 1. Col. 1.)

All vehicles, especially armoured fighting vehicles, should avoid operating, or coming to rest within 400 yards of R.A.F. wireless stations. The R.A.F., you know, will probably be engaged with the real enemy and we want to avoid interfering with their functional efficiency.

With regard to digging and wiring, the orders are that the digging of weapon slits, gun-pits etc. and the erection of wire obstacles will be carried out at all times as in actual battle. Where the ground and tactical siting permit, digging should take place, if possible, along the line of hedges and fences.

All units should take full advantage of the facilities provided, and these special arrangements will add greatly to the realism and training value of the exercise, but the army must demonstrate that it is possible to apply sound common sense to the use of land under these conditions without abusing the facilities provided.

Aircraft of Bomber Command laid mines in enemy waters and bombed objectives in Western Germany.

The Prime Minister has sent a message of good wishes to the Wings for Victory Campaign.

March 1943. Southland — news of the fall of Salisbury. The Bulldog cautions participants to keep out of public houses and not to park near RAF wireless stations, in case this interferes with radar reception. Troop dispositions are not revealed. Information reaching the enemy would provide the Luftwaffe with the locations of targets.

passing to attack, but if we carry the Spartan determination in defence into attack, then the battle will be won." This unusual newspaper is "Not to be published".

There is a reminder that those taking part in the exercise must leave RAF radar stations in peace so that they can carry on with the real war: "All vehicles, especially armoured fighting vehicles, should avoid operating, or coming to rest within 400 yards of RAF wireless stations. The RAF, you know, will probably be engaged with the real enemy and we want to avoid interfering with their functional efficiency."

8 March **Navy lands rescued Germans at Mudeford.**

E-boats failed to ambush a coastal convoy off Devon and escaped eastwards pursued by the Polish destroyer *Krakowiak*, until she pulled in to Poole to refuel. The six-inch coastal batteries then opened up from Brownsea Island, Hengistbury Head and Mudeford, aided by 3.7 inch dual anti-air and anti-ship emplacements and the 40 mm Bofors anti-aircraft guns on the Bournemouth cliffs. There were German losses in Poole Bay; two bodies and four survivors have been brought to Mudeford by the picket-boat *Robert T. Hillary* which is a former lifeboat crewed by the Royal Navy Volunteer Reserve.

9 March **Bouncing-bombs upset the Abbotsbury swans.**

Carrying steel versions of the prototype bouncing-bomb devised for dam-busting operations by designer Barnes Wallis of Vickers-Armstrongs, Wellington BJ895/G returned yesterday to Warmwell Aerodrome and the Chesil Beach bombing range for an extended series of trial runs over The Fleet lagoon. The dummy bombs are skimming the water with the precision that suggests their use as an effective weapon is now feasible. These trials concluded this evening.

Locally, there have been complaints that the Wellington's approach flight, at 300 miles an hour over the West Fleet towards Langton Hive Point, and the uninhabited Herbury peninsula, has been upsetting the breeding at the famous Abbotsbury Swannery.

Footnote   The next set of tests, to determine the handling behaviour of the bomb on choppier water, would take place off Reculver, Kent.

18 March **Hanging parachutist killed in Poole Harbour.**

A Royal Artillery officer fouled his parachute on the airframe of a Dakota in a jump that went tragically wrong today. He found himself hanging from the aircraft, which was from RAF Broadwell, and the pilot headed south to the nearest area of calm sea.

He chose Poole Harbour and circled at a thousand feet over the Wareham Channel. The Dakota then came in low, to within a hundred feet of the harbour, at which point the soldier dropped off. He died as a result of impact with the water.

21 March **Australian Sunderland wrecked in Poole Harbour.**

Sunderland flying boat T9111 of 461 (Royal Australian Air Force) Squadron was wrecked today at 20.55 hours off RAF Hamworthy. The pilot, Flight Lieutenant Manger, had begun lifting off from the 'Trots'—as the sea runways are called—when he found himself losing power.

The flying boat careered into the mud-flats of Poole Harbour and is a total loss but the pilot and his eleven crewmen were able to clamber free and stagger to the shore. They have only superficial injuries.

23 March **BOAC Catalina wrecked in Poole Harbour.**

Having successfully returned to Poole Harbour on the last leg of a trip from Lagos, Nigeria, BOAC Catalina flying boat DA took off again on a training flight.

Everything was routine until the second homecoming of the day. This time, however, it turned to disaster.

It is the second time this week that a flying boat has been lost in landing, though the circumstances are different. The Catalina ploughed into a mass of flotsam. Three crewmen have been killed.

30 March   1st Dorsets leave Malta.

The siege of Malta has been lifted and the 1st Battalion of the Dorsetshire Regiment today sailed for Egypt. It is part of the 1st Malta Brigade which is to be renamed the 231st Infantry Brigade.

Footnote   They were welcomed to Fayid by General Sir Bernard Montgomery: "This morning I have seen some magnificent soldiers. These fine Regular battalions who have been shut up in Malta, and have now joined us, will be an asset to the 8th Army."

March   Hurricane comes down off Green Island.

A Hurricane has crashed into Poole Harbour, off Green Island. Its pilot was picked-up by the Air-Sea Rescue launch *Commodore*.

17 April   Poole Catalinas leave for Trincomalee.

Repainted with the white and blue roundels of the South-east Asia theatre, two BOAC Catalina flying boats are en route from Poole Harbour to Trincomalee, Ceylon, where they will be handed over to the Royal Air Force.

Catalina FM left Poole on 11 April and Catalina FL lifted off today for the same destination.

Footnote   They would survive to become named flying boats *Altair* and *Vega*.

21 April   Australian flying boats leave for Pembroke.

461 (Royal Australian Air Force) Squadron today left RAF Hamworthy and took their Sunderland flying boats to Pembroke Dock in South Wales.

They are being replaced by 210 Squadron which is flying military Catalinas.

21 April   Mine damaged vessel puts into Christchurch.

The United States Coastguard Service vessel *Apache*, bound for Cowes from Boston, Massachusetts, has been forced to put into the River Avon at Christchurch for repairs after having hit a mine in the Channel.

28 April   German craft sunk off St Alban's Head.

Last night the German submarine chaser VJ 140Z was sunk by Hunt-class destroyers, the Royal Navy's main coast protection flotilla from Portsmouth, whilst it was trying to guard Axis Convoy code 37K/MS. It went down off St Alban's Head.

1 May   American daylight raiders cross Dorset.

Elements of the first massed United States Air Force daytime bombing raid against Germany have crossed Dorset on their way to the Channel. The Royal Observer Corps log at Dorchester records: "09.30 hours. 20 Liberators spotted south-west. 10.45 hours. 47 Fortresses flying south." Planes returned individually through the afternoon. The Observer Corps, incidentally, was awarded the 'Royal' cachet on 11 April 1941.

9 May   Exercise Demon in Sherborne's wrecked street.

Bomb-damaged Newland in Sherborne, one of the streets devastated by the air raid of 30 September 1940, has provided a realistic setting for Exercise Demon. Spectators watched from rows of seats on the rise that looks down towards the Black Horse Hotel as troops, firemen, ARP wardens and the Women's Voluntary Service practised their crafts—from street warfare to the arrival of tea urns.

16 May   Halifax bomber crashes at Bransgore.

A four-engined Halifax bomber, DG390 of 295 Squadron, crashed today whilst on a flight from Hurn to the nearby RAF station at Holmsley South [Plain Heath Airfield] on the edge of the New Forest. A mile short of its destination, at Bransgore, it dived to starboard from twelve hundred feet and two of the crew were killed on impact. A Canadian, 21-year-old Flying Officer D.J. Smith, was dragged out of the wreckage alive but died in Boscombe Hospital.

The other dead are Royal Canadian Air Force Flying Officer M.W. Collins, aged 21, and Flying Officer P.S. Thomas, an RAF air gunner.

Footnote   They are buried in Bransgore churchyard.

17 May   RAF moves into Tarrant Rushton.

An RAF advance party has taken control of the aerodrome which from today is RAF Station Tarrant Rushton. They are Station Admin Officer Squadron Leader T.H.W. Pearce, Equipment Officer Flight Lieutenant S.N. Weight, and Accounting Officer Flight Lieutenant C.F.N. Harrison, assisted by 43 other ranks.

The station is operating as part of the Army Co-Operation Command, through No. 38 Wing, but the aerodrome is not yet operational. The Wing is responsible for training aircrew in an army airborne-support capacity.

9 May 1943. Sherborne—Exercise Demon. Firemen arrive in Newland.

9 May 1943. Sherborne—Exercise Demon. Above it is make-believe, the detached eye being courtesy of the butcher. Below is reality, the arrival in Newland of the Women's Voluntary Service with urns of tea.

9 May 1943. Sherborne—Exercise Demon. Newland provided a realistic setting. The Luftwaffe scattered bombs along the street on 30 September 1940.

9 May 1943. Sherborne—Exercise Demon. Mopping up captured Germans, with the uniforms being authentic even if the contents spoke broad Dorset.

17 May **Dambuster bombs were tested in Dorset.**

The earliest version of the bouncing bombs that were dropped last night by Lancasters of 617 Squadron, to breach the Möhne and Eder dams in the Ruhr, were tested in Dorset. Prototypes of the weapon had been developed on a freelance basis by Barnes Wallis of Vickers-Armstrongs, working outside the official Ministry of Aircraft Production's armament programme. They were carried by a Wellington and dropped from sixty feet on to the flat waters of The Fleet lagoon, near Langton Herring.

This part of the Chesil Beach bombing range was used to ascertain that the bombs worked in principle, skimming across the water like a well-thrown stone, though the actual practice runs for Operation Chastise were carried out by the Lancasters over the Elan valley reservoir in the mountains of mid-Wales.

17 May 1943. The Ruhr floods—from an idea that first bounced across Dorset's Fleet lagoon.

Footnote Air Marshal Arthur Harris, Commander-in-Chief Bomber Command, recalled that he "rang up Washington, where Churchill and Portal were at the time, to give them the news. The telephone personnel seemed never to have heard of the White House, and there was some little difficulty. When I did get through I was intercepted and asked for an assurance that the person I was calling was reliable. I don't know whether she was persuaded that Winston Churchill came into that category, but I got through to Portal in the end and told him that the two dams had gone." Eight of the nineteen Lancasters failed to return. The main aim had been to cause a shortage of water for industrial purposes in the Ruhr, rather than sweeping everything away in a flood which is how we tend to remember the exploit. Not that there were many happy farmers in Kassel when two hundred million tons of water spread across their fields.

20 May **Another Holmsley Halifax crashes.**

Another Halifax bomber from RAF Holmsley South [Plain Heath Airfield] has failed on take-off and crashed with the loss of all crewmen. Its pilot, Flying Officer R.M. Reisner, was a Canadian. The aeroplane came down nine miles north-west of the airfield, near Fordingbridge, after it had cast-off a Horsa glider.

23 May 1943. Bournemouth. Firemen fight the flames that have destroyed Beales, Bournemouth's largest department store. Its clock lies amid the rubble on Old Christchurch Road. The bombs fell just after one o'clock but the clock collapsed with the fire. It came to rest on its left side and the hands are seen overlapping at ten minutes past two this Sunday afternoon.

23 May   77 civilians killed in Bournemouth's worst air raid.

This has been Bournemouth's worst air raid. Beales department store was burnt out and West's Picture House, the Central Hotel, Metropole Hotel and Punshon Memorial Church shattered beyond repair as at lunchtime sixteen Focke-Wulf 190s came in low from the sea and bombed the central shopping areas of the Square and Lansdowne.

Seventy-seven civilians are dead, plus a number of Canadian airmen at the Metropole Hotel, with 196 injured, and 3,481 buildings damaged; it is estimated that about forty of these will have to be demolished. But for the fact that the attack came at 13.00 hours on a Sunday, casualties could have been much higher.

Two hours later Sir Adrian Boult, the BBC Orchestra's conductor, took the Bournemouth Municipal Orchestra through the 'Nimrod' passage from Elgar's *Enigma Variations* in memory of those who had died. The bombs marred what had been intended as a celebration—it was the fiftieth anniversary concert of the Bournemouth Orchestra.

**23 May 1943.
Bournemouth. The
Punshon Memorial church
and Central Hotel,
Richmond Hill, devastated
by lunchtime German
bombs. The printing works
of the Bournemouth Daily
Echo, glimpsed to the left,
had a near miss.**

One bomb had exploded beside the omnibus standing area at the Bus Station in Exeter Road. Twenty-five Hants and Dorset buses lost all their glass and some are being sent back into service without any windows. Sacks have been tied across the fronts of the vehicles to reduce draughts. The Shamrock and Rambler coach depôt in Holdenhurst Road has also been devastated.

Bombs fell into residential areas at Bethia Road, Cotlands Road, Dean Park Road, Drummond Road, Howeth Road, No. 248 Holdenhurst Road, Lansdowne Road, Vale Road, Queens Park South Drive, and between Iford Bridge and Pokesdown.

At 14.20 hours Bournemouth ARP control centre requested rescue parties from Christchurch and Poole. A major fire is still burning around Beales, where the bombs fractured the gas main, and twelve pumps are fighting to bring it under control. At the Metropole Hotel the new 100 feet turntable ladders of the National Fire Service were used for the first time, to rescue the surviving Canadian airmen on the upper floors. Thirty-five have been brought out alive.

Five FW190s are reportedly shot down. One has crashed in Grove Road, on the East Cliff.

23 May 1943. Bournemouth. The Hotel Metropole at The Lansdowne, in the triangle between Holdenhurst Road and Christchurch Road. Some rescues were made but many bodies of Canadian airmen are lying in the rubble. 'Room, bath and full breakfast, 10/6d' the sign proclaims. Poole Council workers are helping in the searches.

Footnote   The site of the destroyed cinema, West's Picture House, is now the Burlington Arcade. Falling masonry would kill one of the men who finished the demolishing of Beales.

May   **Catalinas take over RAF Hamworthy.**

Catalina flying boats of 210 Squadron of Coastal Command have moved into the seaplane base at RAF Hamworthy and are operating long-range flights into the Atlantic in the battle against the U-boats.

May   **Hambro heir killed in Tripoli.**

It is reported that Major Robert Hambro, the only son of Captain Angus Hambro of Merley House, Wimborne, and his heir, was mortally wounded whilst serving in a reconnaissance regiment of the 8th Army. He died at Tripoli. Major Hambro was born in 1911.

23 May 1943. Bournemouth. The Pavilion, with the BBC Orchestra's conductor, Sir Adrian Boult, at the rostrum. This is Golden Jubilee day for the Bournemouth Municipal Orchestra. But it is also 'the saddest day in the town's history'. Sir Adrian spoke a few words of sympathy and chose Elgar's 'Nimrod' passage as a tribute to the dead.

24 May 1943. Bournemouth. The burnt-out remains of Beales department store, now a mass of twisted girders and a rubble-filled hole in the ground. It is seen from the tower of St Peter's church in Hinton Road, with 'Brights' sign glimpsed through the wreckage and the flat roof of J.J. Allen below to the right.

1 June   No. 10 Group gets Tarrant Rushton.

Administrative control of the new Tarrant Rushton Aerodrome has been transferred to No. 10 Group Fighter Command but No. 38 Wing remains the operating formation.

12 June   321 more German mines laid off Dorset.

A total of 321 German mines and 84 barrage protection floats have been laid off Dorset and the Isle of Wight in the past week by the combined efforts of the German 2nd, 4th, 5th and 6th Schnellboot Flotillas.   The Royal Naval Mine Sweeping Service has simply noted the areas concerned and is making arrangements to have them cleared as soon as resources and weather conditions allow.

23 June   Dutch vessel blown-up in Poole Bay.

A Dutch craft, the *Leny*, was blown up today by a mine near the Swash Channel at the entrance to Poole Harbour. Only two of its crewmen have been rescued.

25 June 1943. Christchurch. Sub Lieutenant P. M. Lamb wears his hair long because of the scars he gained from landing his Royal Navy Seafire on a Stanpit bungalow. He had lost engine power at the end of a 500 mile delivery flight. Conversion work on the Seafire, the Navy's carrier-based version of the Spitfire, was carried out by Airspeed Limited at Somerford.

25 June Bungalow landing for Christchurch pilot.

19.54 hours. A Royal Navy Seafire, being flown into Christchurch Aerodrome from Donibristle, Scotland, has overshot the runway and crashed into a bungalow, 'Musoka' in Caroline Avenue at Stanpit. The aircraft is number MB315 RN, piloted by Sub-Lieutenant P.M. Lamb who has been taken to hospital with head injuries.

Footnote Lamb was stitched-up, though he had to grow his hair long to cover the scars. "Not my best landing," he wrote in his log, "engine tired of living, fortunately I didn't join it." Seafires were frequently seen over Christchurch as the Airspeed factory converted 160 of them, from standard Spitfires, for use by the Fleet Air Arm.

29 June 5005 Squadron at Tarrant Rushton.

A detachment of No. 4676 Flight from 5005 Squadron has arrived at Tarrant Rushton Aerodrome.

June Thousand rockets pound Studland beach in thirty seconds.

The RCL, a tank landing craft that has been modified at Poole to carry batteries of rocket launchers, has been tested in Studland Bay and at Kimmeridge. It fires more than a thousand explosive rockets in about thirty seconds, delivering them on to a small area of the beach; the aim is to annihilate enemy strongpoints with firepower that is devastatingly concentrated.

June   Gliders leave Hurn: destination Sicily.

No. 3 Overseas Aircraft Despatch Unit is co-ordinating a massive shuttle service from RAF Hurn. No. 13 Maintenance Unit is fitting out Halifax bombers as tow-craft for the Horsa troop-carrying gliders which had been made ready by No.1 Heavy Glider Maintenance Unit. That unit has moved to Netheravon, Wiltshire, and the Halifaxes of 295 Squadron are taking the gliders, built by Airspeed at Christchurch, to Portreath, Cornwall.

296 Squadron has been flying its Albemarle paratroop carriers out of Hurn since 3 June. Twenty-eight had left by 21 June. The squadron was equipped with the Albemarles in February and has been training with the Rebecca radio navigation system.

From Cornwall, the Albemarles and the Halifax-Horsa combinations are flying out, in Operation Beggar, to Sale in Morocco. Then they are being moved eastwards to Kairouan, in Tunisia, where they will be taken over by the 1st Air Landing Brigade Group, who are preparing for Operation Husky.

They are tasked to begin the invasion of Sicily between 22.10 and 22.30 hours on 9 July with a drop west of Siracusa to capture the Ponte Grande over the Anapo River, take out the coast batteries to the north, and also attack a seaplane base. Seaborne landings are to follow with the commandos arriving four hours later and then the main force of 13 Corps.

Footnote   The airborne operation was disrupted by high winds. Some gliders came down in the sea and many paratroops fell a considerable distance from the objective. Few reached the Ponte Grande but they held the bridge heroically for eighteen hours. The seaborne assault proved to be a complete success.

August 1943. Warmwell Aerodrome. Ground crew load a dinghy into a Mark II Spitfire of 276 Squadron for an Air-Sea Rescue exercise. It will be dropped, the original caption says, to airmen 'in the drink'.

10 July 1943. 13 Corps steps safely ashore in Sicily, but for the initial assault last night it was 'C' Company of the 1st Battalion of the Dorsetshire Regiment that had to scramble over the side of a troopship and scale the rocky promontory that juts out between the south-eastern beachheads.

5 July   **1st Dorsets sail for Sicily.**

The 1st Battalion of the Dorsetshire Regiment has sailed into the Mediterranean aboard the ex-P&O liner *Strathnaver* among the armada bound for the beaches of Sicily.

1943. Warmwell. 'Bellows' a Westland Whirlwind of 263 Squadron, was piloted by 22-year-old Flying Officer J.P. Coyne of Manitoba. Coyne had just won the Distinguished Flying Cross.

1943. East Lulworth. Neither side has used poison gas in this war but preparing for the eventuality is part of training at the Gunnery Wing of the Armoured Fighting Vehicles School, Lulworth Camp. Here the gas bomb is dropped on a Sherman tank by a Westland Lysander. The ridge in the distance is Whiteway Hill, in the Purbeck Hills at Tyneham.

10 July   One German E-boat sunk and HMS 'Melbreak' damaged.

An engagement last night off Dorset between the Hunt-class destroyers from Portsmouth and the German 2nd Schnellboot Flotilla on convoy-protection duty has resulted in Axis craft M135 being sunk. HMS *Melbreak* sustained serious damage.

10 July   1st Dorsets take Marzamemi.

'C' Company of the 1st Battalion of the Dorsetshire Regiment, under Captain A.C.W. Martin, went over the side of the troopship *Strathnaver* at 03.00 hours to effect a scramble-landing on a rocky promontory at the right-flank of the projected bridgehead in Sicily. They took the village of Marzamemi and were also able to secure the proposed landing beach to the south.

Tracer shells fired vertically from a Bren gun was the dawn signal of success to the Commanding Officer offshore. The Battalion's 'A' and 'B' companies then landed to establish themselves inland.

Footnote   The Royal Navy lost two submarines in the Sicilian invasion. One was HMS *Saracen*, commanded by Lieutenant M.G.R. Lumby of South Eggardon Farm, Askerswell, who was taken prisoner with his crew.

10 July   Spitfires at Hurn as Flying Fortress escorts.

Thirty-eight Spitfires of 66, 131 and 504 Squadrons flew into RAF Hurn today as the cross-Channel escorts for American Flying Fortress bombers. Spitfire EB687 was wrecked on arrival when it collided with a parked Whitley bomber.

Footnote They were commanded by Wing Commander C.E. Malfroy DFC who would bring the Wing back for similar escort duties on 14 July.

12 July Poole's 'Apple' is killed in Sicily.

One of the heroes who was able to thrill the nation with daring exploits in desperate times, Major Geoffrey Appleyard DSO of Poole commandos, is missing presumed killed in Sicily. He was known in Combined Operations as 'The Apple'. His men had been seconded to the North African Forces, where they were known as the 1st Small Scale Raiding Force, and Appleyard was the deputy commander of the 2nd Special Air Service Regiment. He was 26-years-old.

13 July Turin Lancaster just makes it to Christchurch.

This morning a Lancaster bomber, returning from the mass raid over Turin, crossed the English Channel on an almost empty fuel tank. Pilot Officer B.S. Tomlin then put JA851 down on to the 2,400 feet of grass that is Christchurch Aerodrome.

He brought his aircraft and six crew to a perfect landing. Two-and-a-half hours later he was refuelled and airborne again, after an excellent short take-off, and on the way back to 49 Squadron at Fiskerton, Nottinghamshire.

Bomber Command strays are not uncommon in Hampshire and Dorset but it is the first time anyone can recall a four-engined bomber coming down at Christchurch.

24 July Worth's "Window" is opened at last.

"Let us open the Window," Winston Churchill decided and last night it was done—this being the codename given by the Telecommunications Research Establishment's Superintendent, A.P. Rowe, to what was the parting shot of the Worth Matravers scientists to the war effort before their radar laboratories were moved to Malvern. It comprises thousands of metal strips that create a smoke-screen effect upon enemy radar sets at the onset of a mass bombing raid.

"Window" was perfected in Dorset over a year ago but opposition from Fighter Command and Robert Watson-Watt, radar's British pioneer, blocked its operational use. It had been feared that it might give the Germans the idea at a time when they were still liable to carry out major attacks against Britain.

The scientists and Bomber Command are elated with the results of "Window" in causing confusion and consternation to the German defences. Losses which statistically should have been about 6.1 per cent have been reduced to 1.5 per cent—"Window" last night saved seventy-five aeroplanes and their crews.

July Crew killed as Whitley bomber crashes at Hurn.

The crew of a Whitley bomber were killed when it stalled on take-off at RAF Hurn. The aircraft was on what should have been a routine training circuit.

July Advanced landing ground at Winkton.

Hedges and ditches have been removed across an area of flat farmland to the north-east of Sopley, beside the lane from Winkton to Ripley, for a temporary Advanced Landing Ground. This will enable additional fighter capacity to be brought into the Christchurch area for protection of the Channel convoys and the build-up of invasion shipping.

The runways of RAF Winkton have been laid as sheets of steel mesh directly on to the grass.

There are two runways; one north-south from east of Parsonage Farm to west of Clockhouse Farm, and the other east-west from the Ripley lane to within a third of a mile of the cottages at Bransgore.

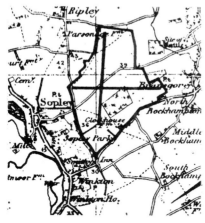

N. f. D.

Zielſtammkarte (L)

ſand: Großbritannien

E n g l a n d (Hampshire)

Ort: **S o p l e y**

Nähere Lage:
   10 km NO Bournemouth

Geogr. **1 ° 45 ′ 45 ″ W**
Werte: **50 ° 46 ′ 30 ″ N**

1. Bezeichnung des Zieles: **Flugplatz**

2. Bedeutung: **Einsatzhafen im Bau**

August 1943. Sopley. Extract from a Luftwaffe target map showing Winkton Advanced Landing Ground—though the Germans failed to notice the RAF's Sopley radar station (at spot-height '42' between Sopley village and Parsonage Farm).

9 August French bombers make it to safety at Hurn.

The Free French bombers of 88 Squadron, flying Bostons alongside those of 107 and 342 Squadrons, headed back across the Channel this morning to the safety of RAF Hurn. The three squadrons had been in action over Rennes, in Brittany, where they had lost two aircraft.

The twenty-one survivors were short on fuel when they landed at Hurn.

14 August 2851 Anti-Aircraft Squadron at Tarrant Rushton.

The main body of No. 2851 Anti-Aircraft Squadron have arrived at Tarrant Rushton Aerodrome from Friston. Their advance party came to Dorset two days ago.

12 August Thirteen killed in Bournemouth raid.

Gas-mains were set alight, water-mains fractured, and 1,455 properties damaged at about 01.10 today when eight high explosive bombs dropped on Bournemouth. Thirteen people are dead and twenty-one receiving hospital treatment.

The bombs fell at the corner of Firs Glen Road and Woods View Road; at the junction of Boundary Road with Beswick Road; at the corner of Wilton Road and Gloucester Road; in Spring Road; Charminster Avenue; and Shelbourne Road.

12 August Christchurch bomb damage.

There was an explosion near the railway, close to Christchurch Station, at 01.10 hours. A high explosive bomb caused widespread damage at Ringwood Road, Walkford, at 01.15. Many houses were shattered and one bed-ridden lady is homeless. Three people were injured. There are also reports of unexploded bombs.

24 August Eight die as Catalina hits Round Island.

Pilot Officer Duff died with seven of his crew when he brought a Catalina of 210 Squadron back to Poole Harbour at 04.25 hours. He descended into thick fog and the flying boat missed the clear waters of the 'Trots' in the channels of the northern harbour.

It crashed into the cord-grass salt-marshes that surround Round Island which is on the Purbeck side of the harbour—a mile south of the safe clearway off RAF Hamworthy. Ratings from the island's naval camp dragged bodies and survivors from the debris. Only four crewmen were rescued from this training flight.

28 August 'Second Front'—Eden, Brooke and Mountbatten fly into Poole.

The Secretary of State for Foreign Affairs, Anthony Eden, together with General Sir Alan Brooke, Chief of the Imperial General Staff, and Admiral Louis Mountbatten, Chief of Combined Operations, landed at 14.00 hours today in Poole Harbour. They were aboard the BOAC Boeing Clipper *Bristol* and had returned across the Atlantic from the Quebec Conference which set the location and timetable for the launching of the Second Front.

The decision has been taken to go for the beaches of Normandy and forgo the need to capture a port by towing across pre-fabricated concrete caissons, codenamed Mulberries, to make two instant harbours. The provisional date for the invasion of Europe is 1 May 1944.

1943. Poole. Entertainments National Service Association performers George Formby and wife Beryl Ingham given a quayside welcome by Seawoman Mollie Skinner of British Airways. They have travelled by flying boat to front-line units in India and Burma.

8 September 1943. The 1st Battalion of the Dorsetshire Regiment arrives at Pizzo in the Toe of Italy.
Bryan de Grineau's sketch, for the Illustrated London News, shows Sergeant W.E. Evans winning a bar to his Military Medal.

31 August Echo of Sedgemoor.

The Daily Telegraph reports that a Lyme Regis hotelier received a stamped addressed postcard from an anxious prospective visitor asking for "the date of the last enemy attack on your town".

The manager sent the card back with the date—"1685".

8 September Dorset mailbag leads the rearguard into Italy.

Support landings at Pizzo, on the Toe of Italy, were carried out just before dawn to establish a rearguard to ease pressure on the Allied troops in the Reggio beachhead.

The commandos went astray, however, and the first craft to beach contained the headquarters unit of the 1st Battalion of the Dorsetshire Regiment. The landing was led—not that he realised it—by an NCO with a mailbag slung over his shoulder.

Later the Battalion's 'B' Company came under heavy counter-attack on the coast road. It knocked out a Mark IV tank but lost one of its two anti-tank guns. Sergeant W. Evans single-handedly immobilised an armoured car with a grenade, killing the crew, and shot a German officer who tried to climb out. The company's left-flank was under infantry attack. This was held off by Lieutenant L.G. Browne's platoon in fierce hand-to-hand fighting which left twenty enemy dead.

At one point the Brigade Commander called up air support and the Kittyhawk fighter-bombers arrived on time. They then confused the British positions for those of the enemy and proceeded to bomb and strafe them, destroying several vehicles. It has been that sort of day.

Footnote Some honour emerged from the chaos. Evans won a bar to his Military Medal and Lieutenant Browne was awarded the Military Cross.

22 September **Twelve Venturas at Tarrant Rushton.**

The last of nine Ventura aircraft from Sculthorpe, Norfolk, arrived today at Tarrant Rushton Aerodrome. Two came yesterday and the main flight of six arrived the day before. That day three other Ventura came in from Stoney Cross Aerodrome in the New Forest, so the total now at Tarrant Rushton is twelve.

23 September **First Albemarle tow-plane at Tarrant Rushton.**

A prototype Albemarle Mark IV was landed at Tarrant Rushton Aerodrome today by Group Captain T.B. Cooper DFC. Its potential is to be assessed in towing trials with a view to using the aircraft as a tug-plane for troop-carrying gliders.

September 1943. Tested at Clouds Hill, in the heathland parish of Turners Puddle, north of Bovington Camp.
The Great Panjandrum
is bizarre in concept and appearance. It has been designed as a method of sending two tons of high explosive careering up a beach to smash holes in the Atlantic Wall of the eastern French coast. The catherine wheels are propelled by rockets, which are in fact smaller than those shown in this drawing. In practice is has proved to be uncontrollable, but its existence may now be usefully leaked—given that the Second Front is not to be launched at the great concrete fortifications of the eastern Channel but across the soft sands of Normandy. This is the decision of the Quebec Conference but considerable efforts will be made to convince the Germans that attention to Normandy is a feint and that the real attack will come in Seine-Maritime or Pas-de-Calais.

September **Great Panjandrum tested at Clouds Hill.**

One of the more bizarre weapons of war, a Great Panjandrum rocket-fired assault wheel, has been tested by Combined Operations commandos from Poole on their explosives firing ground at Clouds Hill, near Bovington Camp. The cylinder at the centre of two ten feet high wheels contains 4,000lb of high explosive.

The rockets are intended to send the wheel out of an invasion landing craft and up the beach to blow a hole in ten feet of concrete of the German Atlantic Wall defences. The rocket propulsion was tried out on the sands of Westward Ho! and Instow, Devon, on 7 and 8 September with unpredictable results. Nevil Shute Norway, the aeronautical engineer and writer, figured out the size of the charges needed to breach the Atlantic Wall and is taking part in the experiments.

Footnote A final trial took place at Westward Ho! in January 1944. It was filmed by motor-racing photographer Luis Klemantaski who had to run for his life as the machine reached a hundred miles per hour and suddenly veered towards him. Onlookers tried to escape up the beach and became entangled in barbed wire. The Panjandrum, meanwhile, wobbled seaward again as rockets spiralled across the beach; one being chased by an Airedale hound, Ammanol. With this the project was abandoned.

One of the wheels of the Clouds Hill Great Panjandrum was discovered in 1946–47 by Bere Regis scouts who were camping nearby in Sare's Wood. Fred Pitfield, then aged fifteen, recalls the terrific fun they had rolling it up and down the hills adjacent to the camp, though even unpowered it still managed to demolish tents, bicycles and billie-cans.

9 October   Sandbanks Air Station closes.

The Royal Navy's seaplane training school at Sandbanks was today disbanded.

10 October   P-o-Ws sent cigarettes.

The following card, written in a camp at M. Stammlager, is typical of those being received by the Society of Dorset Men:

"Kriegsgefangenenlager. Dear Sir, Thank you very much for your letter of September. I have today received a parcel of 200 cigarettes, I believe they are from the Society. Cigarettes to us mean such a great deal. I am a Dorset man, born and bred, and to me it is still the finest little place in the world. Thanking you once again. Yours sincerely, G.W. Harris, 6848."

11 October   India's Viceroy flies out from Poole.

Field Marshal Sir Archibald Wavell, Viceroy of India and Supreme Commander Allied Forces in India and Burma, today left Poole Quay by launch to board a BOAC flying boat bound for Bombay.

11 October   298 Squadron to be formed at Tarrant Rushton.

No. 38 Wing of the RAF, comprising its airborne-forces support units, today changed its name to HQ 38 Group. Today also there were movements on the ground between its two aerodromes in Dorset, from Hurn to Tarrant Rushton. An advance party from 'A' Flight of

1943. RAF Sopley. Aerial Type 7 ground to air radar, positioned above a bunker known as the 'Well'. Here, in the flat fields north of Christchurch, is the key combat radar station for central southern England. Enemy intruders, both raiders and reconnaissance aircraft, are plotted as they approach the coast. 'Starlight' is its night service, as the eyes for the Beaufighters and other specially adapted night-fighters that carry AI (Airborne Interception) radar equipment in their perspex nose-cones. British pilots are talked through the sky from scrambling and given a fix on their target which eventually appears as a blip on the pilot's monitor screen.

295 Squadron moved with its Halifax tow-craft into Tarrant Rushton from Hurn.

They will soon cease to be part of 295 Squadron and are to form the nucleus of the new 298 Squadron which is to be based at Tarrant Rushton. They will be joined by the Stirlings of 196 Squadron.

15 October   Halifax tug-planes arrive at Tarrant Rushton.

Four-engined Handley Page Halifax bombers, converted for use as tug-planes for troop-carrying gliders, have started to arrive at Tarrant Rushton Aerodrome. Their operatives, 'A' Flight of 295 Squadron from Hurn, will soon make themselves at home. The main party arrives on 17 October and the rear party on the 20th. They will then become 298 Squadron.

27 October   Exercise Thresher: three gliders to Wiltshire.

The new 298 Squadron at Tarrant Rushton took to the sky today in Exercise Thresher. Three gliders were towed by Halifax tug-planes and released to land at Netheravon.

28 October   Damaged bomber lands at Tarrant Rushton.

A Mitchell bomber, damaged by German flak off Cherbourg, made a successful emergency landing today at RAF Tarrant Rushton. It was flown by Lieutenant Loeffe of 320 Squadron, from Lasham, near Alton, Hampshire.

1 November   Twenty-three bombs drop on Bournemouth.

Twenty-three high explosive bombs fell on Bournemouth at tea-time. The raid took place at 17.45 and left 1,284 properties damaged but the casualty toll was light, with one dead and twenty-seven injured.

There is widespread damage, at Cecil Avenue, Howard Road, Campbell Road, Borthwick Road, Avon Road, Chatsworth Road, Bennett Road, Orcheston Road, Shaftesbury Road and Shelbourne Road. The bombs at Queens Park Avenue did not do much more than crater the golf links.

6 November   First home leave for the 1st Dorsets since 1936.

Dorset's Regular Army soldiers, the 1st Battalion of the Dorsetshire Regiment, disembarked on the Clyde at Gourock today from the troopship *Durban Castle*. The survivors of the Malta siege and assault landings in Sicily and Italy are looking forward to their first home leave since their transfer to the North West Frontier of India in 1936.

13 November   Fighter Command becomes A.E.A.F.

Psychologically, at least, the war takes its turn today from defence to the offensive. Fighter Command has ceased to exist and is now part of the Allied Expeditionary Air Force, the umbrella command for all British, American and other allied fighting aircraft and air stations in the United Kingdom. Its Commander-in-Chief is Air Chief Marshal Sir Trafford Leigh-Mallory.

13 November   Boscombe adjutant lives by an inch.

There was a shock last night for the Adjutant at the headquarters of the 7th (Boscombe) Battalion of Hampshire Home Guard. A shooting incident occurred shortly before 21.00 hours, as Sergeant G.A. Miller of the 28th Platoon, Headquarters Company, has reported to his

SOUTHERN COMMAND

TRAINING AREA, EAST HOLME, Nr. LULWORTH

IN order to give our troops the fullest opportunity to perfect their training in the use of modern weapons of war, the Army must have an area of land particularly suited to their special needs and in which they can use live shells. For this reason you will realise the chosen area must be cleared of all civilians.

The most careful search has been made to find an area suitable for the Army's purpose and which, at the same time, will involve the smallest number of persons and property. The area decided on, after the most careful study and consultation between all the Government Authorities concerned, lies roughly inside of the square formed by EAST LULWORTH—EAST STOKE—EAST HOLME—KIMMERIDGE BAY. *Including your properties – see overleaf.*

It is regretted that, in the National Interest, it is necessary to move you from your homes, and everything possible will be done to help you, both by payment of compensation, and by finding other accommodation for you if you are unable to do so yourself.

The date on which the Military will take over this area is the 19th December next, and all civilians must be out of the area by that date.

A special office will be opened at Westport House, WAREHAM, on Wednesday the 17th November, and you will be able to get advice between the hours of 10 a.m. and 7 p.m., from there on your personal problems and difficulties. Any letters should be sent to that address also for the present.

The Government appreciate that this is no small sacrifice which you are asked to make, but they are sure that you will give this further help towards winning the war with a good heart.

C. H. MILLER,
Major-General i/c Administration,
Southern Command.

16th November, 1943.

S.C.P. 24. 400. 11/43 S.P. **92944**

16 November 1943. Tyneham, East Lulworth, East Stoke, East Holme and Steeple. Requisition notices have been issued by Major-General Charles Harvey Miller of Southern Command for the military occupation of ten square miles of these parishes in western Purbeck, for tank battle-training in the run-up to the invasion of Normandy.

commanding officer:

"When rifles were being loaded, previous to proceeding to the Operational Patrol, one round was accidentally fired by a member of the patrol, Private G.H. Thomas. The round passed through the ceiling of the guardroom and lodged in the wall of the room above. I am able, fortunately, to report that no one was hurt. The bullet passed within one inch of the Adjutant who was sitting in the room above."

15 November   Hurn now has three squadrons of Albemarles.

Three Albemarle squadrons are now based at RAF Hurn with the formation there today of 570 Squadron. "We launch the spearhead," is the motto chosen for the taxi service of the airborne divisions.

The station's existing 295 Squadron has been re-equipped with Albemarles and re-united with those of 296 Squadron returning from Italy. Three squadrons will co-operate in paratroop drops and in exercises towing Horsa gliders.

A detachment from 570 Squadron is to be based at RAF Stoney Cross in the New Forest.

16 November   Ten square miles requisitioned in Purbeck.

Major-General Charles Harvey Miller, the officer commanding administration at Southern Command, today issued eviction notices to all persons living in an area of ten square miles of western Purbeck. The entire 3,003 acre parish of Tyneham has been requisitioned along with considerable areas of heath and downland in the adjoining parishes of East Lulworth, East Stoke, East Holme and Steeple.

The village of Tyneham and hamlet of Povington will have to be evacuated by 19 December, as will many isolated farms and cottages.

The land is to be used as a live-fire battle-training area for tanks of the United States Army as well as the Gunnery Wing of the Armoured Fighting Vehicles School which has its ranges at Lulworth Camp, next to the requisitioned area.

Practising tank warfare has become a top priority since August, when the Quebec Conference decided that the Overlord plan for the so-called "Second Front" invasion of the Fortress of Europe should be launched against Normandy, with the target date being the spring of 1944.

1943. Worbarrow Bay. Ten square miles of heath and coast are depopulated to make way for tanks and their targets. The pillbox is 1940 invasion-vintage.

16 November   **Paratroop drop near Sixpenny Handley.**

Eight Halifax aircraft from Tarrant Rushton Aerodrome today carried out their Exercise Fledgling in which planes of 298 Squadron dropped men of the 8th Battalion of the 3rd Paratroop Brigade on to Thorney Down two miles south of Sixpenny Handley.

24 November   **Exercise Cumulus puts a cloud over Studland Bay.**

Studland Bay disappeared in a cloud of smoke today. This was Exercise Cumulus in which landing craft were obscured by a dense smoke-screen.

Thirteen Mitchell and twenty-four Boston bombers dropped the canisters. They operated from RAF Hurn for the day. Four Typhoons of 181 Squadron also flew low across the sea to test the effectiveness of the screen against attacking fighters.

1 December   **Hurn and Tarrant Rushton gliders in joint exercise.**

Halifax tug-planes pulling Horsa gliders from 298 Squadron at Tarrant Rushton today met up in aerial formation with similar combinations from their previous aerodrome, 295 Squadron from Hurn, for Exercise Stickies. This also involved aircraft and gliders from Stoney Cross in the New Forest.

8 December   **Americans arrive at Blandford.**

The 184th Auxiliary Anti-Aircraft Gun Battalion is the first unit of the United States Army to arrive at Blandford Camp. It has 716 enlisted men and twenty-five officers. Their task will be to provide protection around the beach landing assault exercise area at Studland.

17 December   **Loaded Horsa gliders towed at Tarrant Rushton.**

Glider lift-offs for the pilots of 298 Squadron at Tarrant Rushton Aerodrome came closer to reality today in Exercise Hasty when their converted Halifax bombers pulled loaded Horsa gliders into the sky.

19 December   **Tyneham villagers are evicted.**

Ralph Bond, the platoon commander of the Tyneham Home Guard and a Purbeck magistrate, has been evicted from his Elizabethan mansion along with his servants, farm labourers and the fishermen of Worbarrow Bay. The whole of the 3,003 acres of the parish of Tyneham plus other land beneath the Purbeck Hills have been depopulated by the order of the War Cabinet. The area will be occupied by the United States Army for invasion training exercises. No mention of this extension of the Lulworth tank gunnery ranges has been permitted in the press and there has been no consultation with the local councils.

Tenancies are, however, being maintained and each occupant has been assured: "This means that when the War Department has no further use for the property and it is handed back, you have every right to return to the property. It should not be assumed by you that, because that War Department has turned you out, you lose the right of occupying the premises again."

The prohibition of editorial mentions of the military take-over has not been extended to the advertising columns. On 2 December the Dorset County Chronicle published notices that the following farmers were quitting: S.G. Churchill (Tyneham Farm), A.E. Cranton (Lutton Farm), A.J. Longman (Baltington Farm), J.H. House (North Egliston Farm), R.J. Cake (West Creech Farm), T.W. Wrixon (Povington Farm), Arthur Cooper (Searley's Farm, Povington), J. Cooper (Jiggiting Corner, Povington), Mrs Vonham (Weld Arms Farm, East Lulworth), Mrs S.P. Damen (The Cat, East Lulworth), H.J. Sampson (Whiteway Farm, East Lulworth), H.C. George

(Broadmoor Farm, West Creech), Frank Cranton (Rookery Farm, West Creech), A. E. Swain (Hurst Mill Farm, West Creech).

Appended is this note: "The Auctioneers wish to draw special attention to the before mentioned sales and sincerely trust that all farmers from over a wide area will endeavour to attend as many as possible, to assist in the dispersal of the stock on offer, all of which is thoroughly recommended by the Auctioneers."

25 December   Glider pilots posted to Tarrant Rushton.

It is a Christmas present for the 1st Battalion of the Glider Pilot Regiment to arrive back in England today from Taranto, Italy. They are to be re-united with their Hamilcar gliders and the four-engined Halifax towing-craft of 298 and 644 Squadrons at Tarrant Rushton, on the edge of the Cranborne Chase chalklands between Wimborne and Blandford.

26 December   Puddletown farmer becomes international broadcaster.

Ralph Wightman, known to the press as "the Dorset farmer" though he never actually farmed, has progressed from his career as Dorset's senior agricultural adviser to being the world voice of the English countryman. He talks into the microphone as if he were having a chat among friends in the village inn at Puddletown, where he lives in a sixteenth century stone-built house.

Last year he was heard on the wireless, in the *Country Magazine*, with established rural pundits such as A.G. Street and S.P.B. Mais. Wightman's dulcet tones, warm humour and practical commonsense immediately appealed to listeners and he was invited back by the BBC to 'star' on the programme.

Tonight he has been given the honour of delivering the Sunday *Postscript* which will be relayed by the Forces broadcasting network to all theatres of the war, as well as across the British Empire and North America.

Footnote Ralph Wightman was to do 290 consecutive weekly broadcasts, describing the countryside at war, for listeners in the United States. He was to compère the bulk of the *Country Magazine* series as well as make regular appearances in *Country Questions, On the Land,* and *Any Questions*. For those who grew up with the wireless he was the best known Dorset man of his generation.

27 December   Paratroop exercises at Tarrant Rushton.

For Tarrant Rushton Aerodrome it has been a Christmas in and out of the clouds. The festivities had to wait for the completion of Exercise James, on Christmas Eve, in which paratroops were dropped. Airborne troops are once more floating down today, in Exercise Wizzer. The year is to end much the same way, with more paratroop dropping in Exercise Novice on 30 December.

29 December   Cross-channel air activity knocks out eight V-I 'Ski-sites'.

Thirty-seven P-47 Thunderbolt fighter-bombers of the United States Army Air Force landed at RAF Hurn today on their return from offensive operations over northern France. So too did two flak-damaged B-17 Flying Fortress bombers. The Thunderbolts had been protecting Liberator bombers that were also returning from raids.

There has been intense activity over the Cherbourg peninsula this month in which Hurn has played its part. On 22 December there were twenty-four Spitfires at the station, from 131 and 165 Squadrons, to escort bombers to Triqueville.

Eight 'Ski-sites' have been accounted for on the Cherbourg peninsula. These were being prepared for the new terror weapon, the FZG76 or Vergeltungs I (Retaliation I) as Germans

1943-44. Burton Cliff, Burton Bradstock. Eyes towards France as American GIs turn south Dorset into a colossal armed camp and prepare to take the war back across the Channel.

have started to call it; this is a flying bomb which requires a concrete ramp, vulnerable to air attack, if it is to be launched with any accuracy.

December   **Flying boats give way to landing craft.**

The Catalinas of 210 Squadron have left RAF Hamworthy to enable its slipway to be used in training exercises to load landing craft with tanks and other heavy vehicles. There is a gathering armada of these vessels dispersed along the creeks and estuaries of the south coast.

December   **'In the Drink' Foss and other stories.**

Perhaps the kindest touch to a war story in the past few months has been that of RAF Sergeant Ronald Foss, from Bridport, who was on a Coastal Command flight over the Bay of Biscay. The first person to know he was missing happened to be his wife, whom he married in April 1942, as she was serving in the operations room of the same air station. Ronald, in fact, was still alive, and was picked up from the sea a week later with enough experience of war to fill a book.

On the other side of the coin, equally human but showing how war could have needlessly tragic consequences, some boys at Portland Royal Navy dockyard mocked a decent self-respecting soldier, of the Buffs, and told him he was no better than a Home Guard. Instantly, in pique, the sentry shot dead John Groves, a seventeen year old of Williams Avenue at Wyke Regis. It was all silly and unintentional, manslaughter rather than murder, and the situation rather than the participants were to blame. Give a man a gun and he may defend his pride as well as his country.

Footnote Regarding the first amazing story, Ronald Foss had in him not one book but three, *In the Drink, Three of us Live,* and *Famous War Stories*. He was to enjoy a long retirement with his wife in London, Ontario.

December   **Eisenhower's deputy is an Old Dorset.**

Air Marshal Sir Arthur Tedder, who is General Eisenhower's Deputy Supreme Commander of Allied Forces Western Europe, began his military career with the Dorsetshire Regiment in the Great War. He served in France in 1915 and transferred to the air service in 1916, rising to become Vice-Chief of the Air Staff in November 1942.

1943–44. Burton Bradstock. Village boy mans A. E. Cheney's pumps, the Red House Garage, as another cleans the windscreen of an American jeep. Either side it is still pastoral Dorset.

1943-44. Burton Bradstock. Petty Officer Podger, recently invalided out of the Royal Navy after serving through both wars, points the way to the canteen for American GI Roy St Jean of Springfield, Massachusetts.

1943-44. Burton Bradstock. Cocoa, in NAAFI cups, bridges another generation gap. Corporal David W. Roberts, from Iowa, leans out of his holiday camp billet to chat with Betty 'Freckles' Mackay, a London evacuee from the Blitz days, and local boy Chris Kerley.

1943-44. Burton Bradstock. The propaganda of this superb series of pictures was every bit as good as the photography — here the subtle inference is that before 1783 Britain and America share a common history. The rector, Rev Arthur Dittmer, points to the inscription on one of his table-tombs.

1943-44. Burton Bradstock. St Mary's church, from the Rectory lawn. Tea is hosted by Mr and Mrs Arthur Dittmer and their tabby cat. Their United States Army guests (also seen opposite) are Lieutenant S.M. Weitzner (left in this picture, right opposite) of Ridgewood, New York, and Major E.M. Beebe of Burlington, Vermont.

1943-44. Burton Bradstock. Blacksmith Benjamin Burton displays a hoof to the Americans. 'US troops are discovering that the Britisher is not as stand-offish as he is said to be' reads the contemporary caption.

1943-44. Burton Bradstock. 'Under the sycamore tree on the village green, a group of US soldiers talk to their friends the village children, and examine a machine-gun belt the children found on the beach.' The troopers are John L. Lawson of Port Jervis, New York; Robert S. Hastings of Azusa, California; Leo H. Pearson of Springville, New York; Corporal Roland Henry of Holland, Pennsylvania.

1943-44. Burton Bradstock. Contemporary caption: 'In the village canteen Gunner Weightman of the British Army, an old habitué, hands round home-made cakes to Corporal James Flower of Walpole, Massachusetts, Private First-class Roy St Jean of Springfield, Massachusetts, and Corporal Allan Decker of Chicago.'

1943-44.
Burton Bradstock.
The GI offensive
began with the
public houses.
Their pint was
beer—darker
but less potent
than the rough
cider of the
locals.
H and G.
Simonds also
had a brewery
at Blandford.
The other
poster makes
an appeal
on behalf
of prisoners
of war.

1943-44.
Burton Bradstock,
at the west end
of the Chesil
Beach. Preparing
for the evening
at an open-air
hair salon on
a boulder in
the shingle.

1943-44. Burton Bradstock. Contemporary caption: 'In 1940 the beach was guarded against invasion, first by Local Defence Volunteers, then by Home Guards. Today, with the tables turned, United States troops can spend their leisure hours on it. Sitting on a concrete blockhouse, behind which Britain's amateur ill-armed soldiers were prepared to sell their lives dearly, Corporal Bert Markowitz of Astoria, New York City, plays his violin. Markowitz was a student at the University of Miami and played with the National Broadcasting Corporation as a studio musician. Listening to him is G.R. Miller of Louisville, Kentucky.'

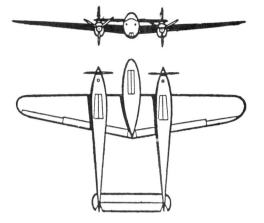

Lockheed P-38 Lightning:
flown by the Americans
from Warmwell.

1944

5 January Battered Flying Fortress makes it to Tarrant Rushton.

A flak-damaged Flying Fortress of the United States Army Air Force limped back across the Channel today after sustaining thirty hits over Mérignac airfield at Bordeaux.

The pilot proudly showed off his shell-shot bomber after he brought it down in a successful forced-landing at RAF Tarrant Rushton. He found himself among the gliders that are preparing for Exercise Nox. This is a major exercise that is to run for almost a week.

13 January Military flying boats return to Hamworthy.

RAF Hamworthy is operating flying boats once more, this time as a station of 44 Group Transport Command. BOAC crews are flying on military secondment.

Their Sunderlands are tasked to operate to Karachi via Gibraltar, Tunis and Cairo, and will carry aircrew personnel who are needed in India and Burma.

14 January Thirteen Halifaxes from Tarrant Rushton cross country.

Exercise Spook took place at Tarrant Rushton Aerodrome today; or rather it began there. Thirteen Halifax bombers of 298 Squadron practised long distance troop-carrying, to Winterton on the North Sea, where 115 men parachuted on to a dropping zone.

The Dorset aerodrome has also been busy, from 5 to 11 January, with Exercise Nox.

20 January Fog-bound Sunderland lands off Swanage.

The coast of southern England was fog-bound as a Sunderland flying boat came in from Gibraltar this morning. Flight Lieutenant Satchwell did not receive a message that he was to divert from Poole Harbour to Pembroke dock in South Wales.

Instead, realising the impossibility of a harbour landing, he brought the Sunderland down into the sea four miles off Swanage. She was located by a launch from Poole which acted as pathfinder for the last ten miles of the journey. The flying boat slowly taxied towards Poole for four hours and was put on its mooring at 13.20 hours.

20 January BOAC air-liner comes to Hurn.

BOAC is transferring its land-planes—as distinct from the flying-boats operating from Poole Harbour—to RAF Hurn. A Mark I Lancaster transporter arrived today for evaluation as an air-liner in tests with a Development Flight unit.

G-AGJI has become the first civilian-flown Lancaster in Britain. It is without gun turrets though it retains wartime camouflage.

Trans-Canada Air Lines operate a similar converted bomber and BOAC is developing a specification for the manufacture of a version of the Lancaster for peacetime needs. Hitherto its solid-runway aircraft have been operating from Lyneham in Wiltshire.

Footnote The first of the post-war civilian Lancasters, to be known as the Lancastrian, was ordered in September 1944.

20 January   **Tarrant Rushton lifts off Canadians and tanks.**

Both specialities of airborne warfare were brought together at Tarrant Rushton Aerodrome today for Exercise Manitoba. It took its name from the participants. Firstly, eight Halifax aircraft of 298 Squadron carried the 1st Canadian Paratroop Brigade to a dropping zone. Then ten Halifaxes, from the same squadron, pulled Hamilcar gliders into the sky. These were loaded with Tetrarch Mark VII light tanks which just fit into a glider. They were released at a thousand feet.

Though now too thinly armoured for normal tank warfare, this 7.5 ton vehicle has a two-pounder gun and a 7.92mm Besa machine gun, which were all that were necessary for taking on German tanks when it was made in 1939. In the scenario of an airborne landing it would hopefully be more likely to find itself in armoured reconnaissance or infantry support rôles rather than facing the fire-power of front-line Panzers.

One Hamilcar and its Tetrarch overshot the landing area and split a Nissen hut apart as the tank shot forward from the debris. Both vehicle and driver survived.

26 January   **Halifax crashes beside Bournemouth Pier.**

Wreckage is being dragged ashore from a four-engined Halifax tug-plane, from RAF Hurn, which crashed today beside Bournemouth Pier.

28 January   **Horsa glider lands on a wet flare-path.**

Two disorientated Glider Regiment pilots of the British 6th Airborne Division were relieved to spot a double line of flares at 20.00 hours this evening. They proceeded to bring their Horsa glider down on to the flare-path of the western flying boat 'trot' in the waters off RAF Hamworthy.

A BOAC Sunderland, waiting to take-off, radioed for a launch to come and take off the pilots. The glider, which had been released on a night- flying exercise, was then towed from the Wareham Channel by a BOAC pinnace and beached on the slipway at Hamworthy.

January   **US Army hospital built at St Leonards.**

An extensive General Hospital of the United States Army is being built on twenty acres of heathland to the south of the main road between Ferndown and St Leonards, near Ringwood. It is being prepared for use as a major surgical centre for casualties brought out of France after the planned invasion of Europe.

January   **Poole yards produce a landing craft a day.**

Round the clock production in the three yards of shipbuilders J. Bolson and Son Limited at Hamworthy, Poole, brings about the completion of one assault landing craft a day. The LCAs are being tethered in Holes Bay. The yards, formerly the Skylark boat business which made yachts and other pleasure craft, also produce air-sea rescue speedboats and minesweepers, and carry out repairs on tank landing craft.

Work practices have been revolutionised. One squad is responsible for the complete production of a single vessel and this has helped Bolson's into their premier position—the largest assault landing craft manufacturers in Britain.

Early 1944. Poole. Rocket-firing landing craft RCL (B) 640 being completed in Bolson and Son's yard.

1 February   RAF Hurn and Tarrant Rushton are AEAF stations.

RAF Hurn and RAF Tarrant Rushton are among the many southern aerodromes where the Allied Expeditionary Force has an inter-service dimension. Joint service chiefs today presented the Supreme Commander, General Dwight D Eisenhower, with their "Initial Joint Plan" at Bushy Park, Teddington, which is the Supreme Headquarters, Allied Expeditionary Force.

Hurn and Tarrant Rushton come under the RAF's 38 Group which is now part of the Allied Expeditionary Air Force, controlled from Stanmore, and Norfolk House in St James's Square. This is the headquarters of the Air Officer Commanding-in Chief, Air Chief Marshal Sir Trafford Leigh-Mallory.

Likewise the 2nd Tactical Air Force of the RAF is working with the Second British Army, which includes the 6th Airborne Division, in the plans for Operation Overlord. British Airborne troops are commanded by Lieutenant-General Frederick Browning. Overall army strategy for the invasion of Europe is being prepared by General Sir Bernard Montgomery who has proposed an assault front comprising two armies with the First United States Army (two divisions) on the west flank and the Second British Army (three divisions, including the First Canadian Army) on the eastern side.

5 February   Germans lose M156.

Enemy boat M156 is effectively out of the war for some time to come having been seriously damaged last night in a lengthy engagement with British destroyers HMS *Brissenden, Tantside, Talybont* and *Wensleydale*. She has been towed by a Vichy French craft into L'Abervrach.

Footnote   M156 was still not safe; at L'Abervrach she was further damaged by bombs from Coastal Command, Calshot.

Early 1944. Weymouth Harbour. Opposite, top, 'Scam' Project 'Swiss Roll' had a heavily laden Bedford lorry driving across the waves.

5 February — Amphibious landings on Weymouth sands.

The 1940 invasion defences provided an authentic backdrop today to the bizarre spectacle of a practice attack by the most unseaworthy collection of craft ever to beach on Weymouth sands. They arrived in a fleet of LTCs, tank landing craft, and splashed down the ramps to wade ashore. The vehicles had to reach land in six minutes. The sea was obligingly flat.

5 February 1944. Weymouth Bay. Opposite, four photographs. A Humber Scout car (bottom, left) drives into four feet of water off Weymouth promenade. It successfully drives through the sea (bottom, right). Next a Humber armoured car drives down the ramp of a tank landing craft (centre, left). And likewise a Daimler scout car.

5 February 1944. Weymouth Bay. The wading exercise continues. Weymouth's anti-invasion defences, dating from 1940, can be seen in the background of these shots. Perhaps the most amazing sight (top, right) was a Stuart tank travelling through six feet of water. Note the depth marker on its exhaust outlet. The other funnel carried air to the engine. Two other Stuarts pass in five feet of water (bottom, left). The timekeeper raises a flag to signal that the time limit of six minutes has expired (bottom, right).

Early 1944. Abbotsbury. Lighting up the night. Star shells fired from two-pounder Pom-poms illuminate the Channel in a 'Scam' project exercise. In that mass of light there are forty or more shells bursting. Silhouetted against the sea are the concrete anti-tank defences of the Chesil Beach, a reminder of the days when the invasion threat was in reverse.

Early 1944. Burton Bradstock. Rope ladders being fired by rockets from assault landing craft to the top of the 150 feet cliff. Grapnels are attached to the rockets. This is one of the better 'Scam' projects for invasion innovations.

12 February   Leigh-Mallory visits Tarrant Rushton.

Air Chief Marshal Sir Trafford Leigh-Mallory, Commander-in-Chief of the Allied Expeditionary Air Force, today visited Tarrant Rushton Aerodrome. He saw preparations for airborne landings and also relevant German aircraft equipment which has been assembled at the station to show flying crews some of the enemy's methods and ideas.

23 February   King visits the 1st Dorsets.

His Majesty the King today visited the 1st Battalion of the Dorsetshire Regiment who are undergoing training at Halstead, Essex. He watched a company attack on a strongpoint, supported by an assault pioneer platoon under Lieutenant W.F. Scott.

February 1944. Bournemouth. General Dwight D. Eisenhower and General Bernard Montgomery at the Carlton Hotel, making plans for the invasion of Europe. They had been watching assault landing rehearsals in Poole Bay.

February **Eisenhower and Monty at Bournemouth's Carlton Hotel.**

The Carlton Hotel on Bournemouth's East Cliff is one of the perquisites of the United States Army's occupation of this holiday coast—they would call it a perk. It is host to the American Forces Bureau of Investigation and some crews of self-propelled guns but still manages to rise to the occasional moments of style. General Dwight D. Eisenhower, Supreme Commander Allied Forces Western Europe, and General Sir Bernard Montgomery, effectively commander-in-chief Allied land forces, though there is no such formal title, have used its facilities and the convenient clifftop view of rehearsals for invasion taking place in the bay below.

These, sadly, have not been without their casualties including soldiers aboard several Valentine DD [Duplex-Drive] tanks which are both amphibious and land vehicles; failings in their 'skirts' whilst carrying out the former role being the cause of the sinkings. These swimming tanks have canvas screens and propeller shafts at the rear. Hundreds of Shermans are being converted into DD tanks for the invasion assault.

Landing craft are now everywhere around, including the bays of Poole Harbour, Christchurch Harbour, and the inlets of the Solent such as Beaulieu River which also conceals the sunken sections of Mulberry Harbours.

February **Massive airfield expansion at RAF Hurn.**

The two main runways at RAF Hurn have been increased in length by half as much again and a square mile of heathland on the north and east sides has been churned into a moonscape of yellow sand, crossed by the curves and frying-pan shapes of a complex network of dispersal areas.

These are being prepared for an armada of day and night-fighters, transport aircraft, tugplanes and gliders.

Early 1944. Hurn Aerodrome. The scale of the expansion is shown by the light areas of disturbed sand. All the dark, tarmac runways are new. North is at the top of the picture and the initial area of the base is shown by the light, concrete shade of the original perimeter taxiway.

1 March   644 Squadron formed at Tarrant Rushton.

Personnel transferred from 298 Squadron, under the interim command of Squadron Leader A.G. Norman, have formed the new 644 Squadron at Tarrant Rushton Aerodrome. As with their parent squadron they will fly Halifax tug-planes with glider combinations in an airborne assault rôle.

7 March   American fliers take over Station 416, A.L.G. Christchurch.

A temporary wire-mesh runway has been laid across the grass at Christchurch Aerodrome which is now an Advanced Landing Ground. It is Station 416 of the 9th United States Army Air Force. Nearly a thousand officers and men of the 405th Fighter Bomber Group have begun arriving by train from Liverpool.

They disembarked from the liner *Mauretania* which had sailed from New York on 27 February.

P-47 Thunderbolts of 509, 510 and 511 Squadrons of the United States Army Air Force will begin arriving next week.

9 March   More Anti-Aircraft Squadrons to guard Tarrant Rushton.

In view of its growing importance and use, the protection of Tarrant Rushton Aerodrome has been reinforced with the arrival today of the main body of 2733 Anti-Aircraft Squadron of the RAF Regiment from North Weald. Their advance party arrived in Dorset on 2 March.

The advance unit of another Anti-Aircraft Squadron, No. 2819 from Marston Moor, arrives on 11 March with its main body to follow on the 13th.

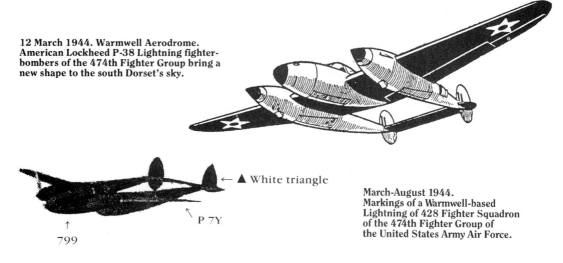

12 March 1944. Warmwell Aerodrome. American Lockheed P-38 Lightning fighter-bombers of the 474th Fighter Group bring a new shape to the south Dorset's sky.

← ▲ White triangle

P 7Y

↑
799

March-August 1944.
Markings of a Warmwell-based Lightning of 428 Fighter Squadron of the 474th Fighter Group of the United States Army Air Force.

12 March   Tragedy mars Warmwell's welcome for the Yanks.

15.00 hours. Tragedy has ended a flying display put on by four RAF Typhoons of 263 Squadron to welcome the 474th Fighter Group of the United States Army Air Force on their arrival at the former Battle of Britain aerodrome at Warmwell. One of the four RAF planes spun out of a low roll and crashed half a mile west of the field. The pilot of HHS MN 129, Pilot Officer Graham Smith, was killed.

The Americans have designated Warmwell as Station 454. They are flying the strangest shape in the sky, the distinctive 400 mile per hour Lockheed P-38 Lightning fighter.

14 March **Hurn changes hands as Albemarles leave.**

RAF Hurn has been transferred to No.11 Group, Air Defence of Great Britain—as Fighter Command is now called—and its three squadrons of Albemarle troop and glider transports have left.

295 and 570 Squadrons have flown to Harwell and 296 Squadron has been redeployed to Brize Norton. Last month they flew supply drops from Hurn to the Resistance forces in occupied France.

Group Captain W.E. Surplice is Hurn's station commander.

17 March **Canadian Typhoons and Hurricanes fly into Hurn.**

143 Wing of 83 Group of the 2nd British Tactical Air Force flew into RAF Hurn today. They are Canadian, with the Typhoons of 438 and 440 (Royal Canadian Air Force) Squadrons, and are to be joined by Hurricanes of 439 (RCAF) Squadron. They will be dive-bombing targets in northern France.

21 March **Worbarrow radar foils an E-boat incursion.**

An attempt last night by the German 9th Schnellboot Flotilla to carry out a raid in Weymouth Bay was foiled by the radar apparatus at Worbarrow Bay which with that on Portland Bill was able to correlate the movements of the enemy craft. As a result the gun-laying by the coastal batteries of the Royal Artillery, from Swanage and Upton Fort at Osmington into the sea off St Alban's Head, was so accurate that S84 collided with S139 as the attack was abandoned in disarray.

21 March **Hurn dog-fight ends in death crash.**

Hurricanes of 439 (Royal Canadian Air Force) Squadron, flying since January from Wellingore, Lincolnshire, returned today to the skies above RAF Hurn, the station where they had been formed. Two American Thunderbolts were unable to resist the temptation of joining their dog-fights.

As Hurricane LD972 levelled off from a manoeuvre it was hit by one of the Thunderbolts, which ripped off the end of the Hurricane's wood and canvas starboard wing. Though Flight Lieutenant Norval E. Pollock was able to pull his damaged Hurricane out of an initial spin he then completely lost control, spiralling to his death in the Avon valley, two miles east of Hurn.

22 March **Hurn Halifax crashes on Moordown.**

The crew of Halifax JP137 and two civilians were killed at 00.35 hours when the bomber crashed on Wimborne Road at its junction with Redhill Crescent in the Bournemouth suburb of Moordown. It had lifted off from RAF Hurn, a mile and a half to the north-east, a couple of minutes earlier.

Either the heavily loaded four-engine Halifax failed to gain enough height to clear the Bournemouth plateau or the pilot, twenty-year-old Dennis Evans, had gathered insufficient speed and the aircraft stalled. The aircraft had come from 1658 Conversion Unit and was on a flight that would have delivered it to an RAF base in North Africa.

23 March **Blandford AA gunners go to London.**

The American 184th Auxiliary Anti-Aircraft Gun Battalion is on the move from Blandford Camp to London to supplement the capital's air defences. Its 'A' Battery has already left, having moved to Essex in January. It is feared the Germans will bombard London with flying bombs.

24 March   Top brass watch Tarrant Rushton mass take-off.

The Halifax tug-planes of 298 Squadron at Tarrant Rushton Aerodrome today put on a show-piece take-off for the benefit of visiting top brass. Air Marshal Sir Douglas Evill had flown in earlier in the day with Air Commodore Francis Masson Bladin.

They watched as four Halifax aircraft, each towing a Hamilcar glider, prepared for a mass take-off. All four were airborne in a hundred seconds.

25 March   Seaplane saves 12 from glider sinking off Swanage.

A Walrus seaplane of 276 Squadron searched successfully for the glider of an airborne forces unit that came down in the sea today six miles south of Swanage. The twelve men aboard were rescued and the Walrus then taxied on the surface for thirty minutes into Swanage Bay. There the soldiers were transferred to a launch.

25 March   Mosquitoes fly into Hurn to defend the night skies.

Mark XVII Mosquito night-fighters have flown into RAF Hurn from Valley in Anglesey. They are with 125 (New Zealand) Squadron and will be controlled by Starlight, as Sopley radar is codenamed, in defensive interceptions over central southern England.

March   Pluto is laid across Poole Bay.

Pluto, the acronym of Pipe Line Under The Ocean, has been laid by the Tweedledrum, a great drum with cone-shaped ends, pulled by HMS *Conundrum* and a tug across twelve miles of Poole Bay to the Isle of Wight. This experiment by the Petroleum Warfare Department is to prove the feasibility of laying an underwater pipeline from a pumping station at Shanklin on the Isle of Wight across the English Channel to the proposed invasion beaches on the coast of Normandy.

March 1944. Studland Bay. One of the more bizarre 'Scam' projects was for a floating airfield, codenamed 'Lily'. It was tried out on a reassuringly flat sea, with a Swordfish 'Stringbag' biplane. The aircraft, loaded to 9,000 lb, is about to use rocket assisted take-off gear to become airborne.

March   'Scam' projects tested in Dorset.

The boffins are trying out their Scam Projects on the Dorset coast. A floating airfield, codenamed Lily, has been tested in Studland Bay by a Royal Navy Swordfish biplane carrying a bomb load and using rockets to enable the exceedingly short take-off.

For the Army there is a floating pier, the Swiss Roll, which has carried heavily laden Bedford lorries across Weymouth Harbour. More practical are the rockets being used to fire grapnels attacked to rope ladders for commandos to scale the 150 feet cliffs beteen Bridport and Burton Bradstock.

March **Swanage Great War VC passes on his experience.**

Chief Petty Officer Ernest Pitcher of Swanage, who won the Victoria Cross in 1917 for staying at his gun in the classic action between an armed merchantman, a Q-boat, and a submarine, is back in uniform in this war at the age of fifty-seven. He rejoined in 1939 and is now training naval gunnery ratings.

Footnote Pitcher died in Gosport in 1946.

1944. Royal Navy Fleet Air Arm shore-establishment HMS Raven (Christchurch Aerodrome). Aircraft delivery girl, First Officer Vera Strodl, an Air Transport Auxiliary, climbs aboard a Fairey Barracuda which she will deliver to an operational base.

4 April   Warmwell airman's heroism in the water.

Corporal Jerry Liroff, an off-duty American serviceman from the 474th Fighter Group at Warmwell, dived fully clothed into the sea off Plymouth today to rescue a drowning child.

7 April   Hurn Mosquitoes on the sidelines as Window opens to the sea.

Mosquito night-fighters of 125 (Royal New Zealand Air Force) Squadron from RAF Hurn have been flanking, at a wide distance, the twenty-five Lancaster and Stirling bombers involved in Exercise Eric. The bombers flew a circuit from Brighton inland to Stockbridge on the Hampshire Downs and then across the New Forest to Lymington.

Here, in the radar hole on German screens that is created by the Isle of Wight, they dropped strips of metallised paper, codenamed Window. This creates deceptive radar images.

The object of the exercise is to practice the dropping of Window in a manner that would suggest to a radar operator that a convoy is approaching steadily at about seven knots. There will have to be a long series of orbits that gradually overlap and which edge towards the enemy coast for a period of five hours. Precision flying will be required to create the illusion of ships rather than aircraft, and the paper will have to be dropped in bundles to simulate objects of the required size.

Footnote   Over a hundred aircraft would take part in the actual deception, in the early hours of 6 June, including two squadrons of Lancasters. One was 617 Squadron of Dambus-

ter fame. The feint was intended to make the enemy think that the D-Day landings were taking place in the area of Boulogne and Cap d'Antifer though the Germans went one better than this and thought the invasion was much further east in the Pas de Calais.

To complete the elaborate diversion the Stirlings of No. 3 Group Bomber Command dropped dummy parachutists and machines that emitted the sounds of mock-battle.

11 April   Christchurch Thunderbolts visit France.

Fifty-five P-47 Thunderbolts of the 405th Fighter Bomber Group of the United States Army Air Force today took off from Christchurch Advance Landing Ground. They assembled fighting formation at 20,000 feet over the English Channel and went on their first day trip to France.

The low-risk sweep of north-western France was intended to familiarise the pilots of 509, 510 and 511 Squadrons with the geography and some of the potential targets of the forthcoming offensive war. All the Thunderbolts returned safely.

March-July 1944. Advance Landing Ground Christchurch (Christchurch Aerodrome) — Station 416 of the 9th United States Army Air Force. P-47 Thunderbolts of 510 Squadron of the 405th Fighter Bomber Group. Opposite is 2Z-M 'Touch of Texas' with her pilot Lieutenant Charles Mohrle, and Thunderbolt 2Z-P visible behind the stack of fuel pods which took them on sorties to France. Below, with the passable imitation of oomph-girl Ann Sheridan, is 'Georgia Peach' and her flier, Lieutenant Curry Powell. Their stories, and all the pictures of Christchurch that appear in this book, are from Leslie Dawson's lavishly illustrated 'Wing over Dorset' which reappeared in an extended edition in 1989.

14 April   **Air-sea Rescue Squadron drafted to Warmwell.**

Another RAF squadron has returned to Warmwell Aerodrome, which is the base for forty-eight P-38J Lightnings of the American 474th Fighter Group. The 275 (Air-sea Rescue) Squadron flies Spitfires in coastal patrols, with an Anson to drop dinghies and a Walrus seaplane for pick-ups beyond the reach of a launch from Lyme Regis, Weymouth, Portland or Poole.

17 April   **Two killed as Halifax crashes at Tarrant Rushton.**

Two Halifax tug-planes of 644 Squadron are tasked tonight for an operation over France but the shock for the squadron came earlier when a routine take-off when wrong. Halifax 'E' stalled and flopped on to the end of the runway, killing the pilot and the rear gunner. It had a glider in tow, but its crew were unhurt.

19 April 1944. Bovington Camp. General Sir Bernard Montgomery arrives as the overall land-force commander of Allied armies in the preparations for Operation Overlord.

19 April   **Montgomery inspects units at Bovington Camp.**

The Driving and Maintenance Wing of the Armoured Fighting Vehicles School at Bovington Camp was today inspected by General Sir Bernard Montgomery, the overall land-force commander of Allied armies in western Europe. He came to Wool in his own train.

19 April   **Bournemouth coast guns in action.**

Royal Artillery coast defence batteries at Hengistbury Head, Mudeford and the Needles opened up last night on the German 5th Schnellboot Flotilla, as they laid electro-magnetic mines in the eastern parts of Poole Bay and off the Isle of Wight.

S64 and S133 of the 8th Schnellboot Flotilla were damaged in a separate engagement last night when a Hunt-class destroyer, HMS *Whitshead*, caught up with them in foul weather.

20 April 1944. Cartoonists have a field day
on the occasion of Adolf Hitler's fifty-fifth birthday.
Der Führer's words of 23 August 1939 are recalled.
How right he is proving to be:
'I am now fifty years old. I prefer a war now
to when I am fifty-five.'

22 April Eisenhower and Leigh-Mallory at Tarrant Rushton.

General Dwight D. Eisenhower, the Supreme Commander of British and Allied Forces in western Europe, today flew into Tarrant Rushton Aerodrome to see the readiness of the British 6th Air Landing Brigade and its associated 6th Airborne Division. He was accompanied by Air Chief Marshal Sir Trafford Leigh-Mallory, Commander-in-Chief of the Allied Expeditionary Air Force, and by Air Vice Marshal Leslie Hollinghurst.

They addressed air crews in the station briefing room. Tarrant Rushton houses over seven hundred men of 298 and 644 Squadrons, and 'C' Squadron of the Glider Pilot Regiment.

19 April 1944. Bovington Camp. General Sir Bernard Montgomery strides through the Armoured Fighting Vehicles School, at home in his Royal Tank Corps beret. His mobile base, his own train — the 'Rapier' — is in a siding at Wool station.

22 April   Warmwell's Lightnings sweep Brittany.

Forty-eight Lightnings of the 474th Fighter Group of the United States Army Air Force, from Warmwell, carried out a three-hour sweep across Brittany today in their first combat air patrol. All the planes returned safely.

22 April   York transport flies from Hurn to Cairo.

Avro York transport MW103, in wartime camouflage but manned by a British Overseas Airways Corporation crew, has taken off from RAF Hurn. It is destined to make the inaugural flight on a service to Morocco and along the southern Mediterranean to Cairo.

24 April   Two dead in Bournemouth fire-attack.

Incendiary and phosphorus bombs fell at about 02.17 and damaged 156 Bournemouth properties—in Stour Road, Avon Road, Gresham Road, Strouden Road, Beatty Road, Portland Road, Charminster Road, West Way, Malvern Road, Shelbourne Road, and Holdenhurst Road. Two people are dead and seven injured.

Footnote   The town's last bombs would be incendiaries dropped around the Roxy Cinema in Holdenhurst Road on 27 May 1944. Bournemouth's wartime casualties totalled 219 dead and 507 injured, from 2,272 bombs of all types. Seventy-five properties were destroyed by direct hits, 171 were so badly damaged that they had to be demolished, and 13,345 required repairs—the vast majority only to windows and replacing slates.

24 April   Three killed in Poole incendiary attack.

Houses were damaged last night in an incendiary attack on the northern parts of Poole and Broadstone. Three people were killed, including firewatcher Arthur Martin, aged 59. Many fires were started but almost all were brought swiftly under control, leaving only thirteen people without homes.

Footnote   B.T. Condon recalled the night for me, in 1987: "I was home on leave from the RAF. When the sirens sounded I decided to go down to the ARP Wardens' Post in the annexe of the Broadstone Hotel to see if I could be of any help to my former ARP colleagues. My way took me past Willis the builders' merchants shop at the side of which was the lorry entrance to their paint store behind it. There I saw Mr Bryant, one of Willis's lorry drivers who lived nearby, and he asked for my help in reeling out a small hosepipe to fight a fire which had been started in the paint store.

"Imagine our dismay when we found that we could get no water through the tap, presumably because the Fire Service were using all the main supply elsewhere. Some of the bombs dropped on that occasion were fiendish 'Ibsens' [Incendiary Bomb Separating Explosive Nose]. These were designed with a delayed action fuse on an explosive device which separated from the fire-bomb on impact and exploded shortly afterwards with the object of maiming anyone fighting the fire caused by the incendiary."

24 April   Hurn Mosquitoes claim three Ju88s.

Last night eight Mosquito night-fighters of 125 (New Zealand) Squadron, flying from RAF Hurn, intercepted a formation of Junkers Ju88 bombers. All the fighters returned safely to the station, with claims that they had shot down three of the bombers, and that two others had been damaged.

28 April   Six hundred Americans massacred off Portland.

Last night a convoy of eight American landing craft, sailing west from the Solent for the big Exercise Tiger practice landings at Slapton Sands, Devon, were intercepted by E-boats as they rounded Portland Bill to enter Lyme Bay. Motor torpedo boats of the 5th and 9th Schnellboot Flotillas ran amok amongst the Americans off the Portland end of the Chesil Beach, which is known locally as Dead Man's Bay from the memory of earlier shipwreck calamities.

A total of 441 United States soldiers have been killed or drowned, together with 197 seamen; LST507 and LST531 are sunk with the loss of twelve tanks; LST289 is damaged by a torpedo.

The coastal gun batteries at Blacknor, Portland, prepared to open fire, but the American commander ordered them not to do so, in view of the number of his men who were in the water. The E-boats withdrew on the arrival of a corvette, HMS *Azalra*, and HMS *Saladin*, followed by HMS *Onslow*.

Footnote   The dead would be stacked in piles on Castletown Pier in Portland Naval Dockyard. Offshore, teams of Navy divers worked for days to recover the identity discs from the other bodies, to account for all the missing and give Allied Naval Headquarters the welcome news that none had been fished out alive from the sea by the Germans and taken prisoner. Confirmation of their demise was accompanied by immense feelings of relief. Some compensation for their misfortune was the assurance that the invasion plans were still secret.

30 April   RAF Hamworthy closes.

The short direct connection with military flying boats has ended at Poole with the closure of RAF Hamworthy. Service flying boats can, however, still be refuelled and oiled at Poole by BOAC.

30 April   Thunderbolt crashes in Highcliffe School playground.

19.03 hours: Police confirm an aircraft has crashed near the Globe Inn, Lymington Road, Highcliffe. Christchurch ARP have had a report of a parachute descending south-east of Hoburne House.

19.20: Damage reported to two houses in Woodland Way.

19.25: Report of damage to Highcliffe School and the ARP store there, as well as water-mains fractured. A rescue party is being sent from Sandhills depôt.

19.35: The aircraft crashed in the playground at Highcliffe School. It was a P-47 Thunderbolt of the 405th Fighter Bomber Group of the United States Army Air Force and had been preparing to land at Christchurch Advance Landing Ground. Its remains lie in a crater and pieces of metal and other debris cover the trees on the other side of the road.

19.40: The American pilot landed unhurt in the nearby recreation ground.

Footnote   Les White of Glenville Road, Walkford, recalls chatting with the 'Snowdrops' (US Military Police) at their road-block between Humphreys Bridge and SRDE (now Plesseys) as the Thunderbolts were landing. "Several were down when we noticed that one was circling at about 3,000 feet and as we watched we saw that the port wing was so badly damaged that it was visibly flapping. A coloured soldier came across the airfield on a bike and told the 'Snowdrops' that the pilot had decided to head out to sea and use his parachute.

"As we watched he baled out and the aircraft, now without any control, was caught by the stiff sea breeze and turned back inland. As my friend and I pedalled our bikes back towards Highcliffe we heard the thud of the crash and arrived on the scene to see the remains of the Thunderbolt lying in a shallow crater in the school yard."

April 1944. Above, Poole Harbour. A line of assault landing craft, built by Bolson's at Hamworthy and Poole, at anchor in Holes Bay. Production is running at one per day. Vast quantities of craft are accumulating in inlets and estuaries along the South Coast as central southern England prepares for the invasion of Europe.

Early 1944. Studland beach. Tanks and beaches don't go well together. Failure (top, left) as the Churchill tank fails to climb one of the steeper parts of the sand dunes. So enter one of Hobart's Funnies (top, right). Major-General Percy Hobart of the 79th Armoured Division designed a series of ingenious machines that could ease the way for tanks, and however strange they looked, his vehicles were to save hundreds of lives in the Normandy campaign. Here, an AVRE lays a carpet from a bobbin, across the soft sand. Next, using the carpet that the AVRE has laid, the Churchill tank repeats its attempt at climbing the dune (above, left). This time it disappears over the top (above, right). On the lefthand side of this picture you can see the deep rut left by its first, unaided, failure.

April 1944. Opposite. Slapton Sands, Devon. In Exercise Fabious landing craft from Portland, Weymouth and Poole joined in the major dummy run for D-Day and the invasion of Normandy. Three tank landing craft are unloading in this sector, protected by barrage balloons from fighter attack.

April   **83 Group has six offensive squadrons at Hurn.**

Rocket-firing Hawker Typhoons of 181, 182 and 247 Squadrons, which form 124 Wing, are now at RAF Hurn. They bring to six the number of offensive squadrons at the airfield that comprise 83 Group of the 2nd British Tactical Air Force.

They are flying regular ground-attack missions across Brittany and Normandy. The rockets have their own propellant and fire clear of the aircraft without recoil. Eight are carried by each aircraft.

April   **Exercise Smash assaults Studland.**

The 1st Battalion of the Dorsetshire Regiment has been back on its native heath, taking part in the repeated mock-invasion assaults of Exercise Smash across the sands of Studland Bay. Unlike normal exercises this one has been distinguished by the widespread use of live ammunition, from small-arms fire to bombs and rockets, and has been studied intently by high ranking officers and a succession of war lords.

From a massive concrete bunker, the Fort Henry observation post built by Canadian engineers on Redend Point, a row of field glasses has lined the slit that looks northward across Studland Bay and the whole of its beach. Users of binoculars have included Prime Minister Winston Churchill, General Dwight D. Eisenhower (Supreme Commander Allied Expeditionary Force), General Sir Bernard Montgomery (effectively, for the assault, commander-in-chief Allied land forces, commanding the British 21st Army Group), General Omar Bradley (commanding the First United States Army), and General Miles Dempsey (commanding the Second British Army).

April 1944. Opposite. The Union Jack will be taken across the Channel, but first it is raised on Slapton Sands, Devon. Exercise Fabious is the major dummy run for D-Day.

1943-44. Studland. Fort Henry at Redend Point. One of Britain's most important relics of World War Two. Length 90 feet, concrete walls almost three feet thick, and recessed observation slit 80 feet long. From it the top brass watched live-fire rehearsals for the Normandy landings. Behind the field-glasses were Churchill, Eisenhower and Montgomery, plus just about all their generals and aides. Post-war sycamores now spoil the view of the sands.

April **Americans bring death to Dorset roads.**

The increase that the United States Army has brought to traffic on Dorset's roads is reflected in this month's accident fatalities, which have risen to seven from only two in April 1943. Colonel Frederick R. Lafferty, the Provost Marshal of 7-Base Section of the US Army, is to instigate five military police patrol groups to control traffic flow at major junctions.

April **Unexploded phosphorous bomb at Holton Heath.**

A five kilogram German bomb packed with phosphorous has failed to explode inside the Royal Naval Cordite Factory at Holton Heath. The contents have been steamed out and it is now on display as a trophy.

1 May **Second Mosquito squadron comes to Hurn.**

604 (County of Middlesex) Squadron arrived today at RAF Hurn. They are the second Mosquito squadron at the station and are led by Wing Commander Gerald Maxwell.

5 May **Hurn Mosquitoes claim two kills.**

Directed by Starlight, as the RAF's Sopley radar station is known, the Mosquitoes of 125 and 604 Squadrons were airborne last night. The Hurn-based night-fighters were successful in making a number of interceptions of Luftwaffe raiders.

125 Squadron claimed a Junkers Ju88 destroyed and an Me410 damaged. 604 Squadron reported a Dornier Do217 shot down and a Junkers Ju88 damaged.

7 May **Warmwell loses two Lightnings in France.**

Two Lightnings from Warmwell, escorting B-26 bombers into France, have been shot down. Lieutenants Merkle and Thacker are missing. The returning planes claimed one probable kill, a Focke-Wulf 190.

Footnote Merkle was killed but Thacker was to surprise his colleagues by escaping into Spain and making it back to Warmwell in June.

13 May **2nd Dorsets lose 75 men to recapture a piece of Burma.**

Having cost seventy-five Dorset lives in fierce fighting against the Japanese that has dragged on for three weeks, the 2nd Battalion of the Dorsetshire Regiment today achieved its costly objective and ousted the enemy from the Kohima Ridge; a second-class hill station at 5,000 feet in central Burma. For the Japanese it is a major strategic disaster but for the West Countrymen it has been hell. Many of the Dorset dead have been left where they fell since 27 April.

The padre held a service on the tennis court near where 'C' Company had sustained the greatest losses in the initial attack. The men were joined by Richard Sharp of the BBC:

"We are still on the six hills in the centre of Kohima. We've mopped up nearly all the Japs on them, and we've taken the famous tennis court. A half-smashed bunker on one of the hills was giving us a good deal of trouble, but we took it at one [13.00 hours] today, and I've seen the hill myself. It's covered with dead Japs. I counted up to forty of them and then stopped. Our men have been sprinkling them with quicklime—a necessary precaution in this weather.

"The men who took it came from a battalion of a West Country regiment. They've been plugging away at that tennis court for sixteen days and they'd become personal enemies of the Japs there, who used to taunt them at dusk, calling across the tennis court:

'Have you stood-to yet?' Today they're on top and they walked on their toes, laughing, among

March–August 1944. Lockheed P-38 Lightnings of the American 474th Fighter Group, flying from Warmwell, are now the commonest aeroplane in the sky over south Dorset.

the bulges in the earth of dug-out roofs; their muscles limber, ready to swivel this way or that in an instant.

"There was a company commander [Captain Clive Chettle], a robust man with a square, black jaw covered with stubble. The skin between his battle-dress trousers and his tunic was bloody, and he swayed as he stood with his legs straddled. But his brain was working at full speed, and he laughed and shouted to his men as they went eagerly from fox-hole to fox-hole with hand grenades and pole charges—that's twenty-five pounds of explosive at the end of a six-foot bamboo."

13 May Eisenhower meets the 1st Dorsets.

The Supreme Commander Allied Forces, General Dwight D. Eisenhower, today visited the 231st Infantry Brigade who are training in the New Forest at Cadlands Camp, Fawley. Representatives of the 1st Battalion of the Dorsetshire Regiment were among those whose confidence he gained.

15 May Zeals Mosquito shoots down Dornier.

A German raider which penetrated Dorset air space in the early hours this morning was tracked by radar along its northerly course, apparently towards Bristol. It was engaged by a Mosquito night-fighter of 488 (New Zealand) Squadron from Zeals Aerodrome, to the west of Mere, which was flown by Flying Officer Ray Jeffs, pilot, and Flying Officer Ted Spedding, the navigator.

Their target, a Dornier 217K, was picked up by Yeovil's searchlights and came into their sights as it crossed into Somerset. They raked it with fire. The Dornier's right-hand engine was blazing and it crashed into the countryside at West Camel.

The pilot, Johannes Domschke (20), died from his wounds but the crewmen, observer Emil Chmillewski (21), wireless operator Waldemar Jungke (22), and gunner Otto Schott (23), parachuted into captivity.

15 May **Four hurt by Purewell bomb.**

Four casualties were rescued from Purewell Hill House, Christchurch, after it had been hit at 02.22 hours by a German bomb. Another fell at West View, Stanpit, about the same time and damaged houses over a wide area. Bombs also dropped behind the OK Garage, Somerford, and at Woolhayes, Highcliffe. The latter failed to explode.

18 May **Mass glider exercises at Tarrant Rushton.**

11.04 hours: twelve Halifax-Hamilcar combinations of 298 Squadron, plus a further twelve of the same type of tug-planes and gliders from 644 Squadron, are lined up beside the main runway at Tarrant Rushton Aerodrome for a mass take-off.

19.00 hours: this morning's exercise is now to be repeated at Tarrant Rushton, this time with eighteen Halifax-Hamilcar combinations from each of the two squadrons, in order to give the pilots experience of mass take-offs and landings at dusk.

Similar large-scale practices will take place on 22 and 29 May.

21 May **American pilot killed at Cheselbourne.**

An American pilot from Warmwell, Lieutenant Kimball, was killed when his Lightning fighter crashed near Cheselbourne.

21 May **Acoustic mine defused in Lyme Bay.**

Lieutenant Commander Bryant and Petty Officer Clark of the Royal Navy have defused one of the new-type acoustic pressure mines that the Germans have laid in Lyme Bay. They were dropped from German Schnellboote S136, S138 and S140 on the night of 18 May.

Conventional mines have also been sown by Schnellboote' S144, S130, S145, S146, S150' and S168 before three Royal Navy destroyers with three motor gun-boats, from Portland, forced their withdrawal to France.

22 May **Another Warmwell Lightning lost in France.**

Lieutenant Usas, an American Lightning pilot from Warmwell, was killed in France whilst on a mission to dive-bomb a strategic target.

23 May **Two Junkers for Hurn's Mosquitoes.**

Both night-fighter squadrons from RAF Hurn were operational over Southampton and Portsmouth last night.

604 Squadron failed to find the German bombers but nine fighters from 125 Squadron came upon them at 00.15 hours. Their first claim was a Junkers Ju88 that was shot down at 00.20, followed by another Ju88 damaged at 00.40. A third Ju88 was then engaged and seen to be crashing to the ground at 00.45.

25 May **Wellington crashes at Christchurch.**

13.00 hours. An RAF Wellington bomber has crashed near Christchurch Aerodrome, on the north side of the railway line.

28 May **Weymouth air raid damages 400 houses.**

At 01.03 hours the air raid sirens warbled at Weymouth but two minutes earlier the bombs had started to drop and they were to damage four hundred houses. Some hundred of them are badly

28 May 1944. Weymouth. Melcombe Avenue as clearing up begins after what will turn out to be the town's last major air raid of the war.

smashed and fire has also damaged Weymouth Hospital and the Christian Science Church. Three Civil Defence volunteers and a junior ATS commander have been killed and thirteen of the injured have been detained in hospital.

Patients from the Weymouth and District Hospital, hit by a bomb and with another still unexploded beneath it, have been evacuated by Colonel Knoblock and Medical Corps of the United States Army to the Emergency Hospital established in Weymouth College.

Footnote The hospital bomb had buried itself twenty-eight feet in the ground and could not be reached and deactivated for several days.

Early in June 1944. Weymouth. Raising the hospital bomb.

28 May German mine-layers driven off.

An attempt last night by the German 5th Schnellboot Flotilla to lay mines off the Dorset coast was seen off by Beaufighters from RAF Holmsley South in the New Forest aided by the Poole Bay coast defence batteries and Royal Navy destroyers from Portland and Portsmouth. The fleeing German boats used their speed to escape but all are taking home some damage.

30 May Mass glider take-off in moonlight at Tarrant Rushton.

Tonight a mass take-off of Halifax-Hamilcar combinations at Tarrant Rushton Aerodrome is to test the station's expertise at mounting an airborne operation in moonlight.

May Paddle-steamers lay hundreds of British mines.

Requisitioned paddle-steamers have joined the mine-layer HMS *Plover* in laying one thousand two hundred mines in defensive barriers to protect the concentrations of invasion craft in Dorset and Hampshire estuaries from enemy E-boats. The Auxiliary Paddle Minesweepers *Medway Queen, Ryde, Whipingham* and *Sandown* and the 10th, 51st and 52nd Mine-Laying Flotillas have been carrying out the task under the watchful eyes of an assortment of escort vessels from the 9th, 13th, 14th, 21st and 64th Motor Torpedo Boat Flotillas.

Footnote These minefields were to claim the richest haul of Axis shipping in the Channel of the whole war; 102 enemy vessels would be accounted for.

May Seven hundred Americans invade Charborough Park.

A United States Army mechanised supply unit of seven hundred men with a hundred heavy six-wheeled vehicles has camped in Charborough Park and dug slit trenches against air attack. The only incident has been caused by a red stag that was nibbling grass and pushed its head into the side of a tent and a sleeping Yank.

The Americans, however, have swiftly developed a taste for young peafowl—not unlike turkey—and those from the Wild West are adept at throwing knives into the trunks of the cedar trees. Admiral Drax's staff have noticed that the Americans drive everywhere, even distances of a few yards, and there is hardly a lawn or patch of grass that isn't being worn bare.

4 June Montgomery: 'The time has come'.

Message to all ranks of the 21st Army Group from its Commander-in-Chief, General Sir Bernard Montgomery: "The time has come to deal the enemy a terrific blow in Western Europe. To us is given the honour of striking a blow for freedom which will live in history."

5 June The invasion—it's on.

04.00 hours. The Supreme Commander Allied Forces Western Europe, General Dwight D. Eisenhower, has given the order that the invasion of Europe is to take place tomorrow. It should have gone ahead today but has been postponed because of the heavy seas. A lull is expected in the winds tomorrow but they are forecast to gather strength again in the evening. This would rule out the 7th, the last day of the present favourable tide cycle, and it is therefore imperative that unless the entire operation is stood-down it must begin at midnight.

5 June Three Warmwell pilots killed on the Seine.

A cloud-base near ground level forced the Lightnings of the American 474th Fighter Group from Warmwell into the trees as they approached their target bridge over the River Seine. Major

Bedford, Lieutenant Coddington and Lieutenant Temple were killed and several of the surviving planes brought back tree boughs in their tails.

5 June Hurn Wing Commander plucked from sea and returned to the sky.

Reg Jones, the chief of scientific intelligence at the Air Ministry, writes in his *Most Secret War* that today he flew over the Solent and realised the invasion was 'on' because the armada that had been in Spithead two days before was no longer there. He flew on to Hurn: "I was silently wishing them good luck when we had a head-on encounter with a whole wing of American Thunderbolts. It was like standing in a butt whilst a covey of enormous grouse is driven past you on all sides. What was more, the Thunderbolts with their big radial engines were climbing, and so none of their pilots could see us.

5 June 1944. 'Touch of Texas' was among the P-47 Thunderbolts of the 405th Fighter Bomber Group of the United States Army Air Force that today buzzed Dr Reginald Jones, head of Air Ministry scientific Intelligence, as he came over their Christchurch base, en route from the Solent to Hurn Aerodrome. This is another of the remarkable series of photographs found by Leslie Dawson for his definitive second edition of 'Wings over Dorset' (Dorset Publishing, 1989).

"We duly landed at Hurn, my main memory being of a Norwegian Wing Commander who had been taking part in the radar strikes. He had been shot down earlier that day, picked up out of the sea by one of the air-sea rescue launches, and had already flown another sortie."

Twenty-eight Typhoons had delivered ninety-six 60lb rockets and seven tons of bombs on German coastal radar stations—taking care to keep that at Fécamp intact so that it could report spoof activity aimed at convincing the enemy that the main thrust of the Allied invasion is further up-Channel, east of the Seine.

Five squadrons of Typhoons and Mosquitoes are now operating from RAF Hurn, as are P-61 Black Widow night-fighters of the 9th United States Army Air Force and B-26 Marauders of the American 97th Bombardment Group.

1 June 1944. South Dorset. V Corps of the First United States Army is the county's army of occupation. It has gathered its tanks into vast fields of armour and the men file behind barbed wire for their briefings. From now on they are to have no conversations with civilians (the notice is at Puddletown; the lesser one reads—'In case of fire call N.F.S. [National Fire Service] Dorchester. Telephone Dorchester 766. You are at D3').
Weymouth Quay, above. The two black lads, Asa Jones and Furrell Browning from Dallas, man an anti-aircraft gun aboard USS 'Henrico'. The preparations for the D-Day embarkations were to go unmolested.

4 June 1944.
Dorchester.
D-Day briefing
for an American
engineer unit.
'The time has
come to deal
the enemy
a terrific
blow' —
Montgomery's
words were
read to all
troops.
Prominent in
the foreground
are Private
Albert V. Ottolino
of Billings,
Montana; Private
First-Class
Howard D. Kraut
of Brush, Colorado;
Private J.H. James
of Woodville,
Texas.

4-5 June 1944. Weymouth. Men of V Corps
(opposite, top) of the First United
States Army, with full kit including
rifles, pass out of the coffee tent:
'From the folks back home
through the American Red Cross.'

1944. Weymouth. United States Military Policeman
Sergeant Daniel Ewton (left) policed the town's
invasion of GIs.

4-5 June 1944. Weymouth. Assault troops, part
of Force O tasked to storm Omaha Beach, relaxing
(opposite, below) with a quayside dance
on the eve of what they know is going to be
the worst day of their lives.

May 1944. Weymouth.
United States Army
Private Ernie Webster
and 20-year-old
Regent Cinema salesgirl
Doris Mockridge,
of 12 Trinity Road.
She sold him a box
of matches and became
a GI bride, their romance
being movingly
recounted by John
Murphy in his own
'Dorset at War'.
By the time of the
wedding, back from
Omaha Beach, Ernie
had lost a leg.

4-5 June 1944. Weymouth Quay. Black 'static' troops of the United States Army load assault landing craft LCA 882 (the centre vessel in the pictures opposite).

4 June 1944. Farewell time, outside the Cove House Hotel, as landlady Mrs Elizabeth Comben (centre) says goodbye to the United States Navy. Their individual stories are told by John Murphy in his 1979 book of this same title, 'Dorset at War'.

4-5 June 1944. Weymouth Quay and the old Ritz Theatre (burnt down in the 1950s and replaced by the Pavilion). Lines of Negro 'static' troops pass down stores to the American assault landing craft which are to lead Force O on to Omaha Beach in Normandy.

4-5 June 1944. Weymouth Quay. Opposite. Royal Navy ratings assist the embarkation of a Ranger battalion of V Corps of the United States Army, due to assault Omaha Beach at H-hour—06.45 hours on D-Day. They will hit the strongest resistance of the Normandy landings, with the Rangers being pinned down on the right flank for several hours and suffering heavy casualties whilst their beachhead lay in the balance.

4-5 June 1944. Weymouth Harbour. Opposite the office of pleasure steamer operators Cosens and Co, landing craft prepare for departure. First Lieutenant Robert T. Eldin (below, left) and First Lieutenant Stanley White look suitably determined.

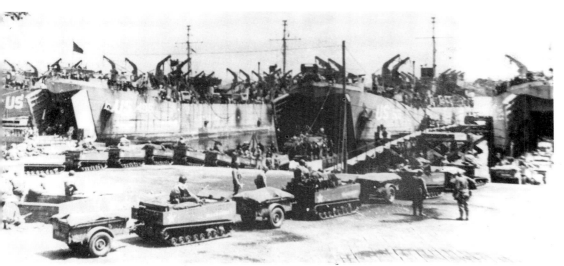

4–5 June 1944. Portland, opposite top, showing a line of American DUKWs beside the Chesil Beach, waiting their turn to go into landing craft at Castletown (above) and to join the armada that is being gathered (below) for the invasion of Normandy.
It is a time for final briefings (opposite, centre) and the march of the GIs southwards along Weymouth seafront (opposite, bottom) for embarkation at the Quay.

4–5 June 1944. Portland and Weymouth. V Corps of the United States First Army, setting off for Omaha Beach and the invasion of Europe. In the pictures opposite, the tank landing craft are at Castletown Dockyard, Portland, and the infantry are filing on to smaller assault craft at Weymouth Quay.
Everywhere in the two ports is a mass of men and equipment (below). For many of the GIs, June 6th would be the longest day of their lives. For the other thousand, however, it will be the shortest.

June 1944. Portland and Weymouth. The emblem that is everywhere around the two ports, and quite common at Poole as well: that of the 14th Major Port of the United States Army Transportation Corps.

4–5 June 1944. Portland and Weymouth. Above, top, an American DUKW reverses into a landing craft at Castletown Docks, Portland. Assault troops are packed like sardines at Weymouth Quay (above) and (right) GIs break into song as they wait to board the USS 'Henrico' at Weymouth.

5 June 1944. Portland Harbour. General Infantrymen of the United States Army aboard the troopship 'Henrico'. This should have been D-Day but turned into a day of standing around waiting when the weather caused the invasion to be postponed until the 6th.

4 June 1944. Portland Harbour. Material was almost as important as men. Supply launches were constantly speeding from the shore to the ships at anchor.

6 June 1944. Mid-Channel. Convoy in the Allied sea armada, protected by barrage balloons from the air attacks that never came. Admiral Sir Bertram Ramsay, commanding the naval support for the greatest amphibious landings in history, described it as 'an air of unreality' because no U-boats were encountered and E-boats were kept in port by bad weather and the elimination of German radar stations. The remarkable series of photographs on this and the previous pages are from the Pentagon and courtesy the United States Army.

5 June **Battleship 'Rodney' in Weymouth Bay.**

Weymouth Bay has its largest gathering of big warships since the Reserve Fleet was dispersed in 1939. The danger of air attack then prevented anything larger than a destroyer operating from Portland Harbour.

Operation Neptune has brought five American and two British cruisers to the bay, plus the strange cut-short silhouette of the 34,000ton battleship HMS *Rodney*. The terrific destructive force of her broadsides is to be used tomorrow in French coastal bombardment—she is preparing to fire her full armament of nine 16-inch, twelve 6-inch and six 4.7-inch guns.

1944. Tarrant Rushton. Training take-off for a troop carrying Horsa glider being lifted by a twin engine Albemarle tug-plane. Such a pair, one of three destined for the French coast at Merville, would be the first to take to the air on 5 June 1944, the eve of D-Day. That is to be a lift-off at dusk, and with grass on both sides of the runway filled with 36 larger Halifax-Horsa combinations. The scene, photographed earlier in the day, appears in the unique sequence that follows. These were assembled jointly by Rodney Legg and Leslie Dawson, principally for the latter's 'Wings over Dorset' which has numerous personal stories from Tarrant Rushton in the run-up to 'the longest day'.

5 June **Gliders ready at Tarrant Rushton.**

Painted with invasion-day stripes, trains of Horsa troop-carrying gliders are being prepared for take-off at Tarrant Rushton. The men are part of the British 6th Airborne Division and will drop to the east of the Normandy beach-heads—at Bénouville, Merville, Randville, Varaville, Bures and Troarn—to hold the bridges on the River Orne and to break those across the River Dives.

In all thirty-nine aircraft are taking part from Tarrant Rushton Aerodrome. Six Halifax-Horsa combinations are involved in Operation Coup de Main. They are carrying a total of

171 troops and are under orders to capture intact the bridges across the Caen Canal and the River Orne to the north of Caen. After releasing the Horsa gliders these Halifax tow-craft will bomb a powder factory to the south-east of Caen to create a diversion.

Another thirty Halifax-Horsa combinations are detailed to carry out Operation Tonga. Their Horsa gliders will be released at point LZ-N, to the east of Caen Canal. The 3rd and 5th Parachute Brigades are involved in this drop, which is to begin about half-an-hour after Operation Coup de Main. Additionally a much smaller force, of only three Albemarle combinations, is tasked to take-out a German coast battery near Merville.

The first three gliders to leave Tarrant Rushton are being towed by twin-engined Albemarles and are those destined for the coast at Merville.

The following six gliders will be towed by four-engined Halifaxes and are also loaded with men from the Oxfordshire and Buckinghamshire Light Infantry, bound for the Orne swing-bridge and canal bridge [codenamed Pegasus]. They are to leave shortly before midnight and are expected to be released about five miles short of their targets, at around 01.30 hours, to glide down on to French soil. Then the other thirty Halifax-Horsa combinations will take-off for Operation Tonga.

Once the infantry have secured the immediate dropping zones the two Halifax squadrons from Tarrant Rushton will return to France, at about 21.00 hours, in Operation Mallard, with a convoy of thirty gliders of the British 6th Air Landing Brigade — the larger Hamilcars with the Division's heavier equipment including Tetrarch tanks, Bren-gun carriers, twenty-five pounder field guns, scout cars and Bailey bridge pontoons.

The gliders are to be released over point LZ-N and eighteen containers are to be dropped at point DZ.

5 June   The gliders lift off from Tarrant Rushton for 'Pegasus' bridge.

22.56 hours. The first Halifax has roared along the central runway at Tarrant Rushton Aerodrome and lifted off, towing a Horsa glider of the British 6th Airborne Division towards France. There are thirty-six Halifax tug-planes and their gliders to be cleared at one-minute intervals. 6th Airborne Division is commanded by 47-year-old Brigadier Richard Gale.

Into the sky has gone the 1st Platoon of 'D' Company of the 2nd Battalion, Oxfordshire and Buckinghamshire Light Infantry. They are commanded by Major John Howard.

He arrived with his men at Tarrant Rushton on 26 May and they have been confined to camp, awaiting the codeword to 'go' which arrived at 09.00 hours on Friday 4 June. To everyone's disappointment this was cancelled because of the windy weather.

This morning Major Howard received the order again and it has been another day of loading and re-checking, leading up to a fat-less evening meal to calm the men's stomachs, at this moment when everyone's faith is in the renowned abilities of the Glider Pilot Regiment. Faces are blackened and all have clambered aboard — for a promised gap in the German flak at Cabourg.

Howard's 'D' Company will be cast off at 5,000 feet to land beside the bridge over the Caen Canal which has been codenamed 'Pegasus'.

Footnote   Operation Coup de Main proceeded smoothly with this section of 6th Airborne dropped near Bénouville as planned and four of the six gliders only yards from their target spot. They were the first Allied soldiers to arrive in France on D-Day and opened the Second Front in the European theatre of war. Both bridges were secured intact.

Operation Tonga encountered more problems. Five of the aircraft failed to release their gliders within the landing zone and Halifax K288 went down with its port wing blazing.

A total of 670 Horsa gliders for the Airborne Divisions were constructed at the Airspeed factory beside Christchurch Aerodrome.

5 June 1944. The British 6th Airborne Division prepares at Tarrant Rushton, Hurn, Holmsley South and other aerodromes to drop in tomorrow on Normandy. Above the graffiti is defiant: 'The Channel stopped you, but not us. Remember Coventry, Plymouth, Bristol, London. Now it's our turn. You've had your time you German …'
The original last word was rubbed out for the benefit of the photographer and eventual readers — but the men were allowed to have 'Swinhunds' instead.

Opposite. The men file towards lines of Horsa gliders painted with D-Day stripes, and a Tetrarch light tank is loaded into the belly of a Hamilcar. The Horsas were manufactured by Airspeed Limited at Christchurch.

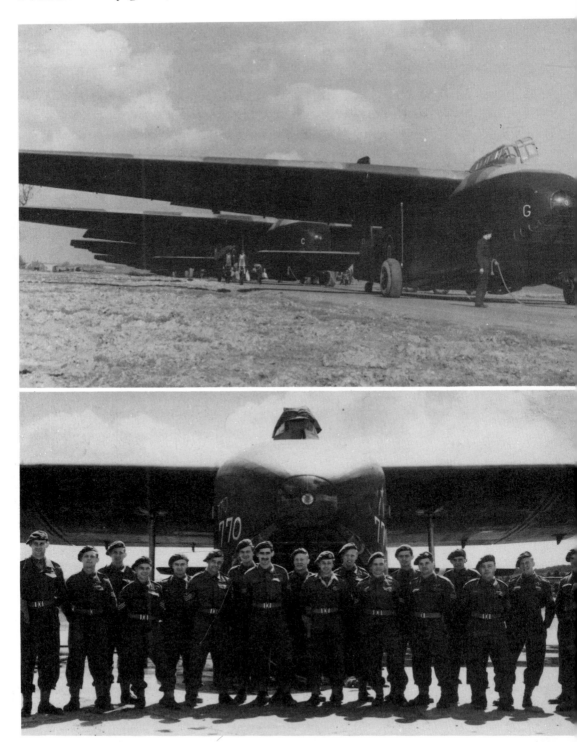

5 June 1944. Above. Hamilcars and in particular number 770, preparing to lift elements of the British 6th Airborne Division from Tarrant Rushton Aerodrome.
Opposite, line-up at Hurn Aerodrome of Horsa troop carrying gliders and their Albemarle tug aircraft of 570 Squadron.

5 June 1944. Tarrant Rushton Aerodrome. British 6th Airborne Division preparations for D-Day.
Above. A Halifax tug-plane of 644 Squadron takes off with a Hamilcar glider.
Below. The Hamilcar (right) is towed by the Halifax over The Cliff escarpment and into the sky above Tarrant Monkton.
Opposite, top. A Hamilcar (right) and Halifax combination over the Crichel Estate woodlands with Badbury Rings (marked 'A') being just discernible. The planes have their D-Day stripes.
Opposite, below. A Hamilcar has its flaps down ready to land back at Tarrant Rushton. The skids on the belly were to help it survive more difficult terrain.

A

5 June 1944. Tarrant Rushton Aerodrome, D-Day minus one: the Halifax
tugs and their Horsa gliders (along the runway) prepare for a midnight date
with history. The photograph is from the north and as on the last page the
Iron Age hill-fort of Badbury Rings has been marked with an 'A'. The planes
are on the east-west runway (actually east-north-east/ west-south-west and
the gliders are facing east-north-east; a south-westerly wind was still blowing
but a lull was forecast, correctly).

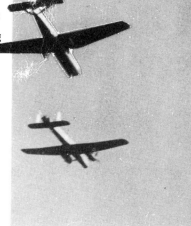

Opposite. The British 6th Airborne Division—airborne in a practice for the
drop on Pegasus Bridge and the other vital crossing points near Caen. The
tugs in this instance are RAF Whitley bombers.

7 June 1944. Major John Howard arrived yesterday with the Horsa gliders from Tarrant Rushton and today the 2nd Battalion of the Oxfordshire and Buckinghamshire Light Infantry control 'Pegasus' bridge over the Caen Canal. Their gliders can be seen on the east bank to the right of the bridge. Any German attack on the Normandy beach-head would had to have come along this road which lies between Bénouville and Ranville, about three miles from the coast.

6 June Invasion Day—the sky fills.

00.15 hours. Victor Swatridge of Dorchester Police was patrolling the town's Victoria Park with the intention of meeting his beat constable there at 00.30 hours. In 1971, Swatridge recalled what happened; he was witnessing the greatest mass movement of aircraft that has ever taken place:

"Britain was still suffering from its black-out and not a glimmer of light dared emit from any house or premises. It was a beautiful clear starlit night, when suddenly I became aware of the heavy drone of aircraft coming from inland. As it drew nearer, the sky lit up: thousands of coloured lights had burst forth and the whole atmosphere exploded into activity.

"It was an amazing transformation as hundreds of bombers towing gliders with their masses of human and vehicle cargo flew overhead and across the English Channel. This huge armada was a continuous procession for more than two hours. It was clearly evident that the invasion of Europe had commenced and I remember how excited I was. But yet the civilian population were still quietly sleeping in their beds; everyone had become immune to the noise of aircraft travelling overhead, yet I venture to suggest if it had been enemy planes, the whole place would have been alive with activity, sirens would have wailed and woken them from their slumber.

"Invasion Day had been very secretively guarded; everyone had been warned that it would be treasonable to give the slightest indication to the enemy that it was about to take place, and the civil population kept that bargain. The police had been warned to expect heavy counter bombing and we were expecting frightening reprisals. We waited but no enemy air action occurred to our utter amazement."

6 June Weymouth wakes up to sound of the air armada.

Twenty-two-year-old Weymouth teacher Miss Barbara Baker writes in her diary: "Early this morning was awakened by the throbbing of low-flying aircraft. Looked out of the window and saw the sky full of bombers towing gliders. Presume airborne troops are being dropped behind enemy lines in France? Heard later that all ships anchored in Weymouth Bay had sailed across the Channel to land troops in Normandy. The long awaited invasion has begun."

The first day back at school after the Whitsun holiday was already on its way into history.

6 June D-Day.

The sea forces deployed today are an armada unequalled in history—138 warships carrying out bombardments; 221 destroyers and other escort vessels; 287 minesweepers; 491 miscellaneous light craft; 441 auxiliaries—quite apart from the more than 4,000 landing craft that they are supporting and protecting. Merchant vessels are also involved in a myriad of support rôles, to a total of 6,488 vessels acting under Admiralty instructions.

6 June 'Fishpond' reveals the Dorset armada.

The armada off Dorset of V Corps of the First United States Army on their way from Weymouth and Portland towards Omaha Beach was such a concentration of steel that it showed on the Fishpond airborne radar set in Roland Hammersley's aircraft. His first report of the blips sent the pilot, Ron Walker, looking for an enemy fighter force, but they saw to their astonishment the flotillas of landing craft heading towards Normandy. What Roland does not realise is that his brother, Walter, is down there on the sea.

Roland Hammersley was born at Swanage and lives at Bovington. He is a gunner with 57 Squadron, and took off this morning at 01.36 hours from East Kirkby, Lincolnshire, on a mission to attack coastal gun emplacements at La Pernelles.

6 June   1st Dorsets among first Britons ashore in France.

Army Operation Overlord/Navy Operation Neptune/Air Force Operation Mallard. Supported by the cruiser HMS *Emerald* and the destroyers HMS *Cottesmore, Grenville, Jervis, Ulysses, Undine* and *Urania*, with the Polish destroyer *Krakowiak*, plus the softening-up efforts of four fighter bomber squadrons, the 1st Battalion of the Dorsetshire Regiment left LCH317 and touched down on the beach to the north-east of the village of Les Roquettes at 07.30 hours. 'A' Company is led by Major A.A.E. Jones and 'B' Company by Major P. Chilton.

They have landed in the Jig Green sector of the Gold Beach bridgehead and with the Hampshires—a thousand yards to the east—can claim to be the first British troops to land in Normandy from the sea.

Captain C.R. Whittington, the Unit Landing Officer, wore a rainbow-coloured battle bowler. He was soon wounded but continued organising the clearing of corridors up the beach. Major Jones was withdrawn wounded and Major Chilton led the crossing of the minefields.

'C' Company [Major R.M. Nicholl] and 'D' Company [Major W.N. Hayes], helped the Hampshires take Asnelles-sur-Mer and proceeded to attack high ground at Point 54. 'C'

6 June 1944.

The invasion of Normandy gathers pace as the tide recedes.

6 June 1944. British Cromwell and Sherman tanks climb inland from the King (Red) sector of Gold Beach at La Riviere.

Company had most of the fighting though the enemy eventually abandoned its four 155mm guns and by 18.00 the Dorsets had found convenient dugouts for Battalion Headquarters on the hillside north of Ryes.

'B' Company moved into Ryes, which had been captured by the Devons.

The Dorsets have achieved all the day's objectives but at the cost of heavy losses—three officers killed; thirty other ranks killed; eleven officers wounded; eighty-four other ranks wounded.

6 June Dorset's Americans get the worst beach.

Dorset's Americans, V Corps of the 1st United States Army—comprising the 29th Division, 1st Division and Ranger Battalions, who embarked from Weymouth and Portland—touched the shore of Normandy at 06.34 hours. These regimental combat teams are Force O for Omaha, as the beach is codenamed.

It lies between Point due Hoe and Colleville to the north-west of Bayeux. Unfortunately for the V Corps they have received the bloodiest reception of the day and for several hours it seemed they might well be thrown back into the sea.

Their misfortune was to find that the coast defences in the Omaha sector had recently been augmented by the German 352nd Infantry Division; a field formation which happened to be holding a stand-to exercise as the American assault began. Extreme sacrifice and gallantry—a thousand dead and twice that wounded—has by nightfall achieved a beachhead a mile in depth.

Footnote The Americans would have lost the beach if the German High Command had not held back their reserve units, thinking that the Normandy assaults were a feint and that the main invasion force would land between the Seine and Calais.

March/June 1944. Poole Bay test for Pluto, and the end result—the Pipe Line Under The Ocean pumping petroleum into a beached tanker on the sands of Normandy.

6 June   Hurn Typhoons notch up 88 sorties.

Air Operation Mallard, the RAF's contribution to Operation Overlord, has been sweeping across the Normandy beachheads all day. The Typhoons of 83 Group of the 2nd British Tactical Air Force have flown eighty-eight cross-Channel sorties from RAF Hurn today in ground support attacks on enemy positions and the railway lines along which their reinforcements would come.

6 June   Warmwell sorties over the Cherbourg peninsula.

Today and for the next nine days the American Lightnings of the 474th Fighter Group from Warmwell will dive-bomb strategic targets in the Cherbourg peninsula and cover convoys of Allied shipping.

Footnote The Americans lost two pilots on these combat air patrols, Lieutenant Doty and Lieutenant Robert Hanson. A second Robert Hanson also flew with the 474th and survived to organise an association of its ex-members.

6 June   HMS 'Lyme Regis' clears Monty's passage.

The minesweeper HMS *Lyme Regis*, paid for and adopted by the west Dorset town in 1941-42, is clearing a safe channel into Sword Beach at the eastern end of the Normandy bridgehead. She is buoying it with French tricolour pennants.

The swept channel is being prepared for the passage into France of General Sir Bernard Montgomery and the Advance Headquarters staff of 21st Army Group.

7 June   Hurn Typhoons fly 138 Normandy sorties.

As the front lines widen in Normandy so the air-war intensifies. Typhoons of 83 Group of the 2nd British Tactical Air Force have been taking off and landing at RAF Hurn all day.

They have logged 138 sorties in support of the Second British Army on the coast north of Caen.

There are many Canadian fliers operating from Hurn and their special interest is with the central beachhead—the Juno sector—where the 3rd Canadian Infantry Division and the 2nd Canadian Armoured Brigade went ashore at Courseulles.

8 June **Surviving rocket-firing craft limp into Poole.**

The first of the returnee vessels from the Normandy landings are a group of LCRs, American rocket-firing landing craft, which have limped into Poole Harbour peppered with shell-holes after their onslaught against the enemy beaches.

10 June **Hurn Typhoons manage a record 154 Normandy sorties.**

The Typhoons of 83 Group of the 2nd British Tactical Air Force have had a record day. They went on 154 sorties from RAF Hurn.

Pilot Officer Grey of 181 Squadron has become the first Hurn fighter pilot to stand upon liberated Europe. He found himself in difficulties and brought his Typhoon down on to a newly-made temporary airstrip. Later he was able to return to Hurn with the story.

13 June 1944. Destroyer HMS 'Boadicia' is sunk off Portland as the German counter-attack picks away at cross-Channel supply convoys.

13 June **HMS 'Boadicea' sinks off Portland.**

HMS *Boadicea*, a Royal Navy destroyer, has been sunk off Portland. The past three days have seen other sinkings off the Dorset coast, as the German 2nd Schnellboot Flotilla evacuated Cherbourg and regrouped in Ostend from where it is concentrating on the supply convoys.

As Supply Convoy S-NS 08 assembled in Poole Bay it was seen by a German reconnaissance plane and intercepted by the Schnellboote in mid-Channel. S177 sank the *Brackenfield*, a 657-ton steamer, and the *Ashanti*, 534 tons. S178 claimed the *Dungrange*, 621 tons. A Norwegian destroyer, the *Stord*, sailed to the aid of the convoy with units of the Royal Navy but the Schnellboote outpaced them and escaped to Boulogne.

Some German losses have been sustained by the E-boat force in the past three days, however, as RAF Beaufighters of 143 Squadron and 236 Squadron, operating from the New Forest, have claimed to have damaged or sunk three Schnellboote, one Raumboot mine-layer, and an M-boat. Two of the fighters failed to return; one being brought down by anti-aircraft fire and the other credited to an Me163 Komet rocket-propelled fighter.

Footnote John Pitfield tells me that a Komet could not have brought down the Beaufighter as these German rocket-propelled planes had a short range and were operational only from German airfields. He says that it was a mistaken identification of one of the other remarkable new planes which the Germans deployed as the war drew to a close, either a Messerschmitt 262 or an Arado 234C. These jets had top speeds of 541 mph and 530 mph respectively. The poor Beaufighter could only do 320 mph.

13 June   **500lb bomb removed from Highcliffe.**

11.50 hours. A 500lb bomb that fell at Woolhayes, Highcliffe, on 15 May has been removed by a bomb disposal unit.

14 June   **Bomber Command soups up the defence of the Channel.**

Bomber Command has supplied some four-engine aircraft to No 19 Group, RAF Coastal Command, who are now hard-pressed to keep the English Channel reasonably safe for the convoys supplying the Normandy forces.

Footnote   By the end of June No 19 Group had sunk fourteen German U-boats in the Channel, three of them in the Dorset sector between Start Point and the Isle of Wight.

15 June   **British frigate torpedoed off Portland.**

A frigate, HMS *Blackwood*, has sunk off Portland Bill after being torpedoed.

15 June   **Portland divers carry out underwater welding.**

To the surprise of American engineer James Spearman and the rest of the unit in LCT1000, major seam repairs to its bottom have been carried out underwater in Portland Harbour. The landing craft turned back for England after cracking across the middle in rough seas.
   She carries a Bailey bridge-building outfit, trucks and pontoons.

Footnote   LCT 1000 was by no means the only casualty of the storm. Unfavourable weather during the first five days after D-Day meant that only thirty-eight percent of the planned tonnage of stores was actually brought ashore on the American sectors.

16 June   **An American bombs Warmwell.**

As an engine cut-out on his aircraft at Warmwell, American pilot Lieutenant Cumbie of the 430th Squadron followed standard procedure and jettisoned his bombs, which—contrary to correct procedure—turned out to be armed. He scored a direct hit on the field's transformer station.
   The pilot returned safely to the airfield, to congratulations from its RAF contingent: "Jerry's been trying to hit that for years!"

21 June   **War interrupts Warmwell's dress parade.**

The American pilots of the 474th Fighter Group, dressed for inspection by General Kincaid at Warmwell when they were to receive medals, instead received an unexpected order to scramble and found themselves back over France. Two of the Lightnings were lost, killing Lieutenant Vinson. The other pilot, Captain Larson, parachuted to safety and lived to receive the medal.

Footnote Three other Warmwell pilots, Lieutenants Gee, Heuermann and Danish were killed in the last week of June as the Americans harried the railway system in northern France. Many of the attacks were on targets of opportunity—"boys, just go over and hit anything that moves" they had been told.

22 June   Airborne rescue turns into a boat trip.

Lieutenant Dumar of 509 Squadron of the 405th Fighter Bomber Group of the United States Army Air Force, flying a Thunderbolt from Christchurch, had three lucky escapes today off the enemy coast. His engine seized over the German side of the English Channel, thirty miles from Cherbourg, and he parachuted into the sea.

He was located and picked up by a Walrus seaplane of the Air-Sea Rescue service. Then the Walrus found itself in difficulties as the choppy conditions prevented it from lifting off.

The crew decided to taxi through the waves and make for home on the surface. The Walrus was nothing more nor less than a sitting duck for the forty-mile slog back into home waters but fortunately no one from the Luftwaffe happened along.

23 June   Hurn Mosquitoes claim six Ju88s over Normandy.

The night prowl of the Hurn Mosquitoes took in the Normandy beachheads last night and the pilots returned with claims of six kills. They had intercepted a formation of Junkers Ju88 bombers.

Squadron Leader Petrie claimed two and Flying Officer Grey three, for 125 Squadron, and Flight Lieutenant Sandemann claimed one for 604 Squadron.

The gale which has raged across the Channel for three days finally eased last night.

23 June   US 3rd Armored Division embarked from Weymouth.

The 3rd Armored Division of the United States Army is now landing on Omaha White Beach, near Isigny, for the tank actions that will decide the Battle of Normandy. The craft had been kept in Portland Harbour for the past four days by a violent gale. Others have crossed from Southampton Water.

The arrivals include the 32nd and 33rd Armored Regiments, supported by the 486th Armored Anti-Aircraft Battalion and the 23rd Armored Engineer Battalion. Headquarters staff and the division's artillery, the 54th, 67th and 391st Armored Field Artillery Battalions, are following tomorrow.

Footnote The 36th Armored Infantry Regiment arrived on the 25th.

24 June   Bridport officer killed in Normandy.

Lieutenant-Colonel J.W. Atherton of Bridport was killed today in Normandy. He was blown up by a shell whilst fighting off a counter-attack by German tanks. Until recently Colonel Atherton was with the 5th Battalion of the Dorsetshire Regiment.

26 June   St Alban's Head battle ends with Germans sent packing.

Last night there was short but fierce naval engagement off St Alban's Head which resulted in German Schnellboote S130 and S168 departing for Dieppe, and S145 sustaining damage and being forced to flee for repairs to the nearest bastion that the enemy still holds; the occupied Channel Island of Alderney.

26 June   Change-over of Typhoons at Hurn.

With the gathering momentum of the siege of Cherbourg, following the capture of its

Maupertus airfield on 23 June, the Typhoons of 124 and 143 Wings from RAF Hurn are now stationed in Normandy. They comprise 83 Group of the 2nd British Tactical Air Force and are being replaced at Hurn by the arrival of 123 and 136 Wings, also with Typhoons.

These, together with 146 Wing which is also coming to Hurn, comprise 84 Group of the Second British Tactical Air Force.

29 June   Sixteen killed as Thunderbolts crash on Mudeford.

Foxwood Avenue at Mudeford, Christchurch, was devastated today by three American P-47 Thunderbolt fighter-bombers in two separate mishaps on take-off from Christchurch Advance Landing Ground. In the first, at 06.45 hours, the pilot survived and no one was hurt on the ground.

Then at 14.00 hours the same pilot tried again to take off. Once more he failed to gain proper height and overshot the runway into a bungalow. His fuel tanks and bombs exploded, bringing down another Thunderbolt, Scarab 2, that was coming off the runway. It was thrown upside down but the pilot, Lieutenant Drummond, escaped unhurt. The three planes belonged to the 509th Squadron of the 405th Fighter Bomber Group of the United States Army Air Force.

As rescue workers pulled the wounded out of the debris another bomb exploded, killing a fireman and wounding others. Sixteen are dead and eighteen injured.

The mortally wounded pilot, 22-year-old Lieutenant Vincent R. James, was comforted by nurse Irene Stevenson. He died in her arms in Boscombe Hospital.

Footnote   Mrs Stevenson became a local councillor and Mayor of Christchurch. Lieutenant James, who was unmarried, is buried at Cambridge American Cemetery. The 405th Fighter Bomber Group, based at Christchurch, lost a total of fifteen pilots during June 1944.

29 June   Hurn Mosquitoes show the Yanks how they do it in the dark.

The Mosquito pilots of 125 Squadron at RAF Hurn are showing the twelve crewmen of six P-61 Black Widow night-fighters of the 71st Fighter Wing of the 9th United States Army Air Force how to carry out blind radar-guided interceptions.

The Black Widows flew in today from Charmy Down, near Bath, and will be taken up on operational night interception flights.

Footnote   The Americans left on 10 July.

2 July   Another Thunderbolt crashes at Christchurch.

Today at 17.00 hours, an American P-47 Thunderbolt landed short of Christchurch Aerodrome and came down in a perimeter field. It bounced on to the adjacent Lymington road and fell to rest upside down. There was no fire and the pilot escaped.

3 July   Twelve Tarrant Rushton aircraft in SOE operation.

Twelve aircraft from Tarrant Rushton Aerodrome are tonight tasked to fly over occupied France for the Special Operations Executive. Men and materials will be dropped to the Resistance. Four Halifax aircraft are being provided by 298 Squadron and four from 644 Squadron.

Additionally the station has on stand-by the four aircraft that have been used on a regular basis for such operations, two Stirlings from 299 Squadron and two from 196 Squadron.

2 July 1944. Christchurch Aerodrome perimeter, on the adjacent Lymington road. This American P-47 Thunderbolt landed short of the airfield, though this time there was no fire or damage to property and the pilot was able to walk away from the wreckage.

5 July Christchurch Yanks give a Brit a Thunderbolt.

The Yanks lent a Brit a plane for the day, sent him out on a combat air patrol over enemy-occupied France, and then had kittens when he failed to return. Lieutenant Harris of the Royal Navy's Fleet Air Arm, a glider-tug pilot seconded to Airspeed Limited at Christchurch which makes Horsa troop-carriers, had talked 511 Squadron of the 405th Fighter Bomber Group of the United States Army Air Force into loaning him a Thunderbolt.

He joined Blue Flight which today lifted off from Station 416, the Advance Landing Ground that is Christchurch Aerodrome, and crossed the English Channel. They beat up the railway system southwards across Brittany to Nantes.

The pilots of 511 Squadron returned to Christchurch for a de-briefing on their targets of opportunity and the bombing of a tunnel. Their fears grew as their British friend failed to join them—the concern was not just for him but that a court martial would result from the unauthorised loan and loss of the aircraft.

Several hours later the panic turned to relief as Lieutenant Harris came home. He had overstayed his flying time in Brittany and had to force-land on an Allied-occupied beach in Normandy. Soldiers found him the petrol to take-off for a nearby captured airfield, where he was refuelled for the return flight to Christchurch.

6 July Christchurch Thunderbolts trap train in tunnel.

A train driver in Lisieux in German-occupied France, on the eastern side of the Allied front line, today took refuge in a tunnel as United States Army Air Force fighter-bombers attacked. His train was safe but their bombs left it trapped. Thunderbolts of the 405th Fighter Bomber Group, which had flown across the Channel from Christchurch, scored direct hits at each end of the tunnel.

6 July Warmwell's two-all air battle over Brittany.

Clear weather saw Warmwell's American Lightning fighter-bombers streaking across north-west France once again but today they met with a flight of more than twenty Focke-Wulf 190s. Though they were able to claim two definite kills the Americans returned across the Channel without Lieutenants Rubal and Jacobs.

Footnote In another bombing run over France, against the rail network, Lieutenant Moore was killed when his plane ploughed into a bridge.

9 July Pigeon post from Normandy to Hurn in seven hours.

Pigeons supplied from Bournemouth lofts have been arriving at RAF Hurn today some seven hours after release from the battle grounds in Normandy. They are helping the front-line troops to keep contact with their air support units; in fact they are proving themselves as an air support unit.

10 July Hurn's 604 Squadron claims its one hundredth kill.

The Mosquito night fighters of 604 Squadron at RAF Hurn have claimed their one hundredth kill. Last night, Wing Commander Gerald Maxwell shot down a Junkers Ju88 and claimed a Dornier Do217 as a probable kill, which took the claims total to its century.

11 July Thunderbolts leave Christchurch for Normandy.

The noise, excitement and danger from bomb-laden crash-landings have ended for the people of Christchurch as the Thunderbolts of the 405th Fighter Bomber Group take off from Station 416 for the last time. They are heading for Airstrip 8, at Picauville, in the Allied-occupied Cherbourg peninsula.

They have left Christchurch Aerodrome to the plane and glider makers Airspeed Limited, and an American flag to the Priory church as a memento of the United States Army Air Force. Their thousand-strong contingent will also leave a certain silence on the ground as the public houses and Bournemouth's places of entertainment clear up after the goodbyes to their liveliest clientele of all time.

14 July Hurn Mosquitoes change-over.

The Mosquito night-fighters of 604 Squadron left RAF Hurn yesterday and were replaced today by Mark VI Mosquitoes flown in by the Canadians of 418 (City of Edmonton) Squadron.

They will work with 125 Squadron in Anti-Diver sorties against incoming flying bombs. The aim is to intercept and shoot down these V-I weapons over the sea eastwards of the Isle of Wight.

18 July Warmwell Americans claim ten FW 190s.

The 474th Fighter Group from Warmwell routed a formation of twenty-five Focke-Wulf 190s over north-west France. They claimed ten, for the loss of three Lightnings. Two of the Americans baled out but the third, Lieutenant Goodrich, died in his plane.

20 July 84 Group Typhoons leave Hurn for France.

The three Wings of 84 Group of the 2nd British Tactical Air Force, flying Typhoons from RAF Hurn, lifted off today to re-group in France.

11 July 1944. The 1st Ballation of the Dorsetshire Regiment fighting in Normandy. Sergeant Turner and Privates Martin, Torrington (a Canadian 'Dorset'), and Smith, with Lance Corporal Wiltshire, are firing a three-inch mortar near Hottot. In the picture below the infantry and anti-tank guns are advancing along a tank track that has smashed through the hedgerows of the Bocage.

27 July **Warmwell pilot killed over Tours.**

Lieutenant Patton, flying a Lightning from Warmwell on a reconnaissance mission over Tours, was killed in an attack by a number of Me 109s.

July **Hurn Mosquitoes bomb the V-3.**

Mosquitoes of 418 (City of Edmonton) Squadron and 125 Squadron, from Hurn, flew together in a bombing raid against the massive concrete emplacement of the German H.D.P. secret weapon project at Mimoyecques, near Calais. The Hochdruckpumpe [High Pressure Pump] is known to British scientific intelligence as the V-3 and is presumed to be a long-range gun.

Footnote Its intended function was not discovered until the site was overrun by the Second Canadian Corps in the last week of September 1944. Fifty smooth-bore barrels of 15 centimetres diameter, 127 metres in length, were pointed towards London and designed to fire finned projectiles, each weighing 300 lbs, at the rate of ten per minute. The technical achievement was a muzzle departure-velocity of 5,000 feet per second, reached by boosting the firing charges with further propellants in side ports along the barrels, but there had been a major hitch in the physics. Above speeds of 3,300 feet per second the shells toppled erratically. Even with more time and less bombing they would have fallen well short of the capital.

July **American Liberator crashes on Furzey Island.**

An American Liberator bomber has crashed in Poole Harbour, hitting Furzey Island, with the loss of all its crew.

July **Wounded American pilots rest at Shaftesbury.**

The American Red Cross are using Coombe House, near Shaftesbury, as a recuperation centre for wounded and exhausted bomber crews.

Footnote In 1945 the Institute of the Blessed Virgin Mary acquired the building and it became St Mary's Convent. The house stands in its own wooded valley, a few hundred yards across the county boundary, in the Wiltshire parish of Donhead St Mary.

1 August **Mosquito night-fighters quit Hurn.**

The Mosquitoes of RAF Hurn were leaving today. Both 125 and 418 Squadrons are being redeployed at Middle Wallop, on the Hampshire Downs, though from there they can still venture into the night skies above Dorset in the unlikely event of German raiders coming this far west.

3 August **USAAF takes over RAF Hurn.**

The B-26 Marauders of 596, 597 and 598 Squadrons of the 97th Bombardment Group of the 9th United States Army Air Force have taken over Hurn Aerodrome from the Royal Air Force.

3 August **Another Warmwell pilot dies in France.**

Lieutenant Chamberlain, flying an American Lightning fighter from Warmwell on a combat air patrol over France, has been killed by enemy action.

4 August   Sea-shell lands in Christchurch.

A shell fell this afternoon in the garden of 36 Seafield Road, Christchurch. Fortunately it failed to explode. It had been fired from the sea.

5 August   Warmwell's Americans move to French base.

The 474th Fighter Group of the United States Army Air Force flew their final patrols from Warmwell today and landed on an airstrip in Normandy. This advance base on the other side of the Channel has been used for the past five days for refuelling and is now the Group's temporary home for the next stage of the war in Europe. Two Messerschmitt Me109s were claimed as kills on their moving day.

14 August   Hurn Yanks blow-up German ammo train.

B-26 Marauders of the American 97th Bombardment Group, flying from Hurn, have returned from a spectacular raid on the railway marshalling yards at Corbeil to the south of Paris.

They caught an ammunition train in the sidings. It was destined for the front-line troops of the German First Army.

18 August   RAF returns to Hurn for Air-Sea Rescue.

Three Walrus sea-planes and six Air-Sea Rescue Spitfires of 277 Squadron have transferred from Warmwell Aerodrome to Hurn. The American B-26 Marauders of the 97th Bombardment Group are due to leave Hurn for France in two days.

Footnote   277 Squadron went back to Warmwell on 29 August.

28 August   Wessex troops first across the Seine.

Eight separate battalion attacks were launched today by the 43rd (Wessex) Division to put the first British troops across the River Seine. Among them were the 5th Battalion of the Dorsetshire Regiment.

Footnote   Lieutenant-General Brian Horrocks, the commander of the 30th Corps, described it as "an epic operation". The logistical support behind the Allied advance had become stupendous and more than sufficient in everything except petrol. The Allies now had two million men and half a million vehicles in France. In tanks their numerical advantage over the Germans was twenty to one.

August   German Panzers to be tested at Lulworth.

Advanced examples of German armour—including Tiger, Panther and PzKpfe tanks of the Panzer Lehr and other divisions of the retreating Panzer Group West—are being shipped to England for evaluation on the gunnery ranges of the Armoured Fighting Vehicles School at Lulworth Camp.

In excess of 650 German tanks and thousands of other vehicles were destroyed during the annihilation of German forces caught in the Falaise-Mortain pocket, the bottlenecked salient of the enemy front-line that was finally closed in the area of Chambois after limited escapes on 20 August. Often the Germans had immobilised themselves in bumper to bumper traffic congestion which provided Allied pilots with their easiest pickings of the war. The wreckage was on such a colossal scale that in places it brought the Allied advance to a halt.

Summer 1944. Lulworth Ranges. Captured German tank, being unloaded for British evaluation, with a backdrop of the Purbeck Hills. It is identified by Lieutenant-Colonel George Forty in his 'Bovington Tanks' (Dorset Publishing) as a Panzer Kpfe III Ausf J, mounting a 5 centimetre gun.

German total losses are now in the order of 1,500 tanks and 3,500 guns destroyed or captured in the Battle of Normandy, plus tens of thousands of other vehicles from armoured car to horse and cart. The Wehrmacht has also lost nearly half a million men. The dead and wounded are estimated to number 240,000 and the number of Allied prisoners has reached 210,000.

Footnote The strategy for the Americans to break-out from the west of Normandy and pivot round towards the Seine, whilst the British and Canadians pinned down German armour east of Caen, was devised by General Sir Bernard Montgomery. His promotion, to Field Marshal, would be confirmed by King George VI on 1 September 1944.

August **Poole blast kills three.**

Three naval ratings were killed and six hurt when ammunition detonated itself in one of the landing craft at HMS Turtle, the Royal Navy's shore-base at Poole. The vessel was destroyed and nearby buildings damaged.

17 September **Tarrant Rushton Hamilcars join Arnhem airlift.**

Nearly a hundred gliders, towed by their Halifax tug-planes, have left Tarrant Rushton this Sunday morning to join the armada of three hundred Allied craft that are to land behind enemy lines in the Netherlands. Operation Market Garden is in the air and the Tarrant Rushton planes are towing the British 1st Airborne Division towards the farthest dropping zone, around Oosterbeek, four miles west of the great bridge over the Neder Rijn, the Lower Rhine at Arnhem.

Footnote This was the bridge too far. The Arnhem landings were a display of euphoric Allied over-confidence in the face of a mass of information that should have caused more than momentary reconsideration. Aerial photographs showed German tanks only a short distance from the drop-zone and Dutch resistance had reported "battered Panzer divisions" in Holland to refit. Furthermore there was an Enigma-coded intercept released two days before the operation was launched, stating that German Army Group B, under Field Marshal Walter Model who was a veteran of the great tank battles in the Ukraine, had moved his headquarters to Oosterbeek, the Tafelberg Hotel to be precise, which lay between the drop-zone and the target—the Arnhem bridge over the Rhine. These were no ordinary enemy troops, they were the 2nd SS Panzer Corps, comprising the crack 9th and 10th SS Panzer Divisions.

All this was known, but Montgomery—in the words of General Bedell Smith, Chief of Staff at SHAEF [Supreme Headquarters Allied Expeditionary Force]—"simply waved my objections airily aside". Eisenhower, the Supreme Commander, admitted in 1966 that "I not only approved Market Garden, I insisted on it". He had on 5 September been so optimistic about the course of the war that he went as far as to declare "the defeat of the German armies is now complete". See the entry for 14 November, for their reaction.

After 17 September 1944. In defeat, defiance—as this picture in the Bundesarchiv proves. One third of the gliders of the British 1st Airborne Division that landed around Arnhem had flown from Tarrant Rushton in Dorset. There were a further 1,900 smaller aircraft involved in Operation Market Garden, with parachutists from the C-47 Dakotas bringing the number dropped at Arnhem to 8,000, and 10,075 as the total for the drop-zones as a whole. Of these, a significant proportion of the 2,490 who escaped back to Allied lines would be saved through the 'matchless heroism' of the 4th Battalion of the Dorsetshire Regiment, part of the 43rd (Wessex) Division.

22 September   Ottawa conference VIPs fly into Poole.

British VIPs returning from the Ottawa Conference have flown back into Poole Harbour aboard a BOAC Boeing Clipper. The party includes the Chief of the Imperial General Staff, Sir Alan Brooke, the First Sea Lord, Admiral Sir Andrew Cunningham, and the Chief of Air Staff, Sir Charles Portal.

29 September   Dorsetmen enter the Reich.

Infantrymen of the 1st Battalion of the Dorsetshire Regiment today formed the first infantry patrol to cross into Germany, though they are disappointed to have been forestalled by Sherman tanks of the Sherwood Rangers who have the distinction of being the first unit of the British Army to enter the Reich.

The Dorsets are operating in aid of the Guards Armoured Division in its breakout from the De Groote bridgehead. Trophies from the cross-border patrol include a German state flag and a black flag of the SS.

This evening, at the invitation of its supporting field battery, the CO of the Dorsets and his second in command fired token shells into Germany. One was painted with a message: "A present for Adolf Schickelgruber."

September   Mudeford mine kills two sappers.

Two members of a Royal Engineers mine-clearance team have been blown up whilst trying to remove a device from the beach at Harbour Run Road, Mudeford.

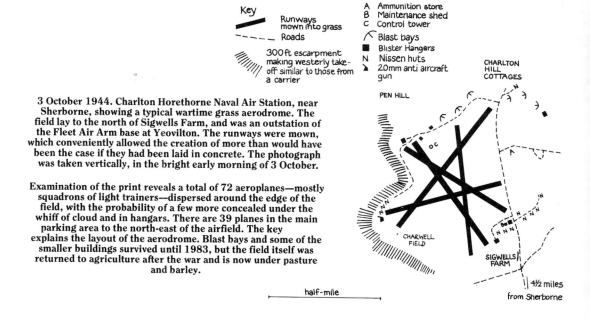

Key

Runways mown into grass
Roads
300 ft escarpment making westerly take-off similar to those from a carrier

A Ammunition store
B Maintenance shed
C Control tower
Blast bays
Blister Hangars
N Nissen huts
20mm anti aircraft gun

3 October 1944. Charlton Horethorne Naval Air Station, near Sherborne, showing a typical wartime grass aerodrome. The field lay to the north of Sigwells Farm, and was an outstation of the Fleet Air Arm base at Yeovilton. The runways were mown, which conveniently allowed the creation of more than would have been the case if they had been laid in concrete. The photograph was taken vertically, in the bright early morning of 3 October.

Examination of the print reveals a total of 72 aeroplanes—mostly squadrons of light trainers—dispersed around the edge of the field, with the probability of a few more concealed under the whiff of cloud and in hangars. There are 39 planes in the main parking area to the north-east of the airfield. The key explains the layout of the aerodrome. Blast bays and some of the smaller buildings survived until 1983, but the field itself was returned to agriculture after the war and is now under pasture and barley.

PEN HILL

CHARLTON HILL COTTAGES

CHARWELL FIELD

SIGWELLS FARM

4½ miles from Sherborne

half-mile

4 October **Dorset troops see the V2s go up.**

The 1st Battalion of the Dorsetshire Regiment, holding what they call "The Island" at Bemmel, which is almost surrounded by Germans and linked only precariously with the main Allied advance, have seen several V2 rockets rise towards London from the enemy-occupied Hook of Holland. They are being launched skywards from positions to the east, north-east and south-east. The rockets go straight up to a height of about ten kilometres before tilting into a 45 degree trajectory. The first to land on London hit Chiswick on 8 September and another fell the same evening at Epping.

Footnote None of the German vengeance weapons fell on Dorset, as the opposite coast had been captured before they became operational. The closest stray was a V1 flying-bomb that dropped on Boldre churchyard in the New Forest.

The Daily Telegraph saw the shape of things to come, if not thankfully to pass: "V2 indicates the kind of weapons with which the Third World War will be fought if there is one."

14 October **Twelve drown in landing craft on Chesil Beach.**

An American tank landing craft, LCT A2454, was washed on to the Chesil Beach at Wyke Regis last night in mountainous seas. The state of the sea prevented the Weymouth lifeboat and a Portland dockyard tug from coming round the Bill to its aid. Ten of the LCT's British crew were drowned despite the desperate efforts of the Fortuneswell Lifesaving Company who had run along the pebble bank from Portland and succeeded in firing a rocket-line into the stricken vessel. Two sailors were rescued by Coastguard Treadwell as a tremendous wave swept most of the crew and everything else that was moveable into the sea.

More lines were fired into the craft but as she shifted across the pebbles these fouled. Treadwell and Captain Pennington Legh were swept away, never to be seen again, as they struggled to free the lines.

The four surviving rescuers also risked their lives to save two more of the sailors. Cyril Brown, wearing a lifebelt, struggled through the waves to get the line to the crewmen, and then had to be hauled ashore himself and taken to hospital. The line broke before the last crewman could be brought ashore and this time it was Albert Oldfield, without any safety line of his own, who managed to wade out to throw another line. The fourth man leapt from the boat and was pulled from the water.

Footnote The four surviving rescuers were awarded the Lloyds' silver medal for lifesaving but one, V.F. Stephens of Wyke Regis, died in a car crash before he could receive it at the reception in Weymouth Guildhall. Cyril Brown, of Portland, also received the Stanhope Medal, for the bravest deed of the year.

18 October **Hurn is RAF Hurn once again.**

Formal control of Hurn Aerodrome was resumed by the Royal Air Force today on its transfer from the United States Army Air Force.

30 October **Poole bullets highlight a problem.**

A Poole refuse disposal stoker had a close shave—a superficial face wound—when a cartridge clip exploded in his furnace. It has highlighted a serious danger and the public is asked to be more thoughtful with the disposal of explosives. Not that dustmen are going to lower their guard. Deadly objects are now lying around all over the country. Inevitably some of the smaller and less noticeable kinds will find their way into the dustbin.

October **Coupon controller approves Christchurch cassock appeal.**

The vicar of Christchurch Priory, Canon W.H. Gay, writes in his monthly parish newsletter: "As some have questioned the legality of my appeal for clothing coupons to refit the choir with cassocks, may I state that the 143 coupons I have received will be sent to the Controller at Bournemouth, who will issue the needed permission to the tailor. I notice that most of the coupons have come from spinsters, widows and bachelors."

1 November **RAF Hurn has closed.**

RAF Hurn has ceased to exist. At 00.00 hours today control passed from the Air Ministry to the Ministry of Civil Aviation and the military station became a civilian aerodrome.

1 November **Poole craft attack Walcheren to free Antwerp.**

Twenty-five Poole landing craft manned by naval crews from the town's HMS Turtle base have landed commandos on Walcheren Island, the German-held strongpoint blocking the approaches to the Dutch port of Antwerp. Nine of the craft, the Support Squadron Eastern Flank, have been sunk and nine are immobilised.

Footnote The British commandos and Canadian ground forces took three days to capture the island. The channel to Antwerp was opened to Allied supply ships on 28 November.

11 November **Dorsetmen are first gunners into Germany.**

The 94th Field Regiment of the Royal Artillery, mainly recruited from Bournemouth and Dorset in 1939, has become the first field gun force to cross the German frontier. It is supporting the Anglo-American offensive in the Geilenkirchen sector.

14 November **4th Dorsets were heroes of Arnhem escapes.**

It became known today that it was largely owing to the matchless heroism of 250 men of the 4th Battalion of the Dorsetshire Regiment, part of the 43rd (Wessex) Division, that 2,400 out of the original 10,075 airborne troops succeeded in withdrawing from the Arnhem bridgehead on the night of 25 September.

Few, however, of the Dorsets escaped—and some of those had to swim the Neder Rijn to do so.

In the salient of the British advance, "The Island" at Bemmel, three Battalions of the Dorsetshire Regiment, the 1st, 4th and 5th, found themselves fighting in adjacent fields for the same "thumb print" on the map—the first time events had brought them together. Other Dorsets were able to give covering fire to men of the 4th Battalion as they rescued the survivors of the 1st Airborne Division and the Polish Parachute Brigade with a shuttle service of assault boats across the Neder Rijn [Lower Rhine].

By dawn on 26 September, at 06.00 hours, the intensity of enemy fire made further rescue crossings impossible.

3 December **The Home Guard stands down.**

With the movement of the war into Europe throughout the second half of this year there have been the inevitable consequences on this side of the Channel and from today the Home Guard is stood down.

26 December **Blandford sees the cost of the Ardennes.**

The news today is that General George Patton has at last been able to lead the tanks of the 3rd

United States Army in the relief of Bastogne. The tide of the great German counter-offensive in the snowy forests of Luxembourg and southern Belgium, the Battle of the Ardennes, has been turned.

It has, however, been an achievement of American grit. The staunch determination of the American soldier since 16 December has prevented the Germans from coming back across the River Meuse.

Casualties are streaming into Dorset. Up to five hundred wounded Americans have been flown into Tarrant Rushton by the Dakotas in a single night, en route for the 22nd General Hospital at Blandford Camp.

Footnote The Ardennes reverses for the Germans were to be worse; estimated losses of 120,000 men with 600 tanks and assault guns, plus dozens of aircraft. There was nothing in reserve for another counter-attack.

29 December **American freighter sinks in Worbarrow Bay.**

The *Black Hawk*, a United States steam-freighter, has sunk in Worbarrow Bay after being hit by a torpedo.

**1944 hero. Captain Lionel Queripel VC,
of the 10th Battalion, the Parachute Regiment,
came from Dorchester.**

December **Posthumous VC for Dorchester's Arnhem hero.**

Captain Lionel Ernest Queripel of Dorchester has been posthumously awarded the Victoria Cross for his gallantry in the battle following the airborne landings at Arnhem. Born in 1920, he was fighting with the 10th Battalion, the Parachute Regiment.

The citation reads:

"At Arnhem on 19 September 1944 Captain Queripel was acting as company commander of a composite company composed of men of three parachute battalions.

"At 14.00 hours on that day his company were advancing along a main road which runs on an embankment towards Arnhem. The advance was conducted under continuous machine-gun fire, which at one period became so heavy that the company became split up on either side of the road and suffered considerable loss. Captain Queripel at once proceeded to reorganise his forces, crossing and recrossing the road whilst doing so under extremely heavy and accurate fire. During this period he carried a wounded sergeant to the Regimental Aid Post under fire and was himself wounded in the face.

"Having reorganised his force, Captain Queripel personally led a party of men against a strong point holding up the advance. This strong point consisted of a captured British anti-tank gun, and two machine guns. Despite the extremely heavy fire directed at him, Captain Queripel succeeded in killing the crews of the machine guns and recapturing the anti-tank gun. As a result of this the advance was able to continue.

"Later in the same day Captain Queripel found himself cut off with a small party of men and took up a position in a ditch. By this time he had received further wounds in both arms. Regardless of his wounds and the very heavy mortar and Spandau fire, he continued to inspire his men to resist with hand grenades, pistols and the few remaining rifles. On at least one occasion he picked up and threw back at the enemy a stick grenade which had landed in the ditch.

"As, however, the enemy pressure increased, Captain Queripel decided that it was impossible to hold the position longer and ordered his men to withdraw. Despite their protests, he insisted on remaining behind to cover their withdrawal with his automatic pistol and a few remaining hand grenades. This is the last occasion on which he was seen.

"During the whole of a period of nine hours of confused and bitter fighting Captain Queripel displayed the highest standard of gallantry under most difficult and trying circumstances. His courage, leadership and devotion to duty were an inspiration to all."

**1944 hero. Lieutenant John Grayburn VC,
of the 2nd Battalion, the Parachute Regiment,
went to Sherborne School.**

December   Shirburnian's posthumous VC for being the hero of Arnhem's bridge.

Lieutenant John Grayburn, a platoon commander with the 2nd Battalion, the Parachute Regiment, has been posthumously gazetted with the Victoria Cross, for three days of gallant fighting on 17-20 September 1944. He went to Sherborne School.

His orders upon landing close to the bridge over the Rhine at Arnhem were to seize it and hold it.

After the north end of the bridge over the Rhine at Arnhem had been captured, Grayburn was ordered to take his platoon and seize and hold the southern end. This they kept attempting to carry out until casualties made further attempts futile: "He directed the withdrawal from the bridge personally and was himself the last man to come off the embankment into comparative cover."

Then, the citation continues, he occupied a house that stood in an almost indefensible position and managed to hold off sustained attack by infantry, mortars, tanks and self-propelled guns: "He constantly exposed himself to the enemy's fire while moving among and encouraging his platoon and seemed completely oblivious to danger."

Fire finally drove them from the building, on 19 September, and then John Grayburn led a fighting patrol back to the bridge to prevent the Germans from laying demolition charges. Despite being wounded in the back he continued to defend an untenable position.

In full view of a German tank he personally directed his men back to safety but stayed on the front-line, wounded and hungry and without having slept for days, and was killed on the night of 20 September.

The citation concludes: "There is no doubt that, had it not been for this officer's inspiring bravery, the Arnhem bridge could never have been held for this time."

December **Henstridge airmen fight the Japs.**

Two Seafire squadrons from Henstridge Royal Naval Air Station, on the Somerset border at Stalbridge, are flying from the aircraft carrier HMS *Indefatigable* in offensive operations against the Japanese forces in the Pacific theatre.

887 and 894 (Fleet Air Arm) Squadrons comprise 24 Royal Navy Fighter Wing. The Seafire is the marine version of the Spitfire.

Footnote On 1 April 1945, HMS *Indefagitable* became the first British carrier to be hit by a Japanese kamikaze plane. Among the pilots of 887 Squadron was Sub-Lieutenant R.Lygo, who would retire as Admiral Sir Raymond Lygo.

December 1944. Bournemouth. The author's parents, Gladys and Ted Legg at 21 Easter Road, Moordown, Bournemouth, received their last Christmas card of the present hostilities from Ted's brother, Arthur Legg, who was having a good war as a dispatch rider in Italy. It gave him a bike and absolute freedom; he always boasted that as far as taxation was concerned he never returned from the Western Desert. Of the Yanks, his lasting memory was the sheer scale and excesses of everything they did—always bringing enough spares to rebuild every piece of equipment half a dozen times. Arthur had more of a sense of humour than the rest of the family put together, myself included. He was in his second childhood and had written: 'The welding went on my silencer at Taranto the other day and now she sounds just like the good old grass track days, and by the way I can't get my licence taken away out here or in Cairo yet. You want to see the speed and the noise we make, especially when on an Immediate Message. I have done 16,000 miles since coming to Italy in January [he wrote this on 14 June 1944, as 'typewriter and radio are tapping away'] and if old Deacon, Roe or Bryon [stuffy Bournemouth neighbours] was anywhere around in the busy streets of Bori, or when I was in Cairo, their hair would stand on end, and I guess I can't get the sack from the job till the Ruddy War is over. One-way streets mean nothing to us DRs [dispatch riders] and the 'Red Caps' [military police] just know we are on SDR [Special Dispatch Riding].' Arthur Legg lies in Talbot Village churchyard. If there is a life after death they will be enjoying something other than peace.

De Havilland Mosquito:
made at Christchurch.

1945

January   Warmwell joyrider takes a Spitfire to Cheselbourne.

Victor Swatridge of Dorchester Police wrote to me in 1971 with an account of an incident on a cold January night, apparently in 1945, when he was called by telephone at 2.45 am by the constable on the Broadmayne beat and told that a Spitfire had been stolen at 02.00 hours from Warmwell Aerodrome.

As there was a blizzard he thought this a little unlikely but the Observer Corps at Poundbury Camp confirmed they had heard a plane overhead at about 2.30 am. The missing plane had been said to have flown west and Poundbury reported the unmistakable sound of a Rolls-Royce Merlin engine. They reported it disappearing about six or seven miles to the north-east.

Moonlight followed the snow and Swatridge went with another officer on to the Dorset Downs around Cheselbourne in the centre of the county:

"At about 5 am on approaching Cheselbourne Water, to our amazement we saw a lighted hurricane lamp in the drive to a cottage. Naked lights were regarded as somewhat treasonable and very much frowned upon, as blackout regulations were strictly enforcible. Even the headlamps of cars were only allowed narrow slotted beams.

"I immediately investigated the reason for this breach and a woman, on answering my call at the cottage, stated that she had heard a plane overhead about two hours previously which appeared to have landed nearby. She went on to say, that she had been expecting her husband home on leave from France and it was the sort of stupid thing he would do, come by any means possible. She had placed the lighted lamp as a guide to him. Amazing as it seemed, we trudged on and clambered on to a high bank overlooking an unploughed cornfield where to our utter surprise we came upon tyre marks. On following them we found the missing fighter plane with its nose embedded in the hedge and bank at the other end of the field, on Eastfield Farm a quarter of a mile north-east of Cheselbourne church.

"Climbing on to the wing we found the cockpit lights burning but the 'bird' had flown. There was no trace of blood inside and we found footmarks in the snow made by the culprit, when walking way from the scene, but they quickly became extinct owing to the drifting snow. To cut a long story short I returned to the divisional station, after leaving a constable to guard the plane and a search party was sent out in daylight and a Canadian airman of the ground staff was arrested, having celebrated too liberally the previous night and in a rash moment embarked on this venturesome journey. There was only slight damaged to the aircraft; the man was concussed and later dealt with by the authorities. So the escapade resolved itself."

25 February   2nd Dorsets cross the Irrawaddy.

The 2nd Battalion of the Dorsetshire Regiment today saw the "flying fishes play" as they crossed the Irrawaddy. Now, in Kipling's words, the British Army is "On the road to Mandalay." This has influenced the Dorsets' current battle cry: "There's a dirty white pagoda to the east of Payadu."

12 March   Burton Bradstock pensioners save crashed pilot.

A Martinet from the Armament Practice Camp at Warmwell Aerodrome today developed engine problems over the Chesil Beach bombing range. The pilot crash-landed at Burton Mere, on the coast between Swyre and Burton Bradstock, but found himself trapped in the wreckage.

Two heroes ignored the flames which were about to engulf the aircraft and untangled the pilot's feet. They were Miss Harriette Evelyn Bendy, aged 68, and Levi Rogers, aged 65, from

Burton Bradstock. As they pulled the shocked airman to safety his aeroplane became an inferno.

19 March   Christchurch Aerodrome goes to Transport Command.

RAF Christchurch was today transferred from 11 Group, Fighter Command, to 46 Group, Transport Command. It is to be a satellite airfield to the major transport base on the western side of the New Forest at Ibsley, between Ringwood and Fordingbridge.

In the past nine months, Christchurch Aerodrome has been used as a diversionary airfield when intended destinations were closed by fog or other bad weather. Incoming flights from across the Channel have brought Allied wounded and German prisoners. Aircraft types visiting Christchurch have included the Boston, Liberator, Stirling and Curtiss C-47.

20 March   2nd Dorsets help take Mandalay.

Having left twenty-seven dead along the road to Mandalay, the 2nd Battalion of the Dorsetshire Regiment have arrived and are mopping up opposition as the Japanese withdraw. General Sir Oliver Leese, Commander-in-Chief Allied Land Forces South-East Asia, visited the men this afternoon and told them they would have to make the next four hundred miles to Rangoon before the monsoon broke—though this time, he promised, they would not have to walk all the way.

Hearing the news of the capture of the ancient Burmese capital, Winston Churchill remarked: "Thank God they've at last got to a place I can pronounce!"

21 March   6th Airborne Division leaves Tarrant Rushton.

The British 6th Airborne Division, with its sixty Halifax tug-planes and their Hamilcar and Horsa gliders, is today leaving Tarrant Rushton Aerodrome for its new location, RAF Woodbridge. This Suffolk airfield is closer to the division's next objectives, on the far side of the Rhine.

Footnote   These landings, Operation Varsity, began at 09.54 hours on 24 March and continued for three hours; 6th Airborne took Hamminkein and the bridges over the River Issel. Fifty-two of the ex-Tarrant Rushton gliders landed successfully.

March   Duchess of Kent visits Blandford.

HRH the Duchess of Kent has visited the 22nd General Hospital of the United States Army, which now works with the 125th, 131st and 140th General Hospitals in a major medical complex across the Anson-Craddock Lines at Blandford Camp. It has received 17,000 patients of the long-term type, many of whom are needing complicated surgery. The commander is Lieutenant Colonel Leonard D. Heaton.

March   Poles sink U-boat in Poole Bay.

Polish pilots have claimed a U-boat in the Channel, sunk in the south-east extremity of Poole Bay, towards the Isle of Wight.

9 April   Warmwell ceases to be an operational airfield.

152 Squadron, who have been operating at Warmwell since the dark days of 1940, have been withdrawn and the station is now only retained for training, by the Central Gunnery School.

17 April   **Puddletown lad loses life for fame in the Argenta Gap.**

Trooper James Legg, aged 21, from Puddletown, serving with the Queen's Bays, has been killed in action in Italy. He drove the first tank to force its way through the enemy's main defensive line in the Argenta Gap.

26 April   **BOAC Lancastrian flies from Hurn to Sydney.**

The first Lancastrian of British Overseas Airways Corporation's new fleet has landed in Australia at the end of a proving flight that lasted fifty-three hours. The airliner, G-AGLF, carried the markings of the RAF's South-East Asia theatre but was on a pathfinding flight to determine the feasibility of a peacetime service.

After flying out of Britain from RAF Hurn on 23 April the airliner touched down en route at Lydda in Palestine, Karachi in India, Ratmalana in Ceylon, and Learmonth in Western Australia.

The pre-war flying boat service from Southampton Water used to take nine days, but though so much faster, the Lancastrian has room for bunks and seats for only six passengers.

4 May   **Dorsets hear there is no longer a war in northern Europe.**

Cipher clerks to the units of the Dorsetshire Regiment in Germany received the signal at 20.50 hours today—"all offensive ops will cease from receipt of this signal." In other words, it's over. "Orders will be given to all troops to cease fire 08.00 hours tomorrow Saturday 5 May. Full terms of local German surrender arranged today for 21 Army Group front follow."

The times are stated in British Double Summer Time and the Instrument of Surrender was signed by General-Admiral von Friedeberg, the emissary of Grand Admiral Karl Döenitz who is exercising command in Schleswig-Holstein in place of Hitler, and General Kinzel, Busch's Chief of Staff. It unconditionally surrenders all enemy forces in northern Germany and was signed at 18.30 hours in the Tactical Headquarters of Field Marshal Sir Bernard Montgomery on Luneberg Heath.

18.30 hours, 4 May 1945. Field Marshal Sir Bernard Montgomery brings the European war to an end. In the next couple of hours the message will be with the troops in the field — that unless they are attacked there is to be no more fighting.

Footnote   Though Hitler was dead, the Allies did not know it at the time.

10 May 1945. Weymouth. U-boat 1023 surrenders.

8 May   VE Day.

15.00 hours. The war in Europe is officially at an end. Street parties, bonfires and church services will mark VE Day this Thursday evening.

9 May   U-boat 249 surrenders at Portland.

U-boat 249 today entered Portland Harbour to surrender.

10 May   Two more U-boats surrender.

U-boat 825 put into Portland and U-boat 1023 came into Weymouth as the surrender of Grand Admiral Karl Döenitz's fleet continues.

12 May   Dorsets in first victory parade.

The 5th Battalion of the Dorsetshire Regiment marched past Lieutenant-General Brian Horrocks, the commander of the 30th Corps, at Bremerhaven today in the first victory parade to be held in Germany.

16 May **Isle of Wight villagers send their prize to Portland.**

Villagers at Freshwater on the Isle of Wight were amazed when a U-boat surfaced offshore and requested someone to take its surrender. Freshwater has a parish councillor or two but it has no mayor or any one of the kind of standing that a German naval officer might respect. Anyway it has no port facilities apart from a beach and the inhabitants considered they were in line for a rollicking from the Royal Navy.

So U-776 was asked to surrender somewhere else and it departed for Portland Harbour. Someone in the Isle of Wight has turned up a splendid opportunity. Think of how he might have answered that inevitable question: "Granddad, what did you do in the war?"

30 May 1945. Blandford Camp. Memorial day for the men of the 22nd General Hospital of the United States Army. They remember the dead of World War Two and the passing of President Franklin D. Roosevelt who died last month, on 12 April.

30 May **Roosevelt Park opened at Blandford.**

The first overseas memorial to the late President of the United States, Roosevelt Park inside the confines of Blandford Camp, was declared open today with an address by Colonel Daniel J. Fourrier of the US Army. A colour party fired ceremonial rounds.

The park is dedicated "to the everlasting memory of our fellow soldiers, at home and abroad, who gave their lives in this war, so that we who live may share in the future a free and better world". It has been provided through voluntary contributions of members of the Army Medical Department with the landscaping being designed by a patient, Private George H. Stuber. Colonel Fourrier handed the park over to Colonel C. Topham of the Royal Engineers who received it on behalf of the British Army.

A six-foot high monument is under construction to enshrine the ideals behind the park permanently in stone.

30 May 1945. Blandford Camp. American colour party at the opening of Roosevelt Park.

6 June   Conservatives hold Dorset but lose Britain.

The Conservative Party smarted today as the landslide of votes in yesterday's General Election is set to oust war-leader Winston Churchill and put a Labour administration in his place. Pre-war memories are blamed for the scale of the socialist success which has surprised the world in its rejection of the country's saviour. It is regarded as an unwarranted dismissal.

Even in Dorset, which must be quite blue, it has been a close-run thing for the Conservatives to hold their seats. The East Dorset constituency returned Lieutenant- Colonel M. Wheatley with 26,561 votes against 25,093 to his Labour opponent Lieutenant-Commander Cyril Fletcher-Cooke, with Liberal Colonel Mander having the remaining 8,975. Out of 80,816 on the registers there was a 60,629 poll, including 8,352 votes from men and women in the armed services.

Footnote Clement Attlee became Prime Minister on 25 July with Ernest Bevin as Foreign Secretary, Sir Stafford Cripps at the Board of Trade and Hugh Dalton as Chancellor of the Exchequer.

June   Gunnery School leaves and Warmwell closes.

The RAF aerodrome at Warmwell closes this month with the departure of the Central Gunnery School for Sutton Bridge, Lincolnshire.

June   Sherborne School's 242 death toll.

The roll of honour published in The Shirburnian school magazine, during the course of the war, has now accounted for two hundred and forty-two lives. It compares with a death toll of two hundred and eighteen in the Great War, but Sherborne School was then far smaller.

The most distinguished of the Old Boys in the present conflict was mathematician Alan Turing who broke the Germans' 'Enigma' cipher codes, and the bravest Lieutenant J.H. Grayburn, of Abbey House, who was posthumously awarded the Victoria Cross for his conspicuous gallantry on the bridge at Arnhem. John's was among the first VCs to be won for the Parachute Regiment and the only one by a Shirburnian in this war.

15 July   Flying Fortress crash-lands at Christchurch.

American aircrew being brought to Bournemouth for a period of leave had a lucky escape today at Christchurch Aerodrome. Flying Fortress 866, carrying men of the 306th Bombardment Group from Thurleigh, Bedfordshire, overshot the western boundary of the notoriously short airfield. It plunged into scrubland. The near-side port engine was ripped out but the aircraft then came to a halt without exploding. No one was hurt.

6 August 1945. Hiroshima's bomb—'brighter than the sun'—but another would be needed to bring about the surrender process.

15 August   Henstridge pilots celebrate VJ Day.

It is Victory over Japan Day. Nowhere in Dorset has the celebration been more heart-felt than in Stalbridge and in particular the Wrens' Quarters on the Dorset side of the Royal Naval Air Station at Henstridge which literally straddles the county boundary with Somerset.

Here a bonfire has been kept burning all night, despite a soaking at 05.00 hours when the rain intensified, having been started a few minutes after midnight when the station Tannoy had roused everyone from sleep: "Attention everybody. Attention. Japan has surrendered." The party began, and is still carrying on in the Swan at Stalbridge.

This was still an operational air station. VE Day had been only half the story. For the young New Zealand pilots and others under training the war was still a going concern and their lives under risk in what was becoming the "forgotten war".

The atomic bombs ended all that. Leaflets dropped on Hiroshima on the 4th warned: "Your city will be obliterated unless your Government surrenders." That blow was delivered from a single United States Army Air Force Boeing B-29 bomber, *Enola Gay* piloted by Paul Tibbets Junior, on the 6th. Then Nagasaki was threatened its "rain of ruin the like of which has never been seen on earth". That was from another B-29, *Bock's Car*, on the 9th.

The third atom bomb, standing-by and probably for Tokyo, did not have to be dispatched. Japan began the surrender process four days ago.

21 August   'Our man in Berlin'—Lindsay is dead.

Sir Ronald Lindsay, of Stepleton House near Blandford, died today. The retired diplomat was born in 1877. He rose through the ranks at the Foreign Office to become an under-secretary in 1920 and progressed to the highest postings in the service—being ambassador to Berlin (1926-28) and Washington (1930-39). When he bowed out the war, as they say, was an extension of diplomacy by other means.

The classical Stepleton House and its park, where Peter Beckford wrote the classic book on fox-hunting, has passed to Sir Ronald's nephew, Lord Crawford.

22 August 1945. Portland. Depressing day in the rain for United States Ambassador Gil Winant, unveiling Portland's tribute to the Americans who fell on Omaha Beach. Winant's life was being destroyed for the love of Sarah Churchill.

22 August   US Ambassador unveils Portland's memorial.

Portland's memorial to the Americans of V Corps who passed through the harbour en route to D-Day and the fierce fighting on Omaha beach was unveiled today by the United States Ambassador, Gil Winant. He was welcomed by the chairman of Portland Urban District Council, A. N. Tattersall, after driving along the newly re-named Victory Road. The stone is in Victoria Gardens and the Stars and Stripes flies above beside the Union Jack. Disappointingly, it has been a very wet Wednesday.

Footnote   "Fine, fine, perfectly fine," was Winant's famous remark of the war; which he kept repeating over the transatlantic telephone when Roosevelt told him of Pearl Harbor. By now, however, he was engulfed in personal problems and would shoot himself in 1947, after his return to the United States. He is said to have set his heart on Winston Churchill's daughter, but Sarah Churchill was unable to reciprocate his love.

31 August   Canford School counts 139 dead.

Canford's School's roll of war dead has closed at a total of 139 lives, from this its first war. As the school was founded in 1923 it happened that all Old Canfordians were of an age to serve and indeed nearly a thousand of them held commissions.

August **Penicillin works wonders at Shaftesbury.**

The apparently miraculous cures brought about at Shaftesbury Military Hospital, Guy's Marsh [now a Borstal] with M&B tablets have now been upstaged by the use of penicillin. This has reversed impossible infections which previously would have certainly killed even the strongest soldiers. It has taken years to bring the drug into commercial production; in 1942 the entire world supply was needed to treat a single case of meningitis.

Remarkable surgery is taking place too. Strabismus is being corrected by an easing of the muscles around the eyeball. Major John Charnley has carried out a hip-replacement operation at Shaftesbury which was as much a feat of carpentry as an exercise of the surgeon's craft.

August **British military back in Blandford Camp.**

The British Army has returned to Blandford Camp—which saw out the war as a major American General Hospital—with the arrival of the 1st and 2nd Searchlight Regiments, Royal Artillery, in the huts of the Craddock and Benbow Lines. These units will train conscripts who have been called up to serve their national service with the Royal Artillery.

18 September **First Jap prisoners arrive home at Poole.**

The first BOAC flying boat to bring repatriated prisoners-of-war home to Britain from Japan has touched down in Poole Harbour, amid sensational press interest in the men's stories of degrading and inhuman treatment.

They were given a civic welcome at a reception on Poole Quay. Many thousands are en route home by sea and air.

18 September **Pan Am Skymaster drops into Hurn from New York.**

An ex-military C-54 Skymaster of Pan American Airways has landed at Hurn Aerodrome from La Guardia Airport, New York, in a proving flight that took seventeen hours. The airliner, carrying nine crew and ten staff as observers, stopped off en route at Gander in Newfoundland and Rineanna in Eire.

This was the first time a four-engined land-plane—as distinct from a flying-boat—has crossed the Atlantic on a civilian flight.

Former Halifax bombers, in conversions known as Haltons, are currently operating from Hurn on the BOAC route to Lagos and the other West African colonies.

3 October **Christchurch colonel fires a V2.**

Colonel Raby, the Director of Signals Research and Development Establishment at Christchurch Aerodrome and Steamer Point, Highcliffe, today test-fired a German V2 rocket which he had reconstructed from captured parts. It has been flown northwards, along the coast from Cuxhaven, near Bremerhaven, into the North Sea off Denmark.

This has been a secret test, codenamed Operation Backfire, and tomorrow another rocket will be fired. Raby's establishment is working on the first British guided weapons.

Footnote A third V2 was fired by the British team on 15 October, 1945; this time the world's press would be invited and bill it as "the first Allied test-firing of a V2 rocket".

October **Blandford hospital staff leave on the 'Queen Mary'.**

The 22nd General Hospital of the United States Army has finally pulled out of Blandford Camp.

The last of its staff are now sailing back across the Atlantic from Southampton aboard the liner *Queen Mary*.

August 1945. Yanks go home. Troopship 'Queen Elizabeth' prepares to sail down Southampton Water for the United States, with tugs at her bow and a flypast salute overhead.

25 November **Five Poole flying boats exit for Argentina.**

Argentina, a Sandringham 2 flying boat which is a Mark V Sunderland powered by American Pratt and Whitney Twin Wasp engines and fitted out for forty-five passengers, lifted off from Poole Harbour today for Buenos Aires. She has been sold to Dodero, the Argentine airline, along with the similar *Uruguay* and three Sandringham 3 flying boats.

These have more spacious accommodation for their twenty-one passengers and are intended for longer flights. They are the *Brazil*, *Inglaterra* and *Paraguay*. Each is being delivered across the Atlantic by a BOAC crew with Argentinians aboard as observers. The flight time is estimated at thirty-six hours.

31 December **Home Guard disbanded.**

Today has seen the last rites for the Home Guard as it is finally disbanded by the War Office. "The spirit of comradeship and service which was brought to life by service to the Dorset Home Guard must never be allowed to die," says its last Commander, General Henry Jackson.

December **Japan's PoWs still in Hell at Shaftesbury.**

The pitiful casualties of this war, beyond the help of surgery and drugs, are the psychologically distressed ex-prisoners of the Japanese who have been brought home from the Far East to recover at Shaftesbury Military Hospital [now Guy's Marsh Borstal]. Many are also emaciated but it is the mental damage that will take longer to correct. They suffer horrific memories when they are awake and lapse into agonising nightmares in sleep.

Such dehumanised wrecks become even more pathetic as they regain their physical strength without a comparable recovery from mental anguish. They are men returned from Hell.

Their ordeal is worse in its way than the more clear-cut cases on life's edge with tuberculosis. These three wards would once have been one-way nursing towards death but here expectations and hope have been transformed as a result of the introduction of the wonder-drug streptomycin.

December **Plaque at Portland commemorates the logistics.**

The 14th Major Port of the Transportation Corps of the United States Army has presented a bronze plaque to Portland dockyard commemorating the logistics of the invasion of Europe:
"1944–1945. The major part of the American assault force which landed on the shores of France 6 June 1944, was launched from the Weymouth and Portland Harbors. From 6 June 1944 to 7 May 1945, 517,816 troops and 144,093 vehicles embarked from these harbors. Many of these troops left Weymouth Pier. The remainder of the troops and all vehicles passed through Weymouth en route to Portland points of embarkation.
"Presented by the 14th Major Port, U.S.Army. Harold G. Miller, Major, T.C. [Transportation Corps] Sub Port Commander. Sherman L. Kiser, Colonel, T.C. Port Commander."

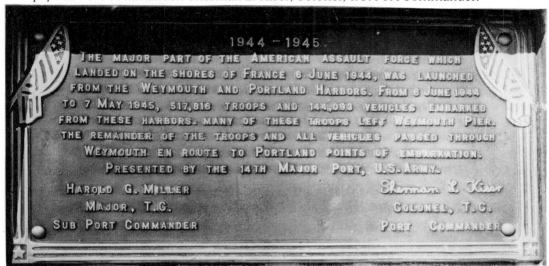

1946

February **War's upheavals bring Uplands School to Parkstone.**

Uplands School, which was founded in 1903 at St Leonards-on-Sea, Sussex, is on the move to Parkstone. It has come via Monmouthshire, where it was evacuated when invasion threatened in 1940, and it had been hoped to return to Sussex in 1944 but the flying bombs caused these plans to be abandoned. Instead it is coming to Parkstone, to the buildings of a sister church school for girls, Sandecotes, which was itself closed in 1940 when the buildings were requisitioned by the military.

1 July **2nd Dorsets on Tokyo's 'Buck House' guard.**

The 2nd Battalion of the Dorsetshire Regiment has been hastily consigned to Tokyo in Operation Primus, to relieve the New Zealanders on ceremonial guard duties in the Japanese capital. The Americans are its army of occupation on the streets. Dorset sentries are preparing for what they call "No 1, Buck House guard"—at the Imperial Palace.
The rosters assume that the battalion's eight hundred men will be able to maintain two hundred sentries at posts around the city.
Footnote Sharing the imperial guard with the Americans was not quite on Buckingham Palace lines, Lieutenant Colonel Geoffrey White recalled in *Straight on for Tokyo*: "It is not easy when your companion on the post allows himself rather a more relaxed form of stand-at-ease, and it is most disconcerting to have a doughnut offered you on the end of a bayonet."

1945-46. Off Brownsea Island, Poole Harbour. Hythe-class Short Sunderland Mark-3 flying boats, formerly RAF transports with gun turrets (above), though these are removed in the second picture (below). They carry Transport Command markings and operate with British Overseas Airways on the Empire route to India, Singapore and Australia. OQZS 'Hanbury' is seen on take-off (above), heading westwards up the Main Channel and destined for Bombay. The passenger launch (below) is speeding away from OQZC 'Hamilton' and OQZH 'Harwich'.

Index of people, Dorset area place-names, ships, aircraft types, and military units.